34TH CONGRESS, } SENATE. { Ex. Doc.
3d Session. } { No. 62.

REPORT

OF

THE SECRETARY OF WAR,

COMMUNICATING,

IN COMPLIANCE WITH A RESOLUTION OF THE SENATE OF FEBRUARY 2, 1857,

INFORMATION RESPECTING

THE PURCHASE OF CAMELS

FOR THE

PURPOSES OF MILITARY TRANSPORTATION.

WASHINGTON:
A. O. P. NICHOLSON, PRINTER.
1857.

REPORTS

UPON

THE PURCHASE, IMPORTATION,

AND USE OF

CAMELS AND DROMEDARIES,

TO BE

EMPLOYED FOR MILITARY PURPOSES,

ACCORDING TO ACT OF CONGRESS OF MARCH 3, 1855:

MADE UNDER THE DIRECTION OF

THE SECRETARY OF WAR.

1855-'56-'57.

THIRTY-THIRD CONGRESS, SECOND SESSION—Chap. 169.

SEC 4. *And be it further enacted,* That the sum of thirty thousand dollars be, and the same is hereby, appropriated, to be expended under the direction of the War Deparment in the purchase of camels and importation of dromedaries, to be employed for military purposes..

Approved March 3, 1855.

IN THE SENATE OF THE UNITED STATES.

February 2, 1857.

Resolved, That the Secretary of War be directed to furnish the Senate with any information in his possession, showing the results of the trial of the camel as a beast of burden and for the transportation of troops; and showing, also, the characteristics and habits of the animal, and the number imported up to the present time.

February 26, 1857.

Read, referred to the Committee on Military Affairs, and ordered to be printed.

February 28, 1857.

Ordered. That five thousand extra copies be printed for the use of the Senate.

LETTER FROM THE SECRETARY OF WAR COMMUNICATING THE REPORT.

WAR DEPARTMENT,
Washington, February 24, 1857.

SIR: In compliance with the resolution of the 2d inst., I have the honor to transmit herewith the correspondence and reports of the officers charged with the purchase and importation of the camel, and its employment for purposes of transportation in the military service of the United States, together with the information obtained from persons who were considered the best authority as to the general characteristics and habits of the animal.

Under the appropriation of $30,000, made on the 3d of March, 1855, seventy-five camels have been imported. The aid furnished by the Secretary of the Navy in the use of a storeship returning from the Mediterranean greatly reduced the cost of transportation, and enabled the department to introduce a much greater number of camels than was originally calculated, and has secured to the government the means of making the experiment upon a scale which will sufficiently demonstrate the adaptation of the animal to the climate and circumstances of our country and its value for military purposes.

The limited trial which has been made has fully realized my expectations, and has increased my confidence in the success of the experiment.

I have the honor to be, very respectfully, your obedient servant,

JEFF'N DAVIS,
Secretary of War.

Hon. JAMES M. MASON,
President pro tem. United States Senate.

TABLE OF CONTENTS.

PART I.

PAPERS RELATING TO THE FIRST EXPEDITION FOR CAMELS AND DROMEDARIES.

	Page.
Letter of Secretary of War to Major Wayne, (instructions,) May 10, 1855	13
Letter of Secretary of War to Major Wayne, May 16, 1855	14
Letter of Secretary of War to Lieutenant Porter, United States navy, May 16, 1855	14
Letter of Major Wayne to Secretary of War, May 18, 1855	16
Letter of Secretary of the Navy to Secretary of War, May 23, 1855, enclosing copy of instructions to Lieutenant Porter	16
Letter of Major Wayne to Secretary of War, June 7, 1855	17
Letter of Major Wayne to Secretary of War, July 4, 1855	18
Letter of Major Wayne to Secretary of War, July 27, 1855, enclosing copy of correspondence with General Daumas	19
Letter of Major Wayne to Secretary of War, August 10, 1855, enclosing copy of correspondence with Consul General Chandler	22
Letter of Lieutenant Porter, United States navy, to Secretary of War, August 13, 1855	25
Letter of Major Wayne to Secretary of War, October 5, 1855, enclosing copy of circular addressed to several gentlemen in the east in reference to obtaining information about camels	26
Letter of Major Wayne to Secretary of War, October 11, 1855	29
Letter of Major Wayne to Secretary of War, October 31, 1855	30
Letter of Lieutenant Porter, United States navy, to Secretary of War, December 12, 1855	32
Letter of Major Wayne to Secretary of War, December 28, 1855, enclosing copy of correspondence in relation to purchase and exportation of camels from Egypt	35
Letter of Major Wayne to Secretary of War, January 3, 1856	44
Letter of Major Wayne to Secretary of War, January 31, 1856, enclosing copy of letter to Consul General De Leon	45
Letter of Major Wayne to Secretary of War, February 8, 1856	46
etter of Major Wayne to Secretary of War, February 11, 1856	48

CONTENTS.

	Page.
Letter of Major Wayne to Secretary of War, April 10, 1856, reporting results of inquiries and observations	49
And enclosing—	
Notes upon the dromedaries of Egypt, by Linant de Bellefonds, Bey	64
Letter of E. De Leon, United States consul general for Egypt, in relation to dromedaries and burden camels of Egypt	72
Letter from Rev. H. G. O. Dwight, Edwin E. Bliss, and W. F. Williams, in relation to camels in Asia Minor, and other portions of Turkey in Asia	76
Notes upon the camel in Algiers, from the official reports of General Carbuccia, by Albert Ray	83
Notes upon the anatomy of the dromedary, from the official reports of General Carbuccia, by Dr. Engles, United States navy	91
Letter of Major Wayne to Secretary of War, May 1, 1856	95
Letter of Major Wayne to Secretary of War, May 5, 1856	95
Letter of Major Wayne to Secretary of War, May 14, 1856	98
Letter of Major Wayne to Quartermaster General, May 17, 1856	99
Letter of Major Wayne to Secretary of War, May 17, 1856, enclosing copy of letter from G. H. Heap to Major Wayne	100
Letter of Secretary of War to Major Wayne, (telegraphic despatch,) through Colonel D. D. Tompkins, May 2, 1856	102
Letter of Major Wayne to Secretary of War, May 21, 1856	102
Letter of Lieutenant Porter, United States navy, to Secretary of War, May 28, 1856. Report of proceedings, journal of events on shipboard, and correspondence with Consul General De Leon in relation to dromedaries presented by the Viceroy of Egypt	103
	133
Letter of Major Wayne to Secretary of War, June 19, 1856	148
Letter of Major Wayne to Quartermaster General, June 20, 1856, (extract)	149
Letter of Major Wayne to Secretary of War, June 28, 1856	150
Letter of Secretary of War to Major Wayne, July 5, 1856	151
Letter of Quartermaster General to Major Wayne, (instructions,) July 14 and 30, 1856	151, 152
Letter of Major Wayne to Secretary of War, July 22, 1856	152
Letter of Major Wayne to Secretary of War, July 28, 1856	153
Letter of Major Wayne to Secretary of War, August 4, 1856	154
Letter of Major Wayne to Secretary of War, August 12, 1856	154
Letter of Major Wayne to Secretary of War, August 12, 1856	155
Letter of Major Wayne to Secretary of War, August 30, 1856	156
Letter of Major Wayne to Secretary of War, September 24, 1856	157
Letter of Major Wayne to Secretary of War, November 5, 1856	159
Letter of Major Wayne to Secretary of War, November 20, 1856, reporting death of camels, and enclosing results of post mortem examinations	160
Letter of Major Wayne to Secretary of War, December 4, 1856	162

PART II.

PAPERS RELATING TO THE SECOND EXPEDITION FOR CAMELS AND DROMEDARIES.

	Page.
Letter of Secretary of War to Lieutenant D. D. Porter, U. S. N., (instructions,) June 26, 1856	188
Letter of Quartermaster General to Lieutenant D. D. Porter, U.S.N., July 14, 1856	188
Letter of Lieutenant Porter, U. S. N., to Secretary of War, September 11, 1856	190
Letter of Secretary of War to Lieutenant Porter, U. S. N., October 8, 1856	192
Letter of Lieutenant Porter, U. S. N., to Secretary of War, November 14, 1856	192
Letter of Secretary of War to Major Wayne, December 13, 1856	193
Letter of Lieutenant Porter to Secretary of War, December 3, 1856	193
Letter of Major Wayne to Secretary of War, January 4, 1857	194
Letter of Lieutenant Porter to Secretary of War, (extract,) January 30, 1857	195
Letter of Major Wayne to Quartermaster General, February 12, 1857	195
Letter of Major Wayne to Secretary of War, February 21, 1857, enclosing statements from Captain J. N. Palmer and Assistant Surgeon Joseph R. Smith, in connexion with acclimation of camels	197
Letter of Captain W. K. Van Bokkelen, February 10, 1857, announcing safe landing of second cargo of camels	200

PART III.

THE ZEMBOUREKS, OR THE DROMEDARY FIELD ARTILLERY OF THE PERSIAN ARMY.

	Page.
By Colonel F. Colombari, Grand Officer of the Order of the Lion and Sun, of Persia, decorated with several other orders, and member of the Geographical Society. Extracted from the "*Spectateur Militaire*," 1853. Translated by Brevet Major H. C. Wayne, U. S. A., 1854	201

ILLUSTRATIONS.

PART I.

No. 1. Nomanieh dromedary, drawn by .... G. H. Heap.
2. Becharieh dromedary, drawn by .... do....
3. "Courier of the Desert," drawn by .... Vernet...
4. Dromedary from Muscat, (female,) drawn by .... Heap...
5. Dromedary from Lower Egypt, (female,) drawn by .... do....
6. Arvana camel from Asia Minor, drawn by .... do....
7. Dromedary from Lower Egypt, (male,) drawn by .... do....
8. Dromedary from Mount Sinai, (male,) drawn by .... do....
9. Female camels and young, drawn by .... do....
10. Wrestling camel, from Asia Minor, (male,) drawn by .... do....
11. Bactrian camel, from Central Asia, (male,) drawn by .... do....
12. Bactrian camel, from Crimea, (male,) drawn by .... do....
13. Bactrian camel, blanketed, from Central Asia, (male,) drawn by .... do....
14. Tuilu, (hybrid, male,) drawn by .... do....
15. Embarkation of camels, drawn by .... do....
16. Camels secured for a gale, drawn by .... do....
17. Burden camel of Egypt, drawn by .... Prisse...
18. Burden camel of Egypt, drawn by .... do....
19. Dromedaries of Egypt, drawn by .... do....
20. Dromedaries of Egypt, drawn by .... do....

PART III.

Sketches of zembourek, or dromedary artillery, of Persia.

PART I.

PAPERS RELATING TO THE FIRST EXPEDITION FOR CAMELS AND DROMEDARIES.

PAPERS RELATING TO FIRST EXPEDITION.

WAR DEPARTMENT,
Washington, May 10, 1855.

SIR: Assigned to special duty in connexion with the appropriation for "importing camels for army transportation and for other military purposes," you will proceed without delay to the Levant, and there make such investigations as, with the knowledge you already possess of the animal, and of the views and intentions of the government in relation to its introduction, will enable you to execute the law of Congress. A storeship, which (after the delivery of stores for the Mediterranean squadron at Spezzia) has been placed at my disposal by the Secretary of the Navy, will leave New York on or about the 20th instant, under the command of Lieutenant D. D. Porter, United States navy, who has been associated with you in the commission. In the prosecution of your duties it may be requisite for one or both of you to go into the interior of Asia; and should you, in such expeditions, visit the government of any state or country with which the United States has no established relations, diplomatic, consular, or commercial, you will present yourselves in your official capacities, as charged by your government with a special commission, and request, in the name of your government, such friendly offices as international courtesy warrants.

On your way to the Levant, you may find, especially in England and France, persons whom it would be desirable to consult on points connected with this special service, such as General Marey Monge, Colonel Carbuccia, and other officers of the French army who were connected with the experiments in Africa, on the use of the camel in the military service of France. You had also better examine for your information the stock, training, and breeding of the Barbary camel, imported into Tuscany some two hundred years ago, and which, by careful breeding, is reported to have been greatly improved, both in size and strength. Leave your address at Spezzia for Lieut. Porter, and indicate the point at which he is to meet you with the vessel.

Report to me as often as you can, giving me full information of your operations, that I may be advised of your course, and, if necessary, furnish you with further and more precise instructions.

In conclusion, it is hardly necessary to mention, but still I do so to impress it upon you, that time is an important element, and that I wish you to be as prompt in the execution of this duty as the security of the experiment will permit, to which, of course, everything else must be subordinate.

During your absence from the United States on this duty, the usual allowances of mileage and commutation of quarters and fuel at Washington rates will be made to you.

Very respectfully, your obedient servant,

JEFF'N DAVIS,
Secretary of War.

Major HENRY C. WAYNE,
U. S. Army, Washington.

WAR DEPARTMENT, *Washington, May* 16, 1855.

SIR: I herewith furnish, for your information and guidance, a copy of the instructions this day given to Lieutenant D. D. Porter, United States navy, who is associated with you in the duty of carrying into effect the law making an appropriation for the importation of camels, &c.

Very respectfully, your obedient servant,

JEFF'N DAVIS,
Secretary of War.

Brevet Major H. C. WAYNE,
Quartermaster U. S. Army, New York City.

WAR DEPARTMENT, *Washington, May* 16, 1855.

SIR: The Secretary of the Navy having detailed you for the command of the storeship Supply, for the purpose of co-operating with the War Department in carrying out the law making an appropriation for the importation of camels, the following instructions are given for your guidance:

Major Henry C. Wayne, who goes out under instructions of this department to purchase the camels and obtain information on the subject, will join you at Spezzia, or some neighboring point. In associating Major Wayne and yourself in this duty, the department expects you will consult freely together, and having placed at your disposal all the facilities you have asked for, will look to you for the success of the enterprise.

The best point for you to proceed to at first will be Smyrna, where you can obtain such information as will guide your future operations. In Salonica, it is said, the camels are of a superior character, and it may be desirable to examine the different points along that coast. If you think the camels at Salonica will suit the purpose, you had better make arrangements to have a number collected there by the time of your return. From Salonica you will proceed to Constantinople, provided there are no serious obstacles in the way, owing to the war in that quarter; and to expedite your voyage it is desirable that you should make arrangements by which you can obtain steam towage through the Dardanelles, up the Sea of Marmora, and into the Black sea, if it should be necessary to go there. It is believed that the best breed of camels is to be found in Persia; and as nothing should be left undone to procure the very best for our purposes, you may find it necessary to take your ship to the nearest point of communication with that country, when Major Wayne and yourself can set out on an expedition inland. If it is found desirable to purchase the camels in Persia, it can be done by shipping them at such port as will best facilitate the operation.

If circumstances occur of such a nature as to prevent communication with Persia by way of the Black sea, you will take your ship to the coast of Syria and disembark the land expedition at Beyrout or such other point as may be most suitable for the purpose. Scanderoon will probably be a good harbor in which to lay up the ship in winter weather, should you be unable to return to the United States this season. By starting from either of the points mentioned, an opportunity will be afforded for examining the quality of the camel in Asia Minor. It might risk the success of the enterprise to import them from a southern climate. Damascus and Palmyra were once celebrated for their dromedaries, and the Kurdistan territory still possesses animals of fine quality. Whenever you meet with fine animals it would be well to procure them. While on the land expedition circumstances and your best judgment must be your guide. In the unsettled state of those countries at present it will be necessary for you to start with a party sufficiently large and well armed to secure you from being molested by wandering tribes. After embarking the camels you will proceed, at the most suitable season of the year, to the United States, stopping at such points as, in your opinion, will be desirable for the purpose of obtaining supplies for the animals. You will proceed to the coast of Texas, and land them at the most convenient point, where Major Wayne, or such other person as may be designated by the department, will take sole charge of them. From that point you will report your arrival to me, and unless further instructed proceed direct to New York.

During your absence report to me whenever you can find an opportunity, giving me full information of your operations. For further information I refer you to the instructions to Major Wayne, a copy of which is herewith furnished. In case of any accident to Major Wayne, by which he might be prevented from carrying out the instructions I have given him, you will proceed alone to fulfil these instructions.

While engaged on expeditions on shore your expenses will be paid; also the expenses of those persons it may be deemed necessary to take with you.

Very respectfully, your obedient servant,

JEFF'N DAVIS,
Secretary of War.

Lieutenant D. D. PORTER,
United States Navy.

NEW YORK, *May* 18, 1855.

SIR: I have the honor to acknowledge the receipt this morning of your letter of the 16th instant, enclosing a copy of your instructions to Lieutenant Porter, of the navy.

I have just returned from an examination of the "Supply," in company with Lieutenant Porter, and am exceedingly pleased with the vessel and with the arrangements made. You know already my estimate of Lieutenant Porter's abilities, but I must add that, in the completeness and thoroughness of the details, he has far exceeded my most sanguine expectations. Everything now has been procured, or is in process of delivery. The revolvers and ammunition for them have not yet been sent over, but I have authorized Lieutenant Porter to receipt in my name for them, as also for the medicines that I requested Colonel Swords, as I advised you this morning, to purchase for the expedition. I sail to-morrow at 12 m., in the Hermann, for Southampton.

With much respect, your obedient servant,
HENRY C. WAYNE,
Major United States Army.

Hon. JEFFERSON DAVIS,
Secretary of War.

NAVY DEPARTMENT,
May 23, 1855.

SIR: I have the honor to transmit herewith a copy of the instructions that have been given by this department to Lieutenant David D. Porter, commanding the United States storeship "Supply," and respectfully request that you will give him such further instructions as may be necessary to carry out the object proposed in your letter of the 11th of April last.

I am, respectfully, your obedient servant,
J. C. DOBBIN.

Hon. JEFFERSON DAVIS,
Secretary of War.

NAVY DEPARTMENT,
May 23, 1855.

SIR: So soon as the United States storeship Supply, under your command, is in all respects ready for sea, you will set sail and proceed direct to Spezzia, and deliver to the naval storekeeper at that place the stores intended for the Mediterranean squadron, taking his receipt therefor. After which you will carry out such instructions as may be given you by the honorable Secretary of War.

Should you fall in with a senior officer, you will show him these instructions, with which he will not interfere, except in a case of great emergency, and he is thereby authorized to afford you any assistance that you may properly require.

I am, respectfully, your obedient servant,

J. C. DOBBIN.

Lieutenant DAVID D. PORTER,
  Commanding U. S. Storeship Supply, New York.

No. 8 PANTON SQUARE, LONDON,
June 7, 1855.

SIR: I have the honor to report my arrival here on Monday evening, the 4th instant, after a passage of fifteen days to Southampton. The next morning (the 5th) I deposited my letter of credit for £4,000 with Messrs. George Peabody & Co., and presented myself at the legation of the United States. Mr. Buchanan received me very kindly, and, upon my informing him of my mission, and my purpose in visiting London in connexion with it, gave me a letter to Professor Richard Owen, F. R. S. of the Royal College of Surgeons, the Cuvier of England. Upon calling at the Royal College yesterday, I was fortunate enough to find the Professor in, and to receive from him, upon the perusal of Mr. Buchanan's note, a cordial greeting, accompanied with manifest interest in the purpose of my visit. My interview with him was very interesting and gratifying, as he gave me the assurance that he could see no difficulty whatever in acclimating and breeding the camel in the United States. As a member of the Zoological Society, he gave me a letter to its secretary, Mr. D. W. Mitchell, whom I found at the society's rooms, No. 11 Hanover Square, and with whom I had a long and animated conversation, closing with an appointment for 10 a. m. to-morrow (Friday, the 8th instant,) at the Zoological Garden, to give me an opportunity of studying the feeding, care, and hygeian of the camels and dromedaries in that institution, where, as I am informed by Professor Owen, five dromedaries have been born and reared. The result of my examinations shall be communicated to you at an early day.

I am, sir, with much respect, your obedient servant,

HENRY C. WAYNE,
Major U. S. Army.

Hon. JEFFERSON DAVIS,
  Secretary of War, Washington city, D. C.

P. S. My address is still, care George Peabody & Co., London.

H. C. W.

PARIS, FRANCE, *July* 4, 1855.

SIR: I have the honor to enclose herewith my account current of the appropriation for introducing the camel into the United States, for the quarter ending June 30, 1855, and to report the result of my researches in England.

As mentioned in my letter of the 7th ultimo, from London, I received from Professor Owen, F. R. S., the most gratifying encouragement in my mission, and, through his introduction to the secretary of the Zoological Society, Mr. D. W. Mitchell, free access to the gardens of that society. To this latter gentleman I am indebted not only for official courtesies and facilities, but for much personal attention and companionship in the prosecution of my examination and inquiries.

In the Zoological Garden are two very fine specimens of the Egyptian camel of burden, male and female, presented by the Pasha of Egypt. They have been in the garden five years, have never been seriously unwell, and have bred two calves since their arrival in England. The first birth was still-born; the second died some months after birth, from an injury to its back. Five camels have been born in the garden, and three reared, within the memory of those connected with it. One imported camel, after being twenty years in the garden in London, was sent thence, three years ago, to the Zoological Garden at Ghent, where he was still living, and well, at the last accounts.

To the stables for the camels—for they are kept separately, though adjacent—are small paved courts, supplied with water, to which they have access at will, except in very severe weather in winter. Then they are confined in their stables, and let out only during sunny hours. Their keeper told me, however, that, on going into the stables in the morning in winter, he not unfrequently found the water left for them frozen over, and that, twice last winter, it was frozen quite solid, yet the camels did not seem to be at all distressed or affected by the cold. During the summer they eat, each, per day, about fifteen pounds of coarse hay, (the coarser and more inferior the quality, the more they like it,) taking occasionally a bite of the oat straw that makes their litter. In winter they receive, each, in addition, per day, two quarts of grain, oats, ground oats, barley, or bran. To a question as to the comparative delicacy of the camel and the horse, and the care necessary to preserve the one and the other, the attendant, who has been connected with this branch of zoology in the garden for some years, replied that he considered the camel to be a very hardy animal, and requiring less care than the coach horse. With regard to the diseases of the animal, I could learn nothing, as none of the camels, within the recollection of the attendants, had ever required medical treatment. As to the difficulty of managing the camel, and the assertion that none but an Arab could do it, the attendants stated that they had never found any difficulty in doing so, and, to satisfy me on that point, the male was led out upon the lawn, where the attendant manœuvred him in walking, pacing, kneeling down, and getting up, with facility, using no severity, and the animal obeying with readiness, and exhibiting no apprehensions.

Mr. Mitchell assured me that no particular care was taken of the camels in the garden, and that he thought they could be transported to, acclimated, and bred in the United States. In this his opinion coincides with that of Professor Owen, who thinks our experiment practicable. Both of these gentlemen, as well as all with whom I conversed in England, regard it with scientific interest, and many measured its commercial advantages, if successful.

I paid frequent visits to the garden, and the result of my researches in it, and in England, may be summed up in a few words, as follows: that the camel stands well the climate of London; that it breeds in it; and that a European can manage the animal as well as an Arab.

With much respect, I am, sir, your obedient servant,
HENRY C. WAYNE,
Major U. S. Army.
Hon. JEFFERSON DAVIS,
Secretary of War, Washington city, U. S. A.

UNITED STATES STORESHIP SUPPLY,
At sea, off Ischia, July 27, 1855.

SIR: Continuing my report, I have the honor to state that I arrived in Paris on the evening of the 20th June, and the next morning presented myself to our minister, Mr. Mason, and delivered the letters, to officials and others, with which I had provided myself before leaving the United States. At the department of war I was informed that General Carbuccia had recently died of cholera at Gallipoli; that General Marey Monge was absent on a distant command; and that the 33d regiment of the line, which, under the above named officers, had been particularly charged with the experiments with camels in Algeria, was also on distant service, and that it was doubtful if any of the officers engaged in those experiments were in Paris. I was further informed, however, that if our ambassador would present me to the minister for foreign affairs, and request an introduction from him to the minister of war, that I would, without doubt, be able to gain access to the bureau of Algeria, and from its files or through its officers obtain perhaps some useful information. Calling upon our ambassador, accordingly, he undertook to put me in connexion with Maréchal Le Vaillant, minister of war, through the minister for foreign affairs, and accomplished it on the 3d of July.

In the mean time I had made the acquaintance of Messrs. Jomard, Maury, and others, gentlemen of science, with whom I discussed freely the possibility of acclimating and breeding the camel on the continent of America. The experiment was regarded by these gentlemen as of doubtful result; but their views were formed upon the camels of Africa, and they had not examined the subject in connexion with the camels of Asia.

Presenting myself to Maréchal Le Vaillant, on the 4th of July, I was questioned by him as to the object of my mission, and if that was the sole purpose of my visit to the east; and was informed that instructions would be given to General Daumas, who had served long in Africa, and was then director of the affairs of Algeria, to correspond with me, and to furnish me, if he could, with the information I desired. From General Daumas I obtained much useful information as to the habits and care of the camel; and enclose herewith a pamphlet by himself, upon the acclimation of the camel in France, which he gave me, and copies of a correspondence between us in relation to my mission.

At the Jardin des Plantes I found but one camel, and that not in appearance a very fine specimen; nor could I obtain from the attendants at the garden anything precise, or that I thought reliable, as to its habits.

Concluding my researches in Paris, I left it on the 17th instant for Pisa, via Marseilles, and on my arrival at Genoa, received a letter from Lieut. Porter, United States navy, informing me of his arrival with the "Supply" at Spezzia, and that while the vessel was discharging he would inspect the camels at Pisa, and obtain all the information on the subject that he could. As this rendered my visit to Pisa unnecessary, I repaired at once to Spezzia, where I arrived on the morning of the 24th, and Lieut. Porter returning from Pisa a few hours afterwards, I embarked with him on board the "Supply."

The pamphlet by General Daumas, on the "Cheval de Guerre," referred to in my letter to him of the 13th of July, I will translate at my leisure, and will forward the translation to you by the first convenient opportunity.

Very respectfully, your obedient servant,
           HENRY C. WAYNE.
            Major U. S. Army.

Hon. JEFFERSON DAVIS,
 Secretary of War, Washington city, U. S. A.

            MINISTÉRE DE LA GUERRE,
              Paris, le 6 Juillet.

MONSIEUR LE MAJOR : J'ai l'honneur de vous addresser une notice contenant les renseignements qu'un long séjour en Afrique, m'a permis de recueillir sur le chameau.

Je me féliceterois vivement si ces quelques pages offraient pour vous de l'interêt, et si elles pourraient aider aux études que vous poursuivez.

Veuillez agréer, Monsieur le Major, l'assurance de ma consideration trés distinguée.

              E. DAUMAS,
       Le Conseiller d'etât, General de Division,
         Directeur des Affaires de l'Algerie.

Monsieur le Major WAYNE,
 Hôtel du Rhin, Place Vendôme.

HÔTEL DU RHIN, PARIS, *July* 8, 1855.

GENERAL: I have the honor to acknowledge the receipt yesterday of your communication of the 6th instant, and to beg you to accept my thanks for your pamphlet upon the acclimation of the camel in France, which it enclosed.

I have read your pamphlet with much interest, and have derived from it information that will be valuable to me in the experiment I am about to conduct. My previous researches led me to nearly the same conclusions in regard to acclimating the African camel in America, and turned me to an examination of the animal in its various conditions in Asia. There I found the Arabian, or camel with one hump, extensively used from China to the Black and Mediterranean seas, and from India to the 50th degree of north latitude, traversing a country very similar in geological structure, in climate, and in changes of temperature, to that portion of America in which we purpose to introduce him. As I proceeded in my investigations I found many parts of Asia Minor and Persia corresponding so closely with portions of Texas, New Mexico and California, in all the essentials for camel life, that to them I have directed my attention, as the region whence the animal may be transported to America with the greatest probabilities of success.

That I may not be misunderstood, I will state that I have adopted the classification of the camel into two kinds: the Bactrian, or camel with two humps, which is found in Tartary and the northern portions of central Asia; and the Arabian, or camel with one hump, which is found in Persia, Asia Minor, Arabia, India, &c.; regarding the word dromedary, as its derivation indicates, as simply the swift courser or racer, in distinction from the camel of burden.

With this classification in view, you will understand me when I say that it is the intention of my government to domesticate, if possible, in America, the Arabian camel, including both the beast of burden and the dromedary. To the appropriation by Congress for the purpose, the President of the United States has added a vessel of our navy, expressly fitted for the purpose, and manned by officers and crew of our navy, the commander being associated with me to superintend the transportation of the animals across the seas. The vessel has been arranged with much care to carry thirty camels, and is now on her way to the Mediterranean, whither I proceed in a few days to join her. As it will not do, in an experiment of this kind, to run any unnecessary risks, it is our intention to avoid transporting the camels to America in the winter or stormy months, but to wait for the more genial season of spring; and in the intervening time to occupy ourselves with a practical study of the animal at Salonica, Beyrout, Smyrna, and as far in the interior of Asia as its present disturbed state will permit.

The experiment possesses much of scientific interest, as well as commercial and political importance. Its object being to introduce a new animal into the heart of our continent, where there are neither navigable rivers nor practicable roads, and by means of it to hold in check the wandering tribes of Indians that are constantly warring upon civilization, to carry on commerce, and to facilitate communication.

Begging you to accept, General, the assurances of my high consideration, I am, with much respect, your obedient servant,

HENRY C. WAYNE,
Major United States Army.

General E. Daumas,
*Conseiller d'etât, General de Division,
Directeur des Affaires de l'Algerie, Paris.*

Paris, *July* 13, 1855.

General: I have again to acknowledge your kindness and to thank you for the pamphlets on the "Camel" and the "Horse for Military Service," (Cheval de Guerre.) The subjects are both of much interest to me, and the latter concerns all military men as of vital importance to the efficiency of an army.

The experiments of France in the breeding and training of horses for her cavalry service have been watched in the United States with interest, and anything in relation to the subject is received by us with eagerness, as we are making exertions to introduce into our country a thorough cavalry system. The useful information contained in your pamphlets will aid me in my studies, and it will give me great pleasure to communicate it to my government. Accept, General, the assurances of my high consideration.

HENRY C. WAYNE,
Major U. S. Army.

General E. Daumas, *&c., &c., &c., Paris.*

United States Storeship Supply,
Off the Goletta, Gulf of Tunis, August 10, 1855.

Sir: On the evening of the 25th July we left Spezzia for Naples, (the cholera at Leghorn closing that port against us,) as Lieutenant Porter desired to procure funds for his ship's expenses, and as we were led to believe that we could procure there, on better terms than at any other port in the Mediterranean, such coin as would be generally current in the east. On our arrival, however, on the 28th July, we found the state of the market to be the reverse of our information, and after conversing with Mr. Owen, our chargé d'affaires, we determined to postpone our money arrangements until we had made inquiries at Malta. Leaving Naples on the evening after, (30th July,) we stretched over to Tunis, where Lieutenant Porter and myself had determined to procure a camel for the purpose of studying the animal and its management on shipboard, and dropped anchor off the Goletta, the port of Tunis, on the afternoon of the 4th August. Calling upon our consul-general, Mr. W. P. Chandler, he suggested an official visit to the new Bey, Mohammed Pasha. As we were the first officers of our country who had visited Tunis since his accession to the throne, and as, under the circumstances of our presence within his regency, he thought it an act of international courtesy that would contribute to the good impressions of the Bey towards our country. A presentation was accordingly arranged, and on the 8th, accompanied by Dr. Engles, Passed Midshipmen Roney and Blake, officers of the "Supply," (Lieutenant Porter being unfortunately detained on shipboard by a slight attack of fever,) I was presented to Mohammed Pasha. On presentation, I requested the consul-general to say to the Bey "that I was glad of the occasion that brought me into the waters of Tunis, as it gave me an opportunity, as an officer of the government of the United States, to pay my respects to him, and to congratulate him, in the name of the President of the United States, upon his accession to the throne; to assure him of the friendly disposition of the President and the people of the United States towards the regency of Tunis, and to express the desire that the amicable relations hitherto existing between his country and my own might, under his wise reign, be continued and extended." To which the Bey replied, "that he thanked me for my visit, and received with sincere pleasure the congratulations of the President; that he wished well to the President and people of the United States, and he hoped that nothing would occur to disturb the harmony at present existing between the two governments, which it was his desire to continue and cherish." Upon retiring from the interview, the consul-general requested from the minister of state, Count Rafo, a *teskorah* (permit) for us to bring off to the ship some live stock for the vessel and the camel I had bought. The Bey, hearing the request, inquired what I wanted with a camel, and if it was a fine one. Upon being informed of the purpose of the purchases, and that I was not yet sufficiently versed in camel knowledge to say whether or not he was a fine one, he promptly desired the interpreter to say to me that he would send me a fine one from his own herds. The gift I accepted in the name of the President and people of the United States, and yesterday we received on board, as the accompanying correspondence will show, *two* camels, (instead of one,) presented to our country by the Bey. We have, then, on board three camels, and they have already demonstrated the admirable fitness of Lieutenant Porter's arrangements for hoisting them on board and for their transportation. We lay about a mile from shore, in a wide gulf, and although the water was not smooth, the animals were transferred from the Tunisian craft, in which they were brought alongside, to their place between the decks of the "Supply," with expedition and without injury. The animals presented by the Bey are both stallions—one grown, the other young—and they are apparently of fine blood. They have been much admired by the resident Americans and Europeans who have seen them, and I have consequently requested our consul-general to procure their pedigrees for me. From this place we go to Malta for letters, and to learn something of the state of the money market, and how to make the best arrangement for funds.

Very respectfully, your obedient servant,

HENRY C. WAYNE,
Major U. S. Army.

Hon. JEFFERSON DAVIS,
  Secretary of War, Washington city, U. S. of America.

Correspondence referred to in the letter of the 10th August, 1855.

MARSA, *August* 9, 1855.

MY DEAR MAJOR: I have just received two camels from his highness. One is of the very finest quality and full grown; the other is a young one. I could not ascertain their exact ages; I send them with my dragoman. You must do the best you can with them, as it will be impossible to refuse.

I am very truly your obedient servant,

W. P. CHANDLER.

Major WAYNE,
  U. S. A., on board U. S. ship "Supply."

UNITED STATES STORESHIP SUPPLY,
Off the Goletta, Gulf of Tunis, August 9, 1855.

SIR: The undersigned, officers of the government of the United States, have received on board this vessel the two camels that his supreme highness, the Bey, has been pleased to present, through them, to the President and people of the United States. In acknowledging such a munificent gift, we beg you to assure his supreme highness that we receive it as an earnest of his kind feeling, and of his desire to maintain the relations of amity and concord which have hitherto existed between the regency of Tunis and the United States; and that we will take the earliest opportunity of making known to the President this instance of his friendship.

We beg you further to renew to his supreme highness the assurances of the friendly disposition of the president and people of the United States towards himself, and to wish him, in their behalf, the enjoyment of health, and a long, prosperous, and happy reign.

With much respect and esteem, we are, sir, very respectfully, your obedient servants,

HENRY C, WAYNE,
  Major U. S. Army.
DAVID D. PORTER,
  Lieutenant Commanding.

Colonel W. P. CHANDLER,
  Consul General of the United States, at Tunis, Marsa.

MALTA, *August* 13, 1855.

SIR: We are about leaving Malta, in the prosecution of our duties, and though, as yet, nothing of importance has been done, it may be agreeable to you to know something of our movements.

We arrived in Spezzia on the 12th of July, being somewhat in advance of the time I allowed to get out there. On my arrival I received a letter from Major Wayne, informing me that he would join the ship in six days. I deemed it advisable to spend that time in taking a look at the camels in Florence and Pisa, and started on the day we received *pratique* on that duty. When I arrived at Florence I found that the greater part of the camels, amounting to two hundred and fifty, had been sent to the grand duke's farm, about eight miles from Pisa, and I proceeded to that place.

I cannot say that I derived any important information from my visit, though I witnessed a practical illustration of the adaptation of the camel to a climate more variable than the one to which we are going to transport them.

The camel has been used in Tuscany for over two hundred years, and has increased and multiplied from a few that were brought from the upper part of Egypt. If the number is limited, it is not because the animals do not breed as freely as in Egypt, but because the demand for them is limited, the grand duke only requiring a certain number for his own use, and not permitting the animal to be used outside of his own grounds, the number he has on hand being sufficient to do the work of one thousand horses.

I found, upon examination, that the camels at Pisa were very much overworked and badly cared for, being supplied with no food whatever, beyond what they could glean from among the pine barrens, and not being housed in winter, in a high latitude, (43° 30',) where they experience severe cold, and a much more trying climate than that of Texas. They are forced to carry seventeen hundred pounds, Tuscan weight, equal to twelve hundred English, and work from sunrise to sunset. With all this they look in good condition, have not deteriorated in regard to size, and would with ordinary care be much better kept than the camels of the east. Under the circumstances, it is a marvel to me how the Tuscans have succeeded in raising the camel at all. The intelligence of our countrymen and their keen perception of their own interest will, I am convinced, bring the breeding of camels to a high state of perfection.

On my return to Spezzia I found that Major Wayne had arrived a few hours before me, and we sailed next day for Naples, for the purpose of procuring money; but we found the rate of exchange so high that we gave up the idea of getting any in that quarter.

Tunis being in our route, we stopped there with the intention of taking on board a camel to keep during the cruise, for the purpose of ascertaining the manner of managing them at sea, and the amount of time they will endure confinement on shipboard, in reference to future shipments. We accordingly purchased an ordinary animal, which we regretted afterwards, as the Bey of Tunis presented Major Wayne with two good specimens; one, indeed, is a remarkably fine one. We have them now on board, and find that they give us very little trouble, very much less than a horse would. They apparently seem as comfortable as if they were on shore.

I find no reason to change any one of the arrangements I have made on board the ship. They suit admirably. Our purpose is to keep these camels on board as long as possible, study their habits and diseases, and be ready to treat those that may hereafter come under our hands. When we have fully satisfied ourselves, we can dispose of two of them, and keep the fine one. No doubt we will derive more experience from practical observation than by reading a dozen books on the subject.

The climate of Tunis is colder in winter and hotter in summer than Texas, and camels ought not to suffer by the change. We stopped in here to fill up with water, and see if we could negotiate bills of exchange on favorable terms, and sail to-morrow morning for Salonica, Smyrna, &c., &c., from whence I shall advise you.

I have the honor to remain, very respectfully, &c., &c.,
DAVID D. PORTER,
Lieutenant Commanding.

Hon. JEFFERSON DAVIS,
Secretary of War.

UNITED STATES STORESHIP SUPPLY,
Constantinople, October 5, 1855.

SIR: I have the honor to transmit herewith my quarterly account current of expenditures on account of the camel appropriation for the third quarter of 1855, and my returns of quartermaster's and ordnance stores in my charge for the same period.

My last report was dated at the Goletta, off Tunis, on the 10th of August, 1855. Since then we have visited Malta, Smyrna and Salonica, and arrived here yesterday evening. From the time of our entrance into the Archipelago we have encountered heavy head gales, causing us much delay and retarding our arrival at this place beyond the time I had calculated upon.

At Malta I took on board ten thousand dollars ($10,000) in silver, as I found that our money arrangements could be made there on better terms than elsewhere to the east of it.

At Smyrna we saw several varieties of the camel, and among them many fine specimens, but no dromedaries. From our consul, Mr. Offley, who gave us every facility for the prosecution of our inquiries, we learned that the price of the animal was at present somewhat higher than usual, owing in a measure to the general effect of the war, but particularly to the demand for the animal as a means of military transportation, the British government having recently contracted for the hiring of eight thousand of them, in addition to the numbers purchased and procured by it during the past year. As far as Mr. Offley could ascertain, the prices now ranged from forty to fifty dollars for the best females, and from seventy-five to one hundred dollars for the best males. On this head, however, as well as on others connected with our expedition, he has engaged to give us more precise information in answer to the circular sent to him by Lieutenant Porter and myself, a copy of which is herewith enclosed. This circular we have addressed to other gentlemen established in the east, and we hope to obtain by it reliable and accurate information to guide us in the discharge of our duty. The replies to it shall be forwarded to you.

At Salonica we found no camels nor dromedaries, the caravans usually visiting it having been diverted to army transportation by the demands of the war. There being no American resident at Salonica, Lieutenant Porter and myself called upon the English consul, Mr. Charles Blunt, who received us very politely, and to whom we are indebted for attentions official and personal.

The three camels taken on board at Tunis on the 9th of August are in good condition, and apparently have not suffered in health from their confinement nor from the pitching and tossing of the vessel in the gales we have gone through. One of them was taken on board much cut (by the moors) and subsequently was attacked by the itch, a disease to which this animal is said to be particularly liable. Both wounds and itch have been cured by the remedies applied in such cases to horses and cows, and he is now in better condition than when received. They consume each from eight to twelve pounds of hay and six quarts of oats per day, and drink once in three days, absorbing at the draught, on an average, (for sometimes they will not drink at all, and at others they drink excessively,) from two and a half to three buckets of water. The camel is undoubtedly a hardy animal, and the diseases it is afflicted with, especially the itch, are most frequently produced, I should say, by hard treatment, and by the filthy state of its skin, no care, by currying, brushing, or other cleaning, being taken of its hide. Patient and humble in its character, it meets with the neglect and oppression usually visited upon meekness.

Two of the hands of the vessel have been employed, at a small additional compensation, in taking care of the three we have, and the result of their attendance satisfies me that Americans will be able to manage camels not only as well, but better than Arabs, as they will do it with more humanity and with far greater intelligence. In conclusion, I will add that observation, so far, of the animal, of the country, and of the climate, confirms my opinion of the advantages to be derived from its introduction into the United States, and of the feasibility of acclimating and domesticating it there, and that the only difficulty in the experiment is that of transportation across the sea.

Very respectfully, your obedient servant,
HENRY C. WAYNE,
Major United States Army.

Hon. JEFFERSON DAVIS,
Secretary of War, Washington city.

[Circular.]

UNITED STATES SHIP "SUPPLY," 1855.

SIR: In executing the duty with which we have been charged by the President of the United States, under a recent act of Congress providing for the introduction of the camel into our country, we deem it important, to the thorough fulfilment of the commission, to obtain, as comprehensively and as accurately as we can, all the information possible as to the different varieties of the animal, their homes, their relative powers of endurance and burden, the climates and soils to which they are subjected, their capabilities of withstanding changes of temperature, &c., &c.

For this purpose we take the liberty of addressing to you the following questions, to which we respectfully invite your attention, requesting such answers as your own knowledge of the subject, and the means of information within your reach, will enable you to furnish to us:

1. How many varieties of the camel are known in ———, and from what parts of ——— or ——— do they respectively come; in what do the varieties differ essentially; what are their different sizes and weights, and how are they named?

2. What are the relative powers of these different varieties as to burden (in pounds weight;) how many days consecutively can they travel with these burdens; what distance per day, (in miles,) and how many hours, without easing them of their packs?

3. What climates, in respect to heat and cold and changes of temperature, are they subjected to in their journeys, and over what kind of country (mountainous, broken, or level) and soils (sandy, gravelly, stony, or rocky) do they travel?

4. What effect do long journeys have upon their feet, especially in traversing rocky ground?

5. How often are camels fed, and what is their food; how often are they watered; are they stabled at all in any seasons of the year, and, in general, how are they treated?

6. What precautions are taken on a journey in loading and unloading camels, and what precautions (if any) to prevent them from falling when travelling in a slippery soil?

7. When does the camel rut; what is the treatment when rutting, and how is copulation managed; is sterility common; are there any males and females reserved expressly for breeding, and, on that account, not put to labor; how soon, after birth, is the mother put to labor?

8. What is the treatment of the calves at birth, and afterwards, and how long are they allowed to remain with the mother; at what age are they accustomed to burdens, and how are they trained to carry them; how many years are they capable of performing labor?

9. What are the diseases to which camels are liable, and what the remedies; what plants are hurtful to them?

10. What are the prices of males, of females, and of females with young nursing by the side (the best?)

11. What varieties known in —— are particularly preferred, and for what reason?

12. Is the dromedary, or swift camel, known in —— as well as the camel of burden; if so, what is its speed and endurance; is it regarded as the same or a different species of camel, and does its treatment differ (if so, in what) from that of the camel of burden?

13. Is the "fighting camel" known in ——; if so, what are its peculiarities, and is it used for burden, or only kept for breeding?

14. Any other information not included in the answers to these questions, and that you may think advantageous.

Very respectfully, your obedient servants,
HENRY C. WAYNE,
Major United States Army.
DAVID D. PORTER,
Lieut. United States Navy.

To —— ——.

UNITED STATES SHIP "SUPPLY,"
Constantinople, October 11, 1855.

SIR: Enclosed is the duplicate of a letter that I forwarded to you on the 6th inst., with the papers referred to in it, by a vessel bound to Boston, the postage upon the package being too high to warrant its transmittal by mail. Since its date we have been making inquiries as to the feasibility of visiting Persia, as I had particularly desired when leaving the United States; but I regret to say that so far the information we have received is against the attempt, on account of the disturbed state of the country from the war in part, but especially on account of the lateness of the season, the snows commencing about the latter part of this month, and blocking up the roads so as to render them impassable until the month of April. We might reach Teheran, but the difficulty, it is said, will be to return. To-day, however, we are to have an interview with the Persian ambassador, accompanied by our secretary of legation, Mr. Brown, in relation to the journey, and to procure facilities for the prosecution of our duties, should we, upon further inquiry, determine to make it. To-morrow we leave for Balaklava, where we are informed that camels, Bactrian and Arabian, are in use by the allies for both burden and draught.

The Crimea is the only place where we shall have an opportunity of seeing the Bactrian camel, and perhaps of procuring a stallion, should we upon observation think it worth while to carry one home, for the purpose of crossing upon the Arabian female, as is done in Persia, to the improvement of the stock for burdens.

Here there are, it may be said, no camels, the caravans being diverted from trade by the war; but yesterday we heard of the arrival of a number of dromedaries for the French army, and saddled for riding one or more men. Inquiries as to the truth of the report, and if true, the place where they may be seen, are now being made by Mr. Heap.

Should we be forced to abandon our trip to Persia, we shall still have open to us Smyrna and the adjacent country, where, I am already satisfied, we can procure an excellent stock of the burden camel. For the dromedary, we must visit Beirout or Cairo.

Very respectfully, your obedient servant,

HENRY C. WAYNE,
Major U. S. Army.

Hon. JEFF'N DAVIS,
Secretary of War, Washington city.

CONSTANTINOPLE, *October* 31, 1855.

SIR: In accordance with my report of the 11th of October, Lieutenant Porter and myself left this place for Balaklava the next day, the 12th, in the British transport steamer, the Imperador, and landed in the Crimea on the 17th. Calling on Major Ross, the deputy quartermaster general at Balaklava, and, further to the front, on General Simpson, the commander of the British forces, we received from these gentlemen kind welcome, and every facility for the prosecution of our duty was promptly afforded to us. I was further fortunate in receiving an introduction to Colonel McMurdo, in charge, under the quartermaster general (General Eyre) of the land transport service in the Crimea, and who, as quartermaster general to General Napier in the expedition against Sinde, had used camels extensively for military purposes. He gave me much interesting information in relation to the military use of the camel, and from General Simpson also, who had served in the same expedition under General Napier, we had additional accounts of the value of the animal, and of the favorable opinion entertained of it by the army, for the services it was capable of rendering. The engagements of Colonel McMurdo were such that I could occupy but little of his time, and in consequence obtained from him only a few material facts without going into details. My thanks are due to him for the moments he devoted to me, pressed as he was with the many and various duties of his position.

We found in the Crimea both the Bactrian or two humped camel, and the Arabian or one humped; but the latter alone seemed to be used for the purposes of military transportation. The former were found in the Crimea at the commencement of the war; the latter were carried there since, from Asia Minor. The former were but little thought of; the latter were highly esteemed; the only objections to them we heard of being the room they occupied in the narrow streets, and their frightening the horses. The two are very distinct species of the same genus, differing from each other as much, I should say, as the buffalo of our western prairies does from the common ox. Doubly humped, the Bactrian is a strongly built, powerful animal, standing not quite so high as the Arabian, of coarser and more shaggy coat, slower in motion, but capable of carrying immense burdens. From the formation of its back (its two humps) there is a difficulty in adjusting to it a pack-saddle, and without one there is always more or less perplexity in loading and securing the load. This I rather think is the principal source of objection to its use, though I believe the opinion advanced to us to be correct, that it is not as serviceable an animal as the Arabian. Its use in the Crimea before the war we understood to be chiefly for draught, and on one occasion we saw two yoked to a Tartar wagon as oxen are, but guided by rope reins. The result of our examination determined us not to procure one, as it would only complicate our experiment without producing such results as we anticipate from the Arabian stock. At some future day, should the camel become domesticated with us, it may then be worth while to import a few males for crossing upon the Arabian females, as it is said is done with advantage in Persia; the issue always taking after the mother, that is being one humped. Sketches of the Bactrian camel were made by Mr. Heap, which will convey very clear ideas of the animal and of its difference from the Arabian.

Colonel McMurdo informed me that in the expedition againts Sinde he had in service about twenty-five thousand camels, and that from his experience he esteemed them highly; so much so, that he had then at Sinope three thousand of them, in addition to the few now in use in the Crimea, in readiness for the campaign next spring.

The loads they will carry depend much, he said, upon the service in which they are employed, rapid movements naturally requiring light burdens; but their average loads, under favorable circumstances, he stated to be about six hundred pounds, and these they will carry easily, without pushing, twenty-five or thirty miles a day. He mentioned the interesting fact, which I do not remember to have heard before, that during the expedition against Sinde, General Napier organized a most efficient corps of one thousand men, mounted upon five hundred dromedaries, two men to each dromedary, the men sitting back to back, one facing the head the other the tail, and both armed with rifles and sabres. The man facing the head was the animal's groom and driver, and the manner of using the corps was as follows: Upon arriving at the scene of operations the dromedaries were made to kneel in square, under the charge of their five hundred drivers, forming as it were a base of operations from which the other five hundred operated as infantry. As the advanced body moved, the square or squares, if more than one was formed, if required, were also moved; and in case of extremity, the square offered a cover under which the one thousand men could find comparative shelter behind the animals, who were prevented from rising by a hobble on the foreleg, and use their rifles most effectively. This corps, Colonel McMurdo informed me, could be readily marched seventy miles in any direction in twelve hours, ($5\frac{5}{6}$ miles per hour,) and rendered throughout the campaign most efficient service.

General Simpson stated that in the same campaign he found the camel so serviceable that he procured five or six for his personal use, and that with them he frequently went seventy miles between sunset and sunrise. To a direct question by Major Delafield, (whom we met at the Crimea,) whether he would not have preferred the best English horses to camels, could he have obtained them, the general answered, No! that he would have preferred the camel, as, packing his baggage upon them in light loads, he could move more quickly and continuously.

In relation to our visiting Persia, the inquiries we have made lead us to the conclusion that, though we might readily get there, our return, owing to the blocking up of the roads by snow, would be impossible until next spring. As this would detain us much beyond the time fixed for our return to the United States, and unnecessarily delay the experiment we are engaged in, we have reluctantly abandoned the journey, though we desired much to see the varieties of the Persian camel, and particularly the zembourek or dromedary artillery. A journey into Persia, with the intention of returning immediately, must be commenced, we find, about May. Our course from this will be, I think, to Syria or Egypt for dromedaries, and then back to Smyrna for burden camels, in the expectation of commencing our return home some time in February.

The inquiries in relation to dromedaries for the French army, reported in my letter of the 11th of October, produced no result.

Very respectfully, your obedient servant,
HENRY C. WAYNE,
Major United States Army.

Hon. JEFFERSON DAVIS,
Secretary of War, Washington city.

UNITED STATES SHIP "SUPPLY,"
Alexandria, December 12, 1855.

SIR: As Major Wayne has so frequently kept you informed of our movements, I have not deemed it necessary to trouble you with my communications. Major Wayne has not, I believe, written to you from this place, and I take advantage of the sailing of the English mail steamer to advise you of what we are about.

Since my last letter we have gone over a good deal of ground where camels are to be found in their best condition, and ample opportunities have been afforded Major Wayne to make his report complete in relation to the future importation of the animals into our country.

As to the treatment of camels and their peculiar habits, I believe we will be as perfectly acquainted with them as it is possible to be.

The camels we took on board at Tunis underwent a long and fair trial; one of them (the only good one) has now been on board "one hundred and twenty days," is in much better order than the day I took him in charge, has never been sick for one moment, nor received a hurt of any kind, although we have been at times exposed to very rough weather. The only food I have allowed him to have has been eight pounds of hay a day, and he grows too large on that.

The experiments I have made with those I have had on board encourage me greatly to hope that I shall have little or no trouble with a number; the only difficulty I see at all in importing camels into the

PURCHASE OF CAMELS FOR MILITARY PURPOSES. 33

United States is the one of transportation, and I hope that the experience we will have gained will set that matter at rest.

I landed two of the camels at Constantinople, one that we bought at Tunis to try experiments with, and one of those the "Bey" of Tunis presented. The latter was rather an ordinary specimen, not worth taking to the United States. I could not very well refuse to take it, as it was presented; but should not have been justified in transporting it to the United States in lieu of a better camel; it was sick when it came on board, and had the itch; but it was cured perfectly, and improved in size, and stood a confinement in the ship of one hundred days, without the least symptom of suffering. While I was absent in the Crimea, the itch broke out on it slightly, and as at that time I anticipated taking on board "four picked camels," (a present from the sultan,) I thought it most prudent to get him out of the ship, so as to run no risk in spreading the disease.

The one we purchased, having no further use for, was also disposed of to the best advantage.

I regret to say I had to sail from Constantinople without taking with me the four camels offered by the sultan. When I went to that port, it was with the expectation of wintering there with the ship, while Major Wayne pursued his journey into Persia; it was not until ten days before we left Constantinople that our destination was changed; circumstances rendering it impracticable to carry out your instructions. After our return from the Crimea, the camels were offered through our dragoman, Mr. Brown, who, not being aware we intended leaving Constantinople, did not advise the Turkish government that we were bound to other places. In the meantime the camels had been sent for into Asia, where it was intended to procure the best from one of the sultan's farms; but as they were not brought over in time, I had to sail without them. The Turkish government authorized Mr. Brown to get four of the best that could be procured, but as there was no particular object in taking any that we were not sure of being without disease, and Major Wayne not thinking favorably of the proposition, I sailed without them.

It would not be desirable to take on board any camels brought up in or about a city, as they are almost always diseased, or crippled; therefore, I do not think we have lost anything by not taking the last four camels that were offered.

My wish was to do nothing that might make the Turkish government suppose their courtesy unacceptable, as I believe they desired to show their good will towards the government of the United States, and would have added to our collection four of the finest camels in Asia, had time and circumstances permitted.

The impracticability of going to Persia by the way of Erzeroom being decided on, I proposed to Major Wayne to go to Alexandria, for the purpose of looking at the trained dromedaries. It is from Arabia that the Persians yearly receive their fine dromedaries, which they use for military purposes, and Alexandria is the point from whence that country and the southern part of Persia can be most easily reached. From Alexandria to the head of the Persian gulf is about eight hundred miles, and it is south of that, in the country of Oman, where the dromedary is procured; though much used in Persia, the best are to be procured in Arabia, and it is found that even in the northern parts of Persia, where it is cold, that the dromedary soon becomes acclimated. Cold is the weather in which camels thrive, and not hot, as is erroneously supposed.

Major Wayne has left, in company with Mr. Heap, for Cairo, where he intends putting himself in communication with Mr. De Leon, the United States consul, and be governed by the information he may get from him. I did not join him in the expedition, as there was no particular object in my going; and, as the winter is coming on, I thought it advisable to stay and look out for my ship. I would not be justified in leaving her in charge of any one under present circumstances.

It is Major Wayne's intention, I believe, to procure ten dromedaries of the swift kind, if the pacha will permit them to be taken out of the country. There is at present an express prohibition against the exportation of any animal without government permission. I trust he may procure animals that have been bred in the country; those brought up in and about the city would be worthless to export. I feel that I should have no difficulty in carrying over safely any number of good camels.

Our trip to the Crimea was an interesting one in many respects, but particularly in enabling us to see the "Bactrian camel," the only place where we could possibly have seen it. They are magnificent looking creatures, and far superior in size and appearance to the one-humped camel, though I do not think them so well adapted to hard work. Those we saw were in fine condition, even after having passed through a hard winter, living as best they might, and exposed out of doors to all sorts of weather. Their humps had, in some instances been mashed down, owing to improper loading, but it did not seem to impair their efficiency. I saw them working in a cart and otherwise, but not in such great numbers as the other camel, which was evidently much more rapid in its motions, but not so strong.

There will be little or no difficulty in finding good camels hereafter. All of Asia Minor, as far south as 35 degrees of latitude, and as far east as 40 degrees of longitude, abounds with them, and can be easily reached. No better place than Smyrna can be found for shipping them, and the best can be procured at a journey of seven or eight days from that place.

There are great differences in the animal, as you will see by the different sketches of them that have been taken. Their appearance depends very much on how they are treated. The Egyptians, the most inconsiderate and cruel camel-masters in the world, have the most wretched looking beasts; while the Turk, more humane in his disposition, keeps his flock in fine order. In our country they would be of such value to any farmer south of thirty-six degrees that they would be fostered with the greatest care. A horse is, in the United States, considered a valuable animal, but he will, in point of worth for labor, in no way compare with a camel, and I hope to see the day when every southern planter will be using the animal extensively. It will be an easy matter at any time for farmers to import a pair of them from Smyrna. The whole cost will not be more than three hundred dollars each.

It is my desire to sail from here as soon as possible, so that we may have plenty of time to pick our camels in the interior of Smyrna, and sail for the United States on the first of March, by which time the rutting season will be over.

It would be impossible to foresee what circumstances may detain Major Wayne, or what difficulties he may have to contend with in procuring the dromedaries. I hope, however, to be able to land the camels in Texas on the sixth of May.

I have the honor to be, very respectfully,
DAVID D. PORTER,
Lieutenant United States Navy.

Hon. JEFFERSON DAVIS,
Secretary of War, Washington.

CAIRO, EGYPT, *December* 28, 1855.

SIR: My last report was from Constantinople, and dated October 31st. Within a few days after our return from the Crimea the itch reappeared upon the camel that we thought we had cured, and entertaining apprehensions that it had been communicated to the animal next to it, Lieut. Porter and myself determined to sell them both, for fear that the disease might be communicated to the third, and that the hold might, moreover, become contaminated and convey it to the others we were to procure. We accordingly landed them and sent them to our consul, Mr. J. P. Brown, who kindly offered to dispose of them for us. Their sale produced one thousand and ninety-six piasters, equal to about forty-four dollars.

Leaving Constantinople on 21st November for Alexandria, Egypt, where we designed procuring ten dromedaries and four camels of burden, we arrived at the latter port in the afternoon of the 29th November. Learning that the United States consul general was in Cairo, but daily expected in Alexandria, I delayed my departure into the interior in the hope of seeing and advising with him in relation to our purpose. The arrival of Commodore Breeze, however, on the 4th instant, (whom Mr. De Leon expected,) and his departure for Cairo on the 7th, determined me to accompany him, as it insured my meeting the consul general.

The harbor of Alexandria, where our ship lay, being a little exposed, Lieut. Porter thought it to be his duty to remain on board. Accompanied, therefore, only by Mr. Heap, I arrived in Cairo on the morning of the 8th December, and was politely received by the consul general, who, in the intervals of his engagements, introduced me to two or three gentlemen, as able to furnish me with useful information. From them I learned that good dromedaries could only be obtained in the deserts, at a distances of from five to eight hundred miles; but that as many as I wanted could, no doubt, be procured in and around

Cairo. The journeys to the points indicated in the deserts by these gentlemen, required, to go and return, from thirty-five to forty days at least, independently of the time necessary for preparation and purchase. This being more time than we could, at present, spare, as it would materially delay our return to the United States, besides the expense for so small a number as we required, I determined to procure such riding camels about Cairo and its neighborhood as I could obtain. The viceroy was also in Upper Egypt, and it was necessary to await his return, daily expected, for permission to export such animals as might be procured. In the meantime, as neither the consul general nor vice consul at Cairo anticipated any difficulty about the exportation, Mr. Heap and myself employed ourselves in looking up burden camels and dromedaries, and succeeded in purchasing five dromedaries, and in making arrangements for the purchase of five more, and nine burden camels, should we, on reflection, determine to take so many of the latter with us; they being so fine in size and strength as to make us hesitate between them and those of Smyrna, whence we had previously thought to draw our principal supply of burden camels.

On the 13th December the consul general accompanied Commodore Breeze to Alexandria, committing me to the care of the vice consul, Mr. C. Kahil. The attention and exertions of Mr. Kahil in furthering our object have been most zealous and active, and I beg leave to present him most favorably to your notice.

The viceroy having returned to Cairo on the 16th December, I requested an interview with the minister of finance and confidential secretary, Zoulfokhar Pacha, to make known to him the purpose of my visit to Egypt, and to request permission to export such animals as I might purchase. On the 22d, the visit was paid in company with Mr. Heap and our vice consul, when the vice consul explained the purpose of my visit, and I preferred my request in the name of our government. The minister replied frankly that there would be difficulty in the matter, as the viceroy objected to the exportation of any animals whatever, and if granted in this case it might be used against him by the consuls of other nations as a precedent for demands of a similar nature. He promised, however, to use his best exertions to secure the fulfilment of our wishes.

The enclosed correspondence, numbered from 1 to 4, will inform you of the result of my application, and of my reason for making it through our vice consul instead of our consul general. It is somewhat of a disappointment to me; but still, four dromedaries landed safely in the United States will enable me to commence so much of the experiment as relates to expresses, to be extended, I hope, by a larger importation next year through Jaffa or Beirout, where there are no restrictions upon exportation, but where we cannot go at this season as they are both open roadsteads affording no secure anchorage.

To-morrow I shall send down under trusty men the five dromedaries I have purchased, hoping to procure permission to carry out the fifth, and on the next day, the 30th, I shall return to Alexandria. Thence, as soon as the dromedaries are on board, we shall sail for Smyrna, to carry out our original plan, and from that place for the United States, touching at the Canary islands. I trust we shall be able to get off from Smyrna about the 15th February or 1st March, and that we shall land at Indianola about the middle of May. Will you give the necessary instructions for the lightering and landing of the animals about that time. The "Fashion," if still in service, seems to me to be adapted to this duty. From Smyrna I shall, if necessary, write more frequently, and give timely notice of the day we will probably leave it, that the arrangements at Indianola may be in readiness for our arrival.

Very respectfully, your obedient servant,
HENRY C. WAYNE,
Major United States Army.

Hon. JEFFERSON DAVIS,
Secretary of War, Washington.

[Translation.]

CONSULATE OF THE UNITED STATES OF AMERICA IN CAIRO,
Cairo, December 24, 1855.

MAJOR: After the conversation we had yesterday with H. E. Zoulfokhar Pacha, minister of finance and confidential secretary of his highness the viceroy, in regard to the permit necessary for the exportation of twenty camels and dromedaries desired by our government, I was informed that there were great difficulties presented to the granting of the permission requested, because there was no precedent for a like concession, and it was deemed desirable not to establish one for the consuls of other nations. In consequence, I thought it my duty to forward your purpose by a formal despatch; and for its further security to follow it up by a personal interview with H. E., the viceroy himself being too much engaged to be seen.

H. E. Zoulfokhar Pacha, fully impressed with the propriety of favoring my request, promised me to lay before the viceroy my despatch and to report to him the substance of our interview, with the assurance that he would second our wishes to the best of his ability. Notwithstanding all this, my dear major, I am truly sorry that the result has not equalled our expectations, an order that I have just received from his highness, with a letter from H. E., authorizing the exportation of two camels only. In the order are stated the motives of the viceroy's action, and that it is only out of regard to our government that even this small concession has been made.

I enclose you herewith, major, the order in question, in the original; and translations of my despatch and of H. E.'s reply, and beg you to accept the assurances of my most distinguished consideration.

Your obedient servant,
C. KAHIL,
*United States Vice Consul in charge of the
United States Consulate at Cairo.*

Major HENRY C. WAYNE,
United States Army, Cairo, &c., &c., &c.

Translation (into French from Arabic, H. C. W.,) of the despatch addressed December 23, 1855, (13 Rabik Akar, 1272) by C. Kahil, vice consul in charge of the consulate of the United States at Cairo, to H. E. Zoulfokhar Pacha, minister of finance and confidential secretary to his highness the viceroy of Egypt.

Excellency: When I had the honor of visiting you yesterday in company with Major Wayne, a distinguished officer of our army, and Mr. Heap, I communicated to you the mission with which these gentlemen were charged, that of having been expressly commissioned by the government of the republic of the United States to procure specimens of camels and dromedaries of different kinds, and from different climates, for the purpose of testing by experiment which of them could most readily be acclimated in the United States; and requested, through the intercession of your excellency, an order from the viceroy to the governor of Alexandria to permit the embarkation upon the vessel-of-war, expressly sent for the purpose, the animals, to the number of twenty, that might be purchased. Your excellency was kind enough to promise me to solicit the permission requested from his highness.

It is, then, with confidence that, under the necessity of the case, I request your kind and friendly influence to obtain, as soon as possible, the permission requested. The vessel-of-war has been now some time anchored in the harbor of Alexandria, awaiting the animals; and persuaded of receiving an answer to my request, in accordance with the liberality with which his highness uniformly treats his friends, the foreign governments, I again press my request upon you, presenting to his highness, in advance, my own personal acknowledgments, and assuring him that the American government will appreciate highly the facilities he may give upon this occasion, and never forget them, granted, as they will be, for an object which has so much merited its attention as to induce it to send out for it a special commission.

I take this opportunity to offer to his highness my best wishes.

C. KAHIL,
*United States Vice Consul, in charge of the
United States Consulate at Cairo.*

Translation from the Arabic of the reply addressed, on the 14th Rabik Akar, 1272, (24th December, 1855,) registered the 16th, by his excellency Zoulfokhar Pacha, minister of finance and confidential secretary to the viceroy of Egypt, to C. Kahil, vice consul, in charge of the consulate of the United States at Cairo.

To our distinguished friend the American consul at Cairo:

In accordance with the communication that you were so kind as to address to me on the 13th Rabik Akar, (23d December, 1855,) in which you ask for the exportation of twenty camels, required by the American government, your request was laid before his highness the viceroy, who replies as follows: That it is contrary to the custom of the country to permit the exportation of animals to foreign countries, but that, out of regard to the American government, he gives his permission for the purchase of two camels, only, and that the necessary instructions have been given to the governor of Alexandria to permit their exportation.

With this communication, sir, I have the honor to enclose the order for carrying out his highness' will.

THE MINISTER OF FINANCE.

Translation from the Arabic of the order enclosed.

To his excellency the governor of Alexandria:

The American consul at Cairo has addressed to me a despatch, dated 13th Rabik Akar, 1272, (23d December, 1855,) requesting permission to export twenty camels, intended for the American government. This request having been laid before the viceroy, he announced that it has never been the custom of the country to permit the exportation of camels to foreign countries, but that, out of high regard for the government in question, he permits the exportation of two camels, only. In conformity with this announcement of his highness, the requisite information has been communicated to the American consul, and this present writing is addressed to you that the necessary instructions and facilities for the exportation of the two camels, above mentioned, may be given by you in obedience to the will of his highness.

THE MINISTER OF FINANCE.

CAIRO, EGYPT, *December* 24, 1855.

SIR: I have the honor to acknowledge the receipt of your communication of this date, from which I learn that his highness, the viceroy, in answer to my application of the 22d instant for authority to export for the United States government, and under its orders, *twenty* camels, has been so kind as to grant permission for the exportation of *two* only.

I am much obliged to his highness for this mark of his good will towards the government of the United States, and although far from desiring to trespass upon his kindness, I feel myself nevertheless constrained by my duty to submit for his further consideration the following statements:

1st. That my mission is of a scientific character, its purpose being to introduce upon the continent of America a new domestic animal, that may prove to be of great usefulness.

2d. That the voyage hence to America is long and tedious, and consequently painful and dangerous to these animals, creating the risk of losing one or both of them, in which event the purpose of the mission would, as far as the camel of Egypt is concerned, be completely frustrated.

The lively interest of the President of the republic, and of the nation at large in this experiment, induced the equipping and sending out a vessel-of-war expressly for the transportation of such animals as might be procured to the United States; and I am sure the enlightened liberality of his highness will not permit, as far as it depends upon himself, the failure of so important an enterprise. I therefore request you, sir, to renew my application to his highness, to extend his order for the exportation to six, or at least four camels, males and females, that the arrival in the United States of at least two living animals may be assured. I further beg your earliest attention to this matter, as the vessel for their reception is now waiting in the harbor of Alexandria, and to assure his highness that the government of the United States will view the act on his part as one of useful friendship.

Begging you to accept, sir, the assurances of my high consideration, I am your obedient servant,

HENRY C. WAYNE,
Major U. S. Army.

C. KAHIL, Esq.,
  Vice consul of the United States,
    in charge of United States consulate, at Cairo.

CAIRO, *December 25, 1855*

MAJOR: Upon the receipt of the request you did me the honor to address to me yesterday, I felt it my duty to forward it immediately to the viceroy, accompanied by a despatch from myself, urging in the strongest manner the extending of the permission to export to six or four camels; and I have the satisfaction of informing you that I have just obtained the consent of his highness to the exportation of the latter number.

I enclose herewith the order to the governor of Alexandria, in the original, this moment received from the viceroy, and as it is therein suggested, (probably by way of precaution,) that a communication from me will be expected when the exportation is made, I enclose also a letter from myself to the same governor. At the same time I send also translations of my despatch and of the reply of H. E. Zoulfokhar Pacha, minister of finance and confidential secretary, as concluding our correspondence in relation to this matter.

Permit me, major, to embrace this opportunity to renew to you the assurances of high consideration with which I sign myself your very humble servant,

C. KAHIL,
  Vice consul United States, in charge
    United States consulate in Cairo.

CONSULATE OF THE UNITED STATES OF AMERICA, *Cairo.*

Translation of the despatch addressed 24th December, 1855, (14 Rabik Akar, 1272,) by C. Kahil, vice consul, in charge of the consulate of the United States, in Cairo, to H. E. Zoulfokhar Pacha, minister of finance and confidential secretary to his highness the viceroy of Egypt.

EXCELLENCY: I received yesterday the communication you did me the honor to address me, with the order in relation to the authority for the exportation of two of the camels required by the government of the republic of the United States. Whilst I hasten to express to his highness, my grateful acknowledgements for the mark of friendly feeling that he has on this occasion exhibited to my government, I must again prefer to his highness another request in relation to it, that has just been sent to me to-day by Major Wayne.

In discharging this important duty by the transmittal herewith of the major's letter, accompanied by this despatch to be laid before the viceroy through the friendly interposition of your excellency, I cannot refrain from soliciting most earnestly, in the persuasion that a just consideration of the circumstances stated in the major's letter, viz: the possible death of one or both of the camels in so long, tedious and painful a voyage, (which would defeat the purpose of my government and all its efforts relative to it,) that his highness will be kindly disposed to obviate the possibility of this occurrence by extending his permit to export to six or four camels.

By this concession, so in accordance with the superior mind that characterizes the viceroy, he will not only contribute to the success of an expedition so interesting to the republic, but he will have contributed also the means of guarding against the defeat of the purposes, efforts and intentions of the American government in this respect. As my solicitations are directed to a purpose purely scientific and of public utility, and consequently, completely in harmony with the protecting interest the viceroy has uniformly accorded to the progress of science, it is with the most perfect confidence that I expect a favorable reply to my request, and which will be, indeed, an effective proof of the friendship of his highness for my government.

C. KAHIL,
Vice consul, in charge of the U. S. consulate in Cairo.

Translation of the reply addressed on the 15th, and registered on the 16th Rabik Akar, 1272, (25th December, 1855,) by his excellency Zoulfokhar Pacha, to C. Kahil, vice consul, in charge of the consulate of the United States of America at Cairo.

To our cherished and distingushed friend the consul for America:

Conformably to your wishes as expressed in your despatch, dated 15th Rabik Akar, 1272, permission is granted to export two male camels and two females. Instructions in accordance herewith have been given to the governor of Alexandria.

THE MINISTER OF FINANCE.

Translation from the Arabic of the order enclosed.

To his excellency the Governor of Alexandria:

You have been written to before in regard to the exportation of two camels by the American consul for the American government. To-day the aforesaid consul desires that the authority be extended to export four. This request having been laid before his highness, he grants it. In consequence, this present writing is sent to you in order that when the four camels, males and females, shall be presented to you in the name of the aforementioned consul with a letter from himself, their exportation will be permitted, as the consul has been this day informed.

THE MINISTER OF FINANCE.

P. S.—These four camels include the two for which permission has been already granted.

CAIRO, *December* 27, 1855.

SIR: I have the honor to acknowledge the receipt yesterday of your note of the 25th instant, informing me that his highness the viceroy, had consented, in answer to my application of the 24th December, to the exportation of four camels, males and females.

This result is gratifying, as I have now some hope of introducing the dromedary into America; and I thank you sincerely for your exertions in carrying out the wishes of our government as made known to you through me. It will give me great pleasure to convey to the Secretary of War copies of your correspondence in relation to the matter, and to represent to him the zeal and activity with which you have assisted me throughout our business, and the vigorous manner in which you pushed with the viceroy the matter of exportation.

I regret the political reasons that have so materially interfered with my original plan, and which I was led in no manner to anticipate; but the number conceded, if safely transported to the United States, will enable me to a certain extent, limited it is true, to carry out the Secretary's views.

I also acknowledge the receipt of the order of the viceroy to the governor of Alexandria, with a letter from yourself to the governor, apparently required by the order, and copies of your despatch and of the minister's reply, enclosed in your note. Thanking you again, my dear sir, for your personal and official exertions in behalf of my mission, and trusting that the government of the United States will long continue in its service one so competent and worthy to represent its interests,

I am, with high consideration, your obedient servant,

HENRY C. WAYNE,
Major United States Army.

C. KAHIL, Esq.,
   Vice Consul, in charge of U. S. Consulate at Cairo.

ALEXANDRIA, *December* 25, 1855.

DEAR SIR: I learn that the viceroy is coming down here on Thursday, I therefore defer my visit to Cairo, as it is necessary to get his permission to export the dromedaries.

If you wish a personal interview with him, come down and I will present you, or if you prefer my obtaining the permit and then joining you at Cairo, I will do whichever is most agreeable to you. Either come down on receipt of this letter, or let me know your wishes. I will await your decision.

Yours, truly,

EDWIN DeLEON.

Major H. C. WAYNE, *Cairo*.

CAIRO, *December* 27, 1856.

MY DEAR SIR: I received this morning your note of the 25th instant, in relation to the viceroy's permit for the exportation of our dromedaries.

By this time you will no doubt have learned that I have already applied for the necessary authority to export, and that the pasha declines permitting me to carry out more than four animals, males and females. I requested authority to export twenty.

It would have given me great pleasure to have had your personal and official influence in this matter, and it was not until Mr. Heap's arrival from Alexandria, on the 20th instant, with the information that your engagements there were such as to render your return to Cairo uncertain, that I felt myself compelled to act through our vice consul here, Mr. Kahil, as time was pressing, it being the anxious desire of the Secretary of War, and also my own, that the practical demonstration of the experiment should be commenced in the United States at as early a day as possible, by the return of the first ship load of animals.

To-morrow I hope to send down five dromedaries that I purchased, under the impression that there would be no difficulty in their exportation, and on my return to Alexandria, I shall be very glad to have your assistance in getting the fifth included in the viceroy's permit. I say "*on my return to Alexandria,*" as in any action you may take in the matter, it will be necessary for you to be advised of the grounds on which the viceroy declined to comply with my request.

I shall endeavor to leave this by the steamer of the 30th December, after giving my dromedaries a couple of day's start.

Very truly, yours,

HENRY C. WAYNE,
United States Army.

EDWIN DE LEON, Esq.
United States Consul General, Alexandria.

ALEXANDRIA, EGYPT, *January* 3, 1856.

SIR: I returned to this place from Cairo, on the 30th ultimo, after having sent off, the day before, the five dromedaries I had purchased, and which arrived here yesterday.

On the 31st December, I learned that a third application had been made to the viceroy on the 30th December, by the consul general, who had succeeded in obtaining permission to export ten camels. Unfortunately this concession comes too late to be of benefit to us, as the time fixed for our departure for Smyrna is at hand, and will not admit of my return to Cairo, and looking up animals again. And, indeed, it is, after all, a matter of little consequence, for the dromedaries I have will enable us to show the riding qualities of the animal to our people, and to commence testing its adaptation to the express service, to be extended next year, as I have before said, in my letter of the 28th ultimo, by an importation of dromedaries exclusively. I was somewhat disappointed at first, I confess, by my want of success in procuring permission to export the full number of animals, twenty that I had asked for, but upon reflection, I think that as it has turned out, it is, perhaps, better than if my request had been granted; for attracted by the size, strength, and fine appearance of the Egyptian camel, I might have, in a measure, jeoparded our experiment by taking from Egypt a larger number than that at first fixed upon, and which would not have been so well adapted to the more rugged climate of Texas, as those from Asia Minor.

Yesterday, at Mr. De Leon's request, I gave him two Minie rifles, as he said he had promised them to the viceroy on the 30th ultimo. To make the gift complete, I added a bullet-mould and a swedge.

As soon as the dromedaries are on board, Lieutenant Porter will take the first fair wind for Smyrna, where I have sent Mr. Heap in advance of us, to make arrangements for procuring camels, as I find that the presence of the vessel, or of Lieutenant Porter or myself, who are now well known to be connected with the enterprise, materially interferes with our selection and purchases, by exciting speculation among a certain class of men resident in all the towns of the east.

We have collected a good deal of positive information in regard to the camel, which will be of practical use to our people, should the experiment be so successful (as I fully anticipate) as to induce the importation of the animal on private account; and we are now about to commence its first difficulty, that of transportation.

Our return to the United States shall be as soon as we can effect it, and I think I may repeat that we shall be off Indianola, early in May, where I hope to find everything ready for lightering and landing the animals. I shall write you now more frequently, advising you of our progress, until the day of our departure for home.

Very respectfully, your obedient servant,

HENRY C. WAYNE,
Major United States Army.

Hon. JEFFERSON DAVIS,
Secretary of War, Washington.

SMYRNA, *January* 31, 1856.

SIR: In my letter of the 3d instant I stated that we would leave Alexandria for Smyrna as soon as the dromedaries bought in Cairo should be embarked. Our departure, however, was subsequently delayed, at the request of our consul general, to receive six dromedaries presented by the viceroy of Egypt, through him, to our government in furtherance of its experiment. The animals were received on board on the afternoon of the 21st of January, and on the succeeding morning (the 22d) we sailed for this place, where we arrived yesterday morning.

The dromedaries presented by the viceroy are all of the common stock, but they seem to be young, sound and healthy. Their riding qualities we had not an opportunity of testing.

Two of those purchased by me in Cairo having, unfortunately, exhibited evidences of the itch after their arrival in Alexandria, though but slightly, I determined to part with them rather than run the risk of contaminating the other animals and of conveying so loathsome a disease with them to our country. We left Alexandria, then, with nine dromedaries and the Tunis camel—in all, ten animals. Of the dromedaries, two of those I bought in Cairo are of fine blood; one a female from Muscat, the other a male from Sennaar. Both are of good descent, and are reputed to be remarkable for speed and endurance. The other seven are of common stock, and are said to have come: one (bought at Cairo) from Mount Sinai, the remaining six (presented by the viceroy) from Siout, up the Nile.

I also engaged the services of three Arabs to accompany me to America, and to serve with the camels for one year. These, with four others (Americans) hired for the purpose, will attend to the animals under the direction immediately of wagon and forage master Albert Ray, well known to the army during and subsequent to the war with Mexico, and who, upon application to me before I left Washington, enlisted with Lieutenant Porter expressly for the purpose. To his particular knowledge of horses and general acquaintance with animals, their habits, and diseases, he has, during the voyage, added some useful information about the camel, acquired by observation and care of those we have had on board, and from the books I have treating of them.

Mr. Heap, I find, has been very active in the duty here that I assigned to him, and has procured four Arabian males, one cross of the Bactrian upon the Arabian, fifteen females, and a fine Bactrian that accidentally came into this part of the country. The purchase of this last was not contemplated in my instructions to him, but I approve it, as it will enable us to carry to America one of that species without difficulty, though it will a little complicate the experiment, not, however, to any very objectionable degree.

The requisite number of animals is now completed, and as soon as the pack-saddles and covers for the animals are finished, which will require perhaps a fortnight, we will leave for Texas, touching at the Canary islands to examine the camels there.

Among the females are some procured, according to my instructions, pregnant, and one with her young by her side. A few nights since one of those purchased pregnant dropped a little one, which is doing well. Some of the females have been also impregnated since purchase, with the hope that they will produce next winter.

Lieutenant Porter is sanguine of transporting all these animals safely to Texas, and it would give us both pleasure, should your public duties permit it, to land them in the United States in your presence, if we are successful, or to explain, satisfactorily, the causes of failure, should we be so unfortunate as to be disappointed in our anticipations.

With much respect, sir, your obedient servant,
HENRY C. WAYNE,
Major United States Army.

Hon. JEFFERSON DAVIS,
Secretary of War, Washington City.

P. S.—Enclosed is a copy of our acknowledgment to Mr. E. De Leon, consul general in Egypt, for the six dromedaries presented by the viceroy.

UNITED STATES SHIP SUPPLY,
Alexandria, Egypt, January 21, 1856.

MY DEAR SIR: We have the honor to acknowledge the receipt on board of this vessel of the *six* dromedaries presented by his highness the viceroy of Egypt, through you, to the government of the United States.

At the same time, my dear sir, we take the opportunity to thank you for the interest you have manifested in our mission, and for the services you have rendered it.

With much respect, we are your obedient servants,
HENRY C. WAYNE,
Major United States Army.
DAVID D. PORTER.

EDWIN DE LEON,
United States Consul General, Alexandria.

SMYRNA, *February* 8, 1856.

SIR: On the 2d instant another Bactrian camel (male) was brought to us from the interior, which I also purchased, to insure, as far as possible, the arrival of one of these animals in the United States. With the aid of Mr. Heap, whose energy in the duty that I assigned to him here, and whose knowledge of the east, its languages, manners, and customs, from long residence in it, have been of the greatest service to me, I have now procured as many camels as Lieutenant Porter says he can conveniently transport, and the *material* necessary for putting them to service as soon after arrival in Texas as their recovery from the effects of the sea voyage will allow.

The animals are being embarked as fast as the weather will permit, and in a few days I hope we shall sail for Texas, commencing the first trial in our experiment. As far as the motion of the vessel is concerned, I am at ease, as, from the experience we have already had with them, I am satisfied that camels are more easily transported than horses, mules, or oxen; and, as I have every confidence in Lieutenant Porter's arrangements for securing them in rough weather or in gales. My apprehensions are of immediate injury to health, or of subsequent detriment to the constitutions of the animals, which may interfere with or affect the succeeding steps in the experiment, (acclimation and breeding,) from the confinement of so many of them for so long a time between decks. These injuries I trust may be avoided by close observation, by the police for them instituted by Lieutenant Porter, by the veterinary skill of wagon-master Ray, and by the practical knowledge of the natives I take with me. I think I may say that every precaution to insure the safe arrival of the animals in the United States has been taken.

When I left Washington, the surgeon general was engaged in preparing for publication a work upon the climatology of the United States, from the observations made by the officers of his corps at our military posts. Will you have a copy of it sent to me at Indianola to aid my selection of a place for acclimation and breeding, and for testing the usefulness of the camel as a beast of burden and of despatch. I shall be glad to receive also, at the same time, any suggestions, from any source whatever, on this point, or on others that you may think will tend to successful results.

Lieutenant Porter has made the proposal to me, that he be permitted to carry on to Washington, and exhibit to Congress, which will then be in session, perhaps, one of the dromedaries. The effect of this expedition will be, he thinks, to induce Congress to grant another appropriation for the importation of camels.

The only objection that occurs to me is, the additional risk to the animal in its transportation from New York to Washington, and from Washington back to me in Texas, and that this risk will necessarily be incurred by one of the only two fine blooded animals that we have, (the mare from Muscat, in all probability,) as, for the purpose proposed, the finest animal should, of course, be selected. I submit the matter to your decision, which I hope may meet me upon my arrival at Indianola. In connexion with this suggestion, that you may have a clear view of it in all its bearings, I will state that, of the *twenty thousand dollars* turned over to me for the purchase of camels in May last, about *twelve thousand dollars* will remain unexpended after paying for all the purchases and expenditures attending this our experimental trip.

In addition to the Arabs already in our service, I have engaged here two Turks as camel conductors. They are well recommended, and are represented as skilful in the management of camels and in making and repairing the pack saddles and other apparatus used with them.

Unless something at present unforeseen should occur to prevent our departure, we shall sail from this place for the Canary Islands within a week, say on the 15th instant, and, after a week's delay at Fuerte Ventura and Teneriffe, continue on our voyage to Indianola, where I hope to arrive about the last of April or first of May. Let me again request that I may find every preparation made for an immediate lightering of the animals upon our arrival off the bar, and a good, clean stable yard for their reception, in which they can be safely kept and attended to, and recruit from the effects of their voyage and confinement on ship board.

My accounts and returns for the fourth quarter of 1855 will be mailed from Indianola, as I have had no opportunity of sending them by a vessel bound to the United States, the only certain and economical manner of transmitting them, as I have been informed.

With much respect, sir, I am your obedient servant,

HENRY C. WAYNE,
Major United States Army.

Hon. JEFFERSON DAVIS,
Secretary of War, Washington.

SMYRNA, ASIA MINOR, *February* 11, 1856.

SIR: Enclosed is a letter to Messrs. Riggs & Co., bankers of Washington, in relation to closing my account with them. In it, you will see that I have requested them to forward their answer to me through you.

This I have done as I am uncertain where my address may be when they shall be ready to close my account with their house.

The camels purchased here are now embarked, and with the first fair wind we sail for the United States with thirty-three, as follows:

1 Tunis camel of burden, male.
1 Sennaar dromedary, male.
1 Muscat dromedary, female.
2 Siout dromedaries, males.
4 Siout dromedaries, females.
1 Mount Sinai dromedary, male.
2 Bactrian camels, males.
1 "Booghdee" or "Tuilu," male, (produce of the Bactrian male and Arabian female.)
4 Arabian camels of burden, males.*
15 Arabian camels of burden, females.
1 Arabian camel 24 days old, male.

To prevent mistake or delay from possible miscarriage of any of my

---

* The words "Bactrian" and "Arabian," applied to the description of the camel embarked, are not used in a *natal*, but in a *specific* sense, to describe the kind of animals according to the division I have adopted and uniformly followed. The Bactrian has two humps; the Arabian only one. The "Booghdee" takes after the mother and has but one hump. A hybrid, it partakes, it is said, somewhat of the character of the mule, being able to produce only an inferior race.

H. C. W.

previous letters, I will again repeat, that I hope to arrive at Indianola about the last of April or first of May, and request that I may find ever preparation made for lightering the animals immediately upon my arrival off the bar, and a clean stable-yard for their reception, in which they can be safely kept and attended to, and recruit from the effects of their voyage and confinement on shipboard.

Should we be so fortunate as to run through the Mediterranean in fifteen or twenty days, we may be off Indianola by the 15th April, as the "Supply" is a fast ship, and as we shall have, after leaving the Canaries, I am told, the advantage of trade winds. The only delay in the voyage anticipated by the officers of the vessel is in the passage hence to and through the Straits of Gibraltar. The run across the Atlantic they seem to regard as a certainty of thirty-five or forty days.

Very respectfully, your obedient servant,
HENRY C. WAYNE,
Major United States Army.

Hon. JEFF'N DAVIS,
Secretary of War, Washington.

UNITED STATES STORESHIP "SUPPLY,"
At sea, April 10, 1856.

SIR: I have the honor to transmit herewith six papers upon the camel, (one a translation accompanying the original French,) as follows:

No. 1. "Notes sur les dromadaries qui se trouvent en Egypte, par Linant de Bellefonds, Bey, Ingeneur en chef des Ponts et chaussées au Viceroi," &c.

No. 2. "Translation of No. 1."

No. 3. "Letter of Edwin DeLeon, esq., United States consul general for Egypt, enclosing one to him from Mr. Ayrtoun, agent for the estates of Il hami Pacha, son of the late viceroy, in relation to the dromedaries and burden camels of Egypt."

No. 4. "Letters from the Rev. H. G. O. Dwight, D. D., the Rev. Edwin E. Bliss, and the Rev. W. F. Williams, American missionaries, in relation to the camels in Asia Minor and other portions of Turkey in Asia."

No. 5. "Notes upon the camel in Algiers, translated from the official reports of General L. L. Carbuccia, by Albert Ray, late wagon and forage master United States army."

No. 6. "Of the anatomy of the dromedary, translated from the official reports of General L. L. Carbuccia, by Dr. S. Allen Engles, United States navy."

The thanks of the expedition are due to all of the above named gentlemen who have contributed to the advancement of its object; but especially to the Rev. H. G. O. Dwight, D. D., for the hearty zeal and energy with which he entered into the views of his government, and to the Rev. Edwin Bliss and Rev. W. F. Williams, for the promptness and care with which they responded to the calls made upon them. From Dr. Dwight's interest in the subject, I anticipate that the department will receive from him still more valuable and useful information.

In forwarding these papers it has occurred to me that it might not be uninteresting, and that it might perhaps serve a useful purpose, to give briefly a synopsis of the information in relation to the camel acquired by reading, and by subsequent observation and inquiry in the east, in executing the special duty to which I was assigned by your order of the 10th of May, 1855; and to accompany the information with such suggestions for procuring the animal as may aid any future projects for its importation into the United States, whether public or private. In doing so, I shall endeavor to avoid making any statements not verified by my knowledge, or acceded to by my judgment.

And it may not be amiss here to pay a tribute of acknowledgment to the general accuracy of the information furnished to the department from various sources, and acquired by our own researches. Where errors have been found they have generally been traceable to one or the other of two common causes of historic inaccuracies: generalization from local particulars, customs, or habits; or the adoption of statements as facts without examining into their accuracy or probability. I am happy to say, however, that the errors detected were not many nor serious.

Your instructions were, to visit Egypt, Syria, Asia Minor, Persia if possible, to examine the zembourek or camel artillery in use there; Salonica, that had been mentioned to you as a suitable place for procuring and shipping camels, and such other countries in the east as might be deemed advisable for the purposes of the mission. These instructions have been executed as far as time and opportunity permitted, and the particulars reported to you in previous communications. Our inability to enter Persia was explained in my letter of the 31st October, 1855, from Constantinople. Syria was not visited on account of the cholera and fever prevailing throughout it during the summer, and from the risk of shipping during the winter months in its ports, which are only open roadsteads, affording no protection to vessels at anchor. Its burden camels and dromedaries, however, are so essentially the same as those of Asia Minor and Arabia, that, in regard to the animals themselves, we should have acquired but little, if any, information beyond that obtained in Smyrna and in Egypt. Fortunately, the Rev. W. F. Williams has supplied any omission by his description (see No. 4) of the camels and dromedaries of the adjoining province of El Tezereh (Algezirim) which are those also of Syria.

You further directed me to visit the Canary islands, on my return, for the purpose of examining the camels used in them, and where they have been in use, according to Humboldt and others, ever since the conquest of those islands by the Spaniard—about four hundred years ago. Unfortunately, this order I was unable to executue, as, after several days of fruitless effort to reach those islands, on account of variable and head winds and a gale, the attempt was abandoned and the ship stood on her course to America. This failure is the more to be regretted, as I had received from Lieutenant Marcy, of our navy, whom I met on board the frigate Congress at Alexandria, a very favorable comparison of the camels of the Canaries with those of Smyrna, instituted from a general observation of the animal in both places. The desired information, though, can be obtained by forwarding to our consul at Palmas, through the State Department, a copy of the circular letter of inquiry, enclosed to you in my communication of the 5th October, 1855, and requesting him to embrace in his replies, particularly, the camels of the four islands, Teneriffe, Gran Canaria, Fuerte Ventura, and Sanzerote. Permit me to recommend this course to your attention, as the comparative nearness of these islands to the United States will render transportation from them proportionably easy, should the quality and power of the animal in them warrant its importation into America. With this preface, I will now proceed to the brief general view of the camel.

THE CAMEL.

Although among the domestic animals earliest mentioned in the history of man,* yet, from its limited use to a small zone of the earth, but little is known in the world at large of the nature, qualities, diseases and anatomy of the camel, and we find many vague and erroneous ideas in regard to it prevailing even among those classes generally well informed in zoology. The limits of "camel land"— that is, where the camel has been known and used—are said by Johnson, in his Physical Atlas, to lie between the 15th and 52d degrees of north latitude, and the 15th degree of longitude west of Greenwich to about the 120th degree east of it. The animal, then, is not one of the torrid zone, as is often supposed, but rather of the north temperate. Indeed, it suffers as much, if not more, from great heat as it does from intense cold.

"Camel land," according to Johnson, embraces the Canaries, Morocco, Algiers, Tunis, Tripoli, the Great Desert back of these countries, and Egypt, on the continent of Africa ; Arabia, Turkey in Asia, Persia, Cabool, Beloochistan, Hindoostan, Birmah, Thibet, Mongolia, a small portion of the southern part of Siberia, and Independent Tartary, in Asia ; the Crimea, and a small tract of country around and near Constantinople, in Europe. For two hundred years the camel has existed also in Tuscany, not in general use, but on the private estates of the Grand Duke at Pisa.†

To this small zone has the use of the camel been confined; and though efforts have been made, as stated by several writers, to extend its usefulness to the western world, even to our own Virginia, as reported by D. J. Browne, esq., as early as 1701,‡ they have all proved

---

*See Genesis xii c., 16 v. "And he entreated Abraham well for her sake ; and he had sheep, and oxen, and he asses, and men servants, and maid servants, and she asses, and camels."

See the pamphlet of Gräeburg de Hemso, for an interesting account of their introduction and use.

See his article on the importation of camels, in the Patent Office Report, part 2d, Agriculture, for 1853, p. 61, and which gives besides much interesting and useful information.

unsuccessful, either from a want of knowledge of their care, or from neglect, superstition, or jealousy on the part of those with whose peculiar avocations it was thought they would interfere.

The English word *camel* (Latin, *camelus*) is, without doubt, originally derived from the Hebrew, *gamal;* or Arabic, *djmel*, *djemel*, or *gimel*, meaning, according to Carbuccia and others, "the riches, or the wealth, or the gift of Heaven." And here, before going further, it will be necessary to determine the exact meaning of a few words, that I may be precise in my narrative, and that it may be clearly understood.

Science has classified the animal into "the camel," or two humped species, and "the dromedary," or one humped group. This division, as Linant Bey justly observes in his "Notes," (see No. 1,) would exclude "the camel" or "gimel" altogether from Africa, and from all of Asia, except a small region about Tartary. Yet, throughout "camel land" the one humped animal is universally known as *gimel*, *djmel*, *djemel*, or *gamal*, and the word *dromedary*, or anything like it, is unknown. Moreover, the word *dromedary*, derived from the Greek δρομευς (dromeus) meaning "a runner," "a racer," "a courser," is really applicable to but one variety of the camel, that devoted to riding purposes; and is actually only so applied by the Europeans living in the countries where that variety is known and used. With the natives of "camel land," the European residents recognize the generic term *camel* or *gimel;* and to the Asiatic and African, terms of *delool*, *devideh*, *hagine*, *herie*, &c.; add also the Greek derivative *dromedary*, to distinguish that particular variety used, as the saddle or riding animal, without regard to its blood, whether it be fine or common.

Guided, then, by the actual nomenclature of "camel land," rather than by what seems to be an arbitrary distinction of science, I shall use the word "camel" as generic, including both the two humped and the one humped species, which I will distinguish from each other by the qualification of the countries from which they are said to have originally come—Bactria and Arabia. I shall call the two humped animal "the Bactrian camel," and the one humped "the Arabian camel;" confining the term *dromedary* to the saddle or riding variety of the Arabian camel, there being no riding animal, as far as I have been able to ascertain, of the Bactrian species.

THE BACTRIAN CAMEL.

This species is found only on the southern border of Siberia, in a portion of Tartary, and in the Crimea, and is a much heavier built, stouter limbed, and stronger animal than the Arabian. From the difficulty of loading it, on account of its two humps, its usefulness as a beast of burden is limited. It is sometimes, however, used for draught, being yoked to a wagon as oxen are. Its great value is as a breeder, for crossing the male Bactrian upon the female Arabian, the produce being a powerful one humped hybrid; and for this purpose it is kept throughout Asiatic northern "camel land" as breeding stallions are with us, where it is called *bouhoum* or *bouhour*, (see No. 4.) It is altogether unknown in Africa, and a Bactrian camel there would be as great a curiosity as it is with us in the United States.

THE ARABIAN CAMEL.

This is the species with which we have particularly to deal. It is found throughout "camel land," and furnishing varieties for both burden and for riding; is one of the most useful, if not the most useful, of the domestic animals of the east. Its powers and hardiness vary with climate and breeding, and, as a general rule, its strength and endurance is greater the further north that it is found. With the many unmixed varieties of this species may be classed the cross of the Bactrian male upon the Arabian female, before mentioned, and which always follows the mother in the number of its humps. This hybrid, known in Persia as the *booghdee,* and in Turkey in Asia the male as the *tinlu* and the female as the *maya,* is, like the mule, incapacitated from continuing its race, or should it produce, its offspring is but feeble and worthless; but combining the power of the Bactrian with the quicker movement of the Arabian, it is peculiarly valuable as an animal of burden.

The names of the different varieties and of the sexes of the Arabian camel vary with the dialects of the several countries and provinces in which is is found. Those given by the Rev. Mr. Bliss (see No. 4) are generally used in and will be recognized throughout Asia Minor.

Meek and docile as the camel is usually represented to be, it will hardly be supposed that numbers are trained for the arena. Yet so it is; and one of the amusements of oriental life is contests between *pehlavans** or "fighting camels," in which one or the other is generally severely hurt, and not unfrequently killed by a dislocation of the cervical vertebrae.

NATURE AND DISEASES OF THE CAMEL.

The camel belongs to the class of ruminants, and in its general character and diseases resembles more the ox than any other division of animals. Its four stomachs, as a ruminant, are distinctly recognized, but much doubt (see No. 6) is expressed as to its possession of a fifth, attributed to it by by some writers to account for its ability to carry within itself a supply of water to meet the exigencies of desert life. Naturally hardy, the camel will undergo much exposure and fatigue without serious inconvenience; and beyond the ordinary ailments of the ox tribe, it has but two diseases of consequence: the "mange, or itch," (see No. 5,) and a violent pneumonitis, or inflammation of the lungs, which is apt to carry it off in two or three days. The first proceeds too often from neglect and dirt; the last from exposure to extreme cold or chilly dampness when heated.

The remedies in the east for the diseases of camels are charms and other superstitious appliances, a free use of tar distilled from a particular resinous shrub, and the more active one of the actual cautery. For strains and internal injuries the actual cautery is ordinarily used; for bruises and sores, an application of tar. Blue

---

* *Pehlavan* means "prize-fighter," "wrestler."

stone and sulphur are sometimes administered, but I rather think principally by Europeans. The treatment for itch is, separation from the rest of the herd, and applications of tar to the parts affected; for pneumonitis, warm covering and purges of rancid butter or olive oil. Our own intelligent treatment, however, of the diseases of other animals will, I believe, be more effectual also with those of the camel than the limited and simple remedies of Arabs and Turks. The itch appears to be particularly a disease of the camel, and easily produced, especially in the southern and warm portion of "camel land," as in Africa, where it is very prevalent, and apparently but little regarded. From observation and inquiry, I suppose it to be rarely fatal, and only when, from neglect and starvation, the blood becomes completely tainted, and the animal's system thoroughly corrupt.

The camel will wade streams, even up to the hump, but reluctantly, and is said by many writers to be unable to swim. Mr. Ayrtoun, though, (see No. 3,) says that it can swim. He is the only authority for this assertion that I have meet with.

The camel belongs also to the class of retromingents.

THE HUMP.

This particular characteristic of the camel, viewed, when its purpose is understood, in connexion with its ability to carry its own supply of water for several days, exhibits one of those wonderful adaptations, by the Almighty, of animals to country that excite our admiration and reverence. Composed of gelatinous fat, it contributes a stock of provision that, by reabsorption, furnishes the animal with sustenance when the nature of the country, or other unfortunate contingency, deprives it of a supply of food sufficient for its exertions. Stored thus, by the wise arrangement of Providence, with water and with food to meet for several days, should necessity or misfortune require it, the exigencies of an arid and unproductive country, the camel has not inaptly been called "the ship of the desert." So well is the use of the hump understood in the east, that the condition of the animal is judged of and its improvement, after a long and severe journey, measured by it. It is not uncommon to see camels come in, after long and painful journeys, with backs almost straight, exhibiting but little of any hump.

Beyond this supplying with food by reabsorption, the hump does not seem to be intimately connected with the animal's vitality; for Linant Bey informed me that he had repeatedly opened, with a sharp knife, the humps of his dromedaries when, from high feeding, they had become so plump as to prevent the fitting of the saddle, and removed large portions of the fat without in any manner injuring or affecting the general health of the animal.

USEFULNESS OF THE CAMEL.

The usefulness of the Bactrian, as far as known to me, has been already mentioned. That of the Arabian will be considered, first generally, and then separately, as an animal of burden and of the saddle.

From its formation, the Arabian camel is calculated for burden, and not for draught, though it is used occasionally for ploughing, and has been harnessed by the English in India in their batteries. Its deep chest and strong fore legs enable it to support well a load placed over them; but its narrow loins, and long ungainly hind legs, deprive it of the force necessary for longitudinal strain. Its additional joint, too, in the hind legs, by which it is enabled to kneel down and take a position particularly suited to the packing of burdens upon its back, and of readily rising with them, indicate unmistakeably its particular qualifications for that kind of service.

Unfitted by the formation of its nostrils and lungs (see No. 6) for violent exertion, its long and regular strides, however, with its capacity for continuous labor, enables it to make extensive journeys in comparatively good time. It is said, and I believe it, that the camel will, on emergency, travel at its regular gait for sixty successive hours without stopping. Formed rather for a level than a broken country, the camel meets, though without inconvenience, a fair amount of mountain and valley, and is not distressed in ascending or decending moderate slopes, though they be long. Those of Asia Minor, Syria, Persia, Cabool, northern Hindoostan, and Tartary, for instance, cross in their journeys, continually, ranges of mountains and high hills, and often at seasons of the year when they are covered with snow and ice.

The foot of the camel, clothed with a thick, tough shin, said by some to be true horn, enables it to travel with facility over sand, gravel, or stones. It will also stand a tolerable degree of volcanic debris or rocky soil; and aided by art (provided with a shoe of hide, iron shod at the bottom, and which is attached around the fetlock joint) it traverses these impediments without difficulty, and also ice and snow. In wet, clayey and muddy soils the camel moves with embarrassment; as it is apt to slip and slide in it without the ability to gather itself quickly, and is often, it is stated, split up by the straddling of its hind legs, for which there is no cure, death soon following the accident, over such spots it should be driven cautiously; and the straddling of the hind legs is sometimes prevented by hoppling above the gamble joint.

The flesh of the camel is good for food, resembling beef, though said to be more delicate and tender. Its resemblance to beef is such that it can be readily imposed for it upon the unsuspecting without detection. Its milk is good to drink, and is not distinguishable from that of cows. I have used it in my tea every morning for some weeks, knowing it to be camel's milk, without perceiving any difference in color or taste. The pile of the camel also, though course, is applied to the manufacture of many useful articles, as carpets, coarse cloths, and ropes, but not to any of fine texture; not even to that particular commodity, the desire and pride of the fair sex, the shawl, to which it has falsely given its name, but which is really made from the fine, delicate hair of a particular kind of goat.

Another recommendatory characteristic of the camel is its pasturing upon almost every shrub and plant that grows, even the thistle, prickly pear, and other thorny vegetables, and thereby reducing materially the obligation of providing it with food. A little, besides—thanks to its hump—goes a great way, so that, in comparison with other animals of burden or draught, it requires a less provision of forage; an economy at any time, but materially an advantageous arrangement for a journey. The camel can also, on emergency, travel three, four, even seven days without water or food; and it is serviceable from four to twenty-five years of age.

As an animal of burden, the power of the camel depends upon its stock, and, measurably, upon climate; those of Central Asia being ordinarily stronger and more vigorous than those of Africa or India. I have seen, though, in Egypt many noble camels capable of carrying as heavy loads as any that I saw or heard of in Asia. From the most reliable information, confirmed by observation, a very strong camel will carry for short distances, say from one part of a town to another, about from 1,000 to 1,200 pounds. I have heard much heavier loads mentioned, but I placed no reliance upon the statements for two reasons: first, because the loads of camels are not weighed, but only as much put upon them as they can rise under: and secondly, because the oriental habit of amplification prevails in every word spoken by an inhabitant of the east. I do not mean by this to allege intentional moral obliquity, but only the habitual indulgence of a prolific and vivid imagination.

On journeys the loads for the strongest camels range from 450 to 600 pounds, and of the common kinds from 300 to 450 pound; and these they will carry from eighteen to thirty miles a day according to the character of the country, whether broken or level, over which they travel, and moving for the usual daily travelling time of from eight to ten hours. With lighter loads they will travel somewhat faster.

The average travelling load of camels of the different countries and provinces may be stated as follows: of Morocco, Algiers, Tunis, and Tripoli, from 300 to 400 pounds; of Egppt, from 350 to 550 pounds; of Asia Minor, Syria and other portions of Turkey in Asia, of Persia, and of Tartary, the strongest including löks or males, and the hybrid booghdee, or tülus and mayas, from 500 to 600 pounds; and the common stock, including the arvanas or breeding females, from 300 to 450 pounds; of Cabool, Beloochistan, Hindoostan, Birmah, Thibet and Mongolia, from 300 to 400 pounds. The camels around Constantinople being imported almost altogether from Asia Minor, not bred there, from 300 to 600 pounds according to quality.

As a saddle animal, or dromedary, the capacity of the camel for burden is little, its conformation to qualify it for riding being necessarily lighter, but it compensates by speed for its comparative want of power. The average load for a dromedary ranges from 150 to 300 pounds, and this he will carry continually, travelling from eight to ten hours a day, about fifty miles a day. On emergency they will make from seventy to ninety miles a day, but this only for a day or two, and over a level country, (see Nos. 1 and 3.) Instances of greater speed being kept up for several successive days are related, but they are few and far between. Wonderful stories are told by the Arabs of the speed of the *mhari, el herie, delool, &c.;* Linant Bey's comment upon such traditions (see No. 1) is very expressive. Colambari also, in his account of the zembourek or camel artillery, gives the following good reason for discrediting these marvellous tales: "that, on account of the insecurity of person and life in Persia, every native of consequence keeps in his stable a fast horse (whose qualities are known only to himself and a confidential groom) to be used in extremity; that dromedaries would undoubtedly be retained for this purpose were their combined speed and endurance really what Arab tales represented them to be; but that during his long residence and service in Persia he never heard of a dromedary being kept for such an exigency."

Many and contradictory accounts are given of the gait of the dromedary, some describing it as smooth and pleasant, while others represent it to be rough and disagreeable, not unfrequently producing nausea. This discrepancy proceeds from the habit of generalizing from single instances. The gait of the dromedary, like that of the saddle horse, depends upon breeding, the structure of the individual animal, and upon training.

COPULATION, GESTATION, AND PARTURITION.

It has been stated that the camel cannot copulate without the aid of man, and this has been brought forward as a reason why we do not hear of the animal existing in a wild state. It has also been further asserted that, because of its retromingency, connexion is made backwards. I have even heard these statements from intelligent persons residing in the east, whose occupations, however, did not lead them to any particular observation of the animal, and who only uttered the erroneous impressions of uninformed writers, or of vulgar tradition. Neither the one nor the other is correct. The animal does not require the aid of man, though as in the case of stallions it is advisable sometimes to guide the organ of generation. The organ in erection pushing back the sheath, returns to the front, and connexion is made in the usual manner, with this exception, that the female kneels down in the position for receiving a load, and the male covers her, squatting down upon his hind legs to come to her.

The female generally conceives in December, January, or February, this being the usual rutting season of the male, and carries her young about twelve months. She brings forth lying upon her side, without much apparent labor or pain. The young one, according to climate and local custom, is at times, immediately upon birth, swathed in cloths or blankets, except its hump, to prevent its taking cold. For the same reason a blanket is occasionally thrown over the mother. Within the first day the calf will learn to take the teat; and in seven days it will be strong enough in its legs to follow its mother about. It suckles for a year or more; and between three or four years old its training, whether for burden or for the saddle, is commenced. In regard to working a female camel about to calve, the same judgment and management should be exercised as in the case of a mare with colt.

In the rutting season the male becomes rather fierce, obstinate, and unmanageable, and not unfrequently dangerous to all but his keeper. This excitement is often marked by a peculiar projection from his mouth of a loose, membranous lining of the throat, in the form and with the appearance of a bladder, accompanied by a loud, bubbling noise from the passage of the air with which it is inflated.

Barrenness among camels is rare, but miscarriages are not unfrequent, owing usually to overloading and rough treatment while breeding.

WHERE CAN THE BURDEN CAMEL AND DROMEDARY BE BEST PROCURED, AND AT WHAT PRICES?

These questions must be answered now with deference to more enlarged, precise information, to be derived from future direct inquiry, or importation from various places, and with reference to the coast of America, whether the Atlantic or Pacific, which is considered in connexion with the inquiry.

If the Atlantic coast is in contemplation, importation should be from Morocco, or from some point on the Mediterranean, in Africa, or Asia. Burden camels may be procured of the relative qualities previously mentioned on the coasts of Morocco, Algiers, Tunis, Tripoli, and Egypt, and in the country back of them, but the restrictions upon trade in Morocco, Tunis, Tripoli, and Egypt, require that the permission of the sovereign or viceroy should be obtained for their exportation. This, unless previously procured by treaty or special agreement, would be apt to embarrass, if not prevent, any attempt to carry out many, as the naturally suspicious temper of the east and despotic sway have a tendency to induce the arbitrary exercise of power. Of Algiers, I can give no information, as I have not ascertained the mind of the French government in regard to the matter.

From the Asiatic ports on the Mediterranean or Black seas, or on the channel between them, all of which are immediately under the control of the Porte, and from Constantinople, exportation is permitted. It only remains, then, to be seen where the animals can be best procured and shipped. For vessels bound up the Black sea or to Constantinople, burden camels, but no dromedaries, can be had at any point almost of the coast, or by penetrating into the interior, from Samsoun westward to the castles of Europe and Asia. But as at Smyrna, or from the country back of it, the same quality of burden camels are to be readily procured, there would be no object in sending a vessel beyond it upon the longer and uncertain voyage through the Dardanelles; uncertain from the strength of the current flowing through that strait into the Mediterranean, at the rate of two and a half to three miles an hour, against which a vessel cannot beat, and which, in consequence, not unfrequently causes a detention at its mouth of days, and sometimes of weeks.

At Smyrna, or from the country around it, in any direction, as far as it may be desirable to go, every variety of burden camel known in Asia Minor—Löks, Pehlavans, Arvanas, Tiulus, or Mayas, and Bactrian males for breeding—can be purchased, but not dromedaries.

From Smyrna, along the coast, southward and eastward, towards

Syria, and back from it, good burden camels, but no dromedaries, are to be had. At Konieh, in the province of Karamania, the breed of burden camels is represented as particularly fine, but for shipment it would be necessary to drive animals purchased there to Adalia, upon the gulf of that name, to Smyrna, or to an intervening port.

In Syria a very good breed of burden camels, and from Arabia adjoining it, fine dromedaries are to be obtained. Through Syria and its ports burden camels and dromedaries from Egypt may also be imported, there being no prohibition upon exportation by land from Egypt, and the ports of Syria being, as before stated, under the control of the Porte.

It would not be worth while to attempt to import camels or dromedaries to the Atlantic coasts of America from beyond the limits of Turkey, in Asia, on account of the time (months) that would be required to penetrate so far into the interior, and to return to the seacoast, and the expenses that would necessarily attend the collection and driving of the animals, besides the probable loss of some of them in so long a journey.

Taking a general view of the subject, I have no hesitation in recommending Smyrna as the best point for procuring burden camels and Bactrian breeders, and Jaffa and Beirout as the best points through which to obtain dromedaries from Arabia, and burden camels and dromedaries from Egypt, (unless the viceroy of Egypt will withdraw his restriction upon exportation from Alexandria;) but shipments from these two last ports must be made, I am informed, on account of their being open roadsteads, between May and November.

Of any point in Europe I say nothing, as the only one where camels, and only of burden, are to be had is Constantinople, where there are comparatively few, and those few imported from Asia Minor as wanted, it not being customary to breed them there. The war at present closes the Crimea against any exportation from it of Bactrian breeders.

The prices of camels vary, as will be seen by the papers transmitted, and, as I have found from experience, as do those of horses with us, according to breeding, size, training, soundness, &c., &c., and range from $15 to $1,000. In Egypt, sound burden camels, capable of carrying from 400 to 600 pounds, may be purchased for from $50 to $100 and $130; and dromedaries for from $45 to $1,000, common stock for from $45 to $150, blooded animals for from $150 to any fancy price within the limit stated. In Arabia, prices are about the same, with perhaps a trifling diminution. In Asia Minor the prices of burden camels may be set down as follows: males and Tinlus and Mayas at from $75 to $200; females at from $50 to $120; Bactrian breeders at from $300 to $600. In Morocco, Algiers, Tunis, and Tripoli, the prices of burden camels and dromedaries are reported at about the same as those of Egypt, in some instances a little lower. At present the prices are much enhanced by the general effect of the war in the Crimea, and especially by the demand for the animal on account of it and the war in Asia Minor. But war or no war, the stranger Frank who trades in the east must make up his mind to pay for his alienage, whether he deals with Mahomedan, Jew, or

Christian. The prices stated by residents are generally the minimum of those asked among themselves, and not those demanded of strangers. The burdens above mentioned are those for journeys, and not short lifts.

If regard is had in importation to the Pacific coast of America, I can give no positive information beyond indicating the countries where the different varieties of the camel can be obtained, as neither by reading nor personal experience have I had any opportunity of ascertaining either the restrictions upon exportation from them, nor the ranges of prices in them.

Burden camels and dromedaries can be obtained from Egypt and Abyssinia. Good burden camels and the finest dromedaries from Arabia. Dromedaries from Persia bordering upon the gulf, and good burden camels from northern Persia, if the distance and temper of the intervening tribes will permit of their being driven to the gulf. Burden camels and dromedaries are to be had in Cabool, Beloochistan, Hindoostan, and Birmah. The best burden camels of these four last mentioned countries, however, are not able from all accounts to carry more than 400 pounds. The Bactrian breeder could only be obtained from Asia Minor or northern Persia by driving down to the Persian gulf.

TRANSPORTATION.

Whether the importation be to the Atlantic or Pacific coast of America, the camel should, for protection against the weather, be carried under shelter. At certain seasons of the year the animals might perhaps be transported upon deck in secure houses built for them, but this is a nautical possibility beyond my experience to determine; in either case, whether between or on deck, six feet from breast to tail, and four feet from breast to forehead, should be allowed for the average length of the animal, and from six feet eight inches to seven feet for the average height from top of hump to ground when standing.

From some practical experience and much observation of the transportation of horses and mules during our war with Mexico, in vessels of all kinds and sizes, I have no hesitation in saying that the camel is much more easily transported than either, and with less trouble. At the time of this writing, one of our camels (from Tunis) has been on board, without ever leaving the vessel, eight months, and the others from three to two months, during which time they have experienced much rough weather and three severe gales. The vessel, moreover, even in smooth seas has, and deservedly, a very bad character for rolling. I have had, therefore, fair opportunity for comparison.

It is only necessary at the commencement of rough weather or of a gale to make the animals kneel down and so secure them to prevent them from rising. In this position they will remain patiently until released, and after the first fear from the unusual motion has subsided, will eat their food and chew the cud with almost as much complacency as if on shore.

The odor from a number of camels between decks is about the same

PURCHASE OF CAMELS FOR MILITARY PURPOSES. 61

as that of a like number of horses or mules, and proceeds principally from corporeal exhalations; the urine passed being but little, and the dung, or *argols*, as named by Father Huc, being round and hard like that of sheep's, though in size larger, averaging an inch and a half in diameter. For these last reasons, also, camels are much cleaner to transport than horses or mules.

The ingenious arrangements of Lieutenant Porter for embarking the animals and for securing them in gales, and which have answered excellently the purposes for which they were intended, belong particularly to his branch of the expedition, and will no doubt be fully described by him. I shall therefore say nothing in relation to them.

FOOD OF THE CAMEL.

Barley, wheat and beans, ground and made into a thick paste or dough with other grains of the east, and cut straw, form the usual nourishment of the camel. It takes also very readily and kindly to good hay, timothy and clover, and to oats. I give also the names of certain shrubs and plants, mentioned by General Daumas, in his pamphlet, "upon the acclimation of the camel in France," as constituting its habitual grazing. "Many of them," says the general, "are known, some are not." As I have no botanical work, or friend at hand, I must trust to future opportunity, or to your assistance to obtain as far as possible their common names.

SHRUBS.

Arabic name.	Botanical name.	Common name.
Ed-djefen	Radix vitis	
El guezahh	Seminis cepae	
Ez-zit	Oleum olivarum	
El-belbal	do	
El-igthan	do	
El-ghares	do	
El-guethof	Androsoemum	
En-nasi	Cardui species	
Es-Saliân	Herbœ sen oleris species	
Es-sefar	Herbœ spinosae	
Er-regni	do	
El-koubar	do	
En nagad	Anthemis	
Ech-chabrag	Planta rubros fructus habens et rerbrum lignum quocum sanguis occisorum comparatur.	
Teskir	Hyoscyamus	
El-fil	do	
Ed-djelâh	do	
El-ferou	do	
El-djad	do	
El-bethom	Terebinthus	
Larth	do	
Es-sad	Cyperus	
El-alned	do	
La zal	do	
El-merakh	Cynanchum viminale	
Er-rabi	do	
Et-tafeh	do	

SHRUBS—Continued.

Arabic name.	Botanical name.	Common name.
Er-reteum	Genista frutex	
Es-sedra	Zizyphus lotus	
El-gueteum		
Et-tharf	Tamarix	
El-kelokh	......do	
El-Arfedj	Arboris Spinosæ species	
Ed-djedar	Nomen herbæ crescentis in arenis.	
El-karteum	......do	
El-meker	Herniaria	
El-yanthite Yathithar	......do	
El-hadj	......do	
El-zateur	......do	
El-khorchef	Artichauts sauvages	
Zeboudje	Oliviers sauvages	
El-dereuf	......do	
El kuerterm	......do	
Ed-doum	......do	
Tiguentense	......do	
El-nedjil	......do	
El-koddar	......do	
Chihh	......do	
El-kuesol	......do	
El-guetof	......do	
El-oursera	......do	
El-adjerem	Nomen herbæ crescentis in arenis.	

PLANTS.

Arabic name.	Botanical name.	Common name.
El-knarneb	Brassica	
El-bedjig	......do	
El-heulm	Herba arnoglossa albicans foliis et lanuginosa.	
Er-regigue	......do	
Es-samhari	......do	
Ticheret	......do	
El-demrâne	......do	
El-baguel	Olus, speciatim portulaca	
Ed-drine	......do	
Er-reumt	......do	
El-Chegâa	......do	
Ez-zafzâf	Zizyphum	
El-mrar	Absynthum	
Es seluse	Cardui species	
El-hama	......do	
El-mechith	Polypodium crenatum	
El-khend	......do	
El-garthoufa	Olus	
El guelgelâne	Dolichos cuneifoleus	
El-guiz	......do	
Lezoul	......do	
Ech-cheliath	......do	
El-ghebri	Ruellia Guttata	
El-kuikoute	......do	

PURCHASE OF CAMELS FOR MILITARY PURPOSES.

PLANTS—Continued.

Arabic names.	Botanical name.	Common name.
El-aarich	Scabiosa	
Oudene-en-nadja	Oreille de brebis : mot à mot	
Ledene	do	
El-Aademe	Zizamia	
El-ksibeur	do	
El-khebri	Malva	
Dil-el-far	Queue de rat : mot à mot	
Ed-delnef	do	
El-khanfeur	do	
Afli	do	
El halfa	do	
Hamimeuch	do	
Ben-naamân	Coquelicot	
El-bine	do	
El-harmel	Pegamem harmala	
En nequig	do	
Sor	do	
El-adjerem	do	
El-kerat	do	
En-netil	do	
El-metnâm	do	
El-melahh	do	
Et-tâlem	do	
El mak	do	
Bon-nagar	do	
Deu bâl	do	
El-aâknif	do	
El-oucham	Plantæ germen	
El-guehonân	Anthemis	
Sag-el gherabe	La patte du corbeau	
El-khemoun	Cuminnim	
El-reguime	Malva	
El mourar	Species arboris seu planta amara (sic.)	
Azbian	do	
El-bibache	do	
Ech-cherirah	do	
Ez-zagzag	do	
El-hhar	do	
El-haref	do	
El-kerkaz	do	
Ed djemir	Ficus sycomorus	
Bon-kharis	do	
En-nedjem	Nomen plantae (sic dans le dictionnaire.)	
Es-sigue	do	
Es-senagh	do	
Lella	do	
El-âzir	do	
Drâa	do	

CONCLUSION.

The drawings by Mr. G. H. Heap, who accompanied the expedition in its employment, and which will be forwarded to you from New York, upon the Supply's arrival at that port, are good likenesses of the particular camels they are intended to represent, and, with the papers transmitted, will materially aid in the formation of correct ideas of that animal in some of its varieties. Much positive knowledge remains yet to be determined. Some of it, I hope, may be acquired by experience and observation of the race among ourselves in its future use and propagation in America.

Trusting, my dear sir, that our efforts to introduce this domestic animal into the heart of our continent may be successful, and that our anticipations of its usefulness to our country may be fully realized,

I am, with much respect, your obedient servant,

HENRY C. WAYNE,
Major United States Army.

Hon. JEFFERSON DAVIS,
Secretary of War, Washington, D. C.

Notes upon the dromedaries met with in Egypt by Linant Bellefonds, (Linant Bey,) Engineer in Chief of dykes and bridges to the Viceroy of Egypt.

[Translated by Major Henry C. Wayne, United States army.]

According to Buffon, the camel has two humps, and the dromedary only one, and this is the only characteristic distinguishing the two races. Adopting this definition, the camel would not be known in Egypt, and would be found only in Asia about Tartary, whilst the dromedary would be the animal which we meet with in Cairo, Asia Minor, Turkey, Arabia, and throughout Africa. But the Arabs and the Egyptians distinguish, by the word *gimel*, all the animals of this genus, and do not know the word *dromedary*. Among the species with one hump met with in Egypt, Arabia and Africa, those which carry burdens are the *gimels*, called by Europeans *camels;* whilst those used only for riding are termed *hagine*, or by Europeans the *dromedary*. Thus, the species with one hump called (by Buffon) dromedary, furnishes both beast of burden and riding animals. Indeed, it is precisely the same as with horses, some being for draught and others for the saddle. I use, then, the word *dromedary* to designate the riding animal with one hump, which the Arabs call *hagine*.

The diffierent breeds of dromedaries found in Egypt came from two primitive stocks.

The first is from Noman, (Oman, H. C. W.,) near Muscat, on the Persian Gulf, and called thence *Nomani*.

The second is found among the Bicharieh (pronounced Bee-sha-ree-eh, H. C. W.) Arabs residing in the territory of *Bajah* or *Abyé*, lying between the parrallels of Sarratim, on the Red sea, and of Assouan, on the Nile, and comprised between the Red sea and the Nile. This breed is called *Bicharieh*, from the name of the tribe possessing it.

It has not been decided yet which of these two breeds is the best, or which furnishes the swiftest dromedaries. Some prefer the Bicharieh, others the Nomanieh. The truth is, that most excellent animals are found in both breeds.

Although these two breeds are the most celebrated, there are yet others of less pure blood which furnish very good animals; but all these secondary races proceed from crosses of the two primitive stocks, and partake of their qualities, respectively, in proportion as they are found in regions neighboring those of the primitive stocks.

There is sometimes met with, but very rarely, another breed of dromedaries, belonging to the tribes inhabiting the country to the southwest of the Atlas mountains and adjacent to the kingdom of Morocco. I have seen only a few of these dromedaries, but they seemed to me to be fully as good as either the Nomanieh or the Bicharieh, though of lighter build.

The Nomanieh is generally of heavier form than the Bicharieh, and almost always more thickset. Its hair is also longer, and it is always of a fawn color more or less deep.

The Bicharieh is very slender, with longer and more delicate limbs. Many are fawn colored. Many are of lighter colors. And some entirely white, with very short hair.

The difference in the movement of the animals of these two breeds is, also, very marked, and notwithstanding the assertion, I am satisfied that it does not proceed only from the difference in raising and training. Natural qualities and conformation contribute much to their respective gaits, and although I have often tried to teach a young Bicharieh dromedary to move like Nomaniehs, and though, moreover, they had never before been ridden and were quite young, I have never been able to succeed; nor in giving to the Nomanieh the gait of the Bicharieh.

The Nomanieh generally in moving carries the four feet directly in line, one after the other, which gives a quick step without jolting. They always carry the head very low and move as steadily as a machine. They are made to carry the head low by means of a long switch hooked at the end, called *matrak*.

The motion that the rider feels is one simultaneously from right to left and from rear to front, which often wearies the chest and does not seem to be an easy gait. At this quick pace the Nomanieh will make from six to eight miles an hour. To go quicker, it must trot, and then they move the two feet on the same side almost at the same time.

The Bicharieh, in its pace, has a shorter and slower step than the Nomanieh, and the movement of the feet though similar is less regular, which gives to the rider rather a single motion from rear to front. For the pace the Nomanieh is preferable; but for the trot, it is different; the Bicharieh is then at home, its legs almost ambling are thrown out with boldness and suppleness at the same time, and its feet are put down so lightly that the motion felt by the rider is far less rude or rough than that felt on a trotting horse.

The Bicharieh at the pace can only make about three miles an hour; its best gaits are the short and full trot, and with these its swiftness can be varied. They gallop also, but only for a short time, and it is not a gait supportable either by the dromedary or his rider.

In mounting a Nomanieh, the halter, which serves as a bridle, is always slackened. On the contrary, when a Bicharieh is mounted, the halter around the neck is drawn tight, and the *zeoman* (a cord fastened to a ring, H. C. W.) through the left nostril is also slightly tightened, which gives support to both the rider and the animal, and by making the dromedary carry his head up gives him a high spirited and mettlesome air, which the Nomanieh never has.

Besides these two principal breeds of which I have been treating, there are several others in Arabia and in Africa, in the desert between the Nile and the Red sea, which perhaps are less celebrated, though they produce also excellent animals, but in small numbers.

I think the Nomanieh dromedary would be less likely to succeed in America than the Bicharieh, as the country in Africa in which this last breed is found seems to me to be more analogous to that in America where it is intended to use them, than the country of the Nomanieh. For this reason I will treat more of the Bicharieh.

Among the Bicharieh Arabs the dromedaries of the different small tribes composing the great tribe are not equally esteemed.

I will mention those I prefer, which are the most celebrated, and I will give also the mark of each of the tribes possessing the best animals. This mark is burned upon the animal with a red hot iron.

All the dromedaries of a Bicharieh tribe have the mark called *akal* upon the right fore leg. This, without exception. In addition, each small tribe has its own particular mark.

The best breeds of the Bicharieh are the *Ammadabieh*, the *Mahomed hourabieh*, the *Amitirah* and the *Balgah*.

Among the Ababdieh Arabs, which are found to the north of the Bicharieh towards Cosier and called *Achab*, are seen dromedaries of the best stock of the Bicharieh, and as highly esteemed as the pure Bicharieh breed; they are, however, rare.

Among the *Menacir* Arabs, a tribe now separated from the Bicharieh, are found also very fine dromedaries. These Arabs live in the desert between Coroscos and *Abou Ahmed* towards the west, near the Nile.

Among the *Mahazi* Arabs, who occupy the desert between the Nile and the Red sea, from Cosier to Suez and Cairo, are also found good dromedaries.

And finally, among the twelve tribes composing that of the *Ca-*

warah, residing in the peninsula of Mount Sinai, good dromedaries are found, resembling both the Nomanieh and the Bicharieh.

TO CHOOSE A GOOD ANIMAL.

To avoid deception in the choice of a dromedary, one must be very much a connoisseur of the animal, for I think it is more difficult to be skilled in dromedaries than in horses. One must have lived with Arabs and their dromedaries to appreciate either the one or the other. It may be conceived, then, how difficult it is to designate clearly what constitutes a good dromedary.

A dromedary should not be too tall, nor its legs too long, which would give it a gaunt appearance; nor should the chest be too wide nor too heavy.

The fore legs should not touch the callosity upon the breast.

The two rowels or mullets (molettes) of the fore feet should be far from touching each other when the animal walks.

The belly should be round without being puffy, and the hump should not be too big.

The neck should be rather wide than narrow; the head well set on; the eye large and the lips closed.

In walking the animal should show suppleness in the neck and have a wavy movement of the head. The more suppleness there is in this motion the easier will be the gait.

To be highly esteemed a dromedary should not cry when touched; and when bridled (haltered, H. C. W) or saddled it should give utterance only to a low grumbling.

A dromedary should not be taken that has been seriously hurt near the shoulders where the saddle rests; though it does not indicate disease, but proceeds only from the little care the Arabs give to keeping their saddles in repair. In a female this is less objectionable, for in giving birth, if her wounds have caused any disease, it is almost always cured.

Five marks (cautery, H. C. W.) on either side of the callosity on the breast, or on the belly near the naval, indicate always internal incurable disorders.

The hind legs should not be too angular but rather straight.

The hump should not be too much to the front, rather to the rear is better, as then the saddle is more easily adjusted.

The hair should not be too short, as then the animal is more easily injured.

The feet should be small; the nails and the hair around them black rather than white.

Fawn colored dromedaries are more highly prized than those entirely white.

When mounted the dromedary should instantly and quickly rise and start off.

When the dromedary moves it should be with such spirit that the rider is obliged to hold him in. This supports both. To urge him on kick him on the shoulder with the foot.

It is very difficult to find a dromedary uniting in itself all these requisite qualities, and very rarely can such an one, especially if it is a female, be purchased; for the Arabs love their fine blooded dromedaries as much as they do their horses, and it is only as presents, or else at enormous prices, that the choicest animals can be obtained.

A first rate Nomanieh is worth in Cairo from five to six hundred dollars; but those ordinarily met with there sell for from one two hundred dollars.

The Bichariehs sell for less; good ones, that is to say, such as are for sale, may be had for from sixty to one hundred dollars. At nearly for the same prices as for the Bicharieh can be purchased also the other breeds of the *Mahazi, Cawarah,* and *Ababdi.*

I will remark here that the Bicharieh dromedaries do not carry as heavy burdens as the Nomanieh. These last carry a saddle called *gabit,* fitted with pads and with saddle bags, termed *Krourque,* that hang down on both sides of the saddle and carry the baggage, provisions, &c., of the rider and of the dromedary.

The Bicharieh carries a wodden saddle laid over two small pads which are not fastended to it. This saddle is called *Kyapah, maralouf,* &c., &c., according to its shape. Saddle bags cannot be carried over it on account of its form; but behind it a small sack of hide called *Biba,* in which a little baggage can be packed, may be attached after the manner of a valise or portmanteau.

Often in expeditions a servant or follower rides behind upon the dromedaries of the two breeds, both riders carrying their arms. In a word, the Nomanieh generally carries from two hundred to two hundred and thirty pounds; the Bicharieh one hundred and eighty; at the utmost their burdens are three hundred and fifty, and three hundred pounds.

A dromedary well equipped, well ridden and in good condition, can easily make in a day, over suitable ground, level and a little sandy, about ninety miles, that is, between the morning and the evening, but it cannot keep on at that rate. It can make fifty miles a day for fifteen or twenty days, and for a long journey can be counted upon for that. I have myself travelled upon one ninety miles in eleven hours, and gone twelve miles in forty minutes.

If reliance could be placed upon the stories told by the Arabs of the swiftness of dromedaries, whose deeds as well as names have been traditionally preserved, they would have been capable of performing prodigies; but I have never seen any such miracles.

SADDLES.

Fig. 1. The saddle of the Bicharieh is made of the wood of the mimosa, a very heavy and hard wood. The several parts are connected together by strings of raw hide. The pads are of skin, stuffed with wool or horse hair (fig. 2;) the girths are woolen, and the breast-strap is of leather thongs, plaited.

Fig. 3. The saddle of the Nomanieh is of white jujube wood. The connexion of the several parts is also made with hide thongs, not a nail being used. The pads are of skin, and stuffed with wool.

It was for a long time asserted that dromedaries copulated in a manner different from that of other animals, that is to say, by coming together backwards, because the organ of the male, in its ordinary

70 PURCHASE OF CAMELS FOR MILITARY PURPOSES.

state, is directed towards the animal's rear. But with the camel, as with other animals, the lion among others, the organ, at the moment

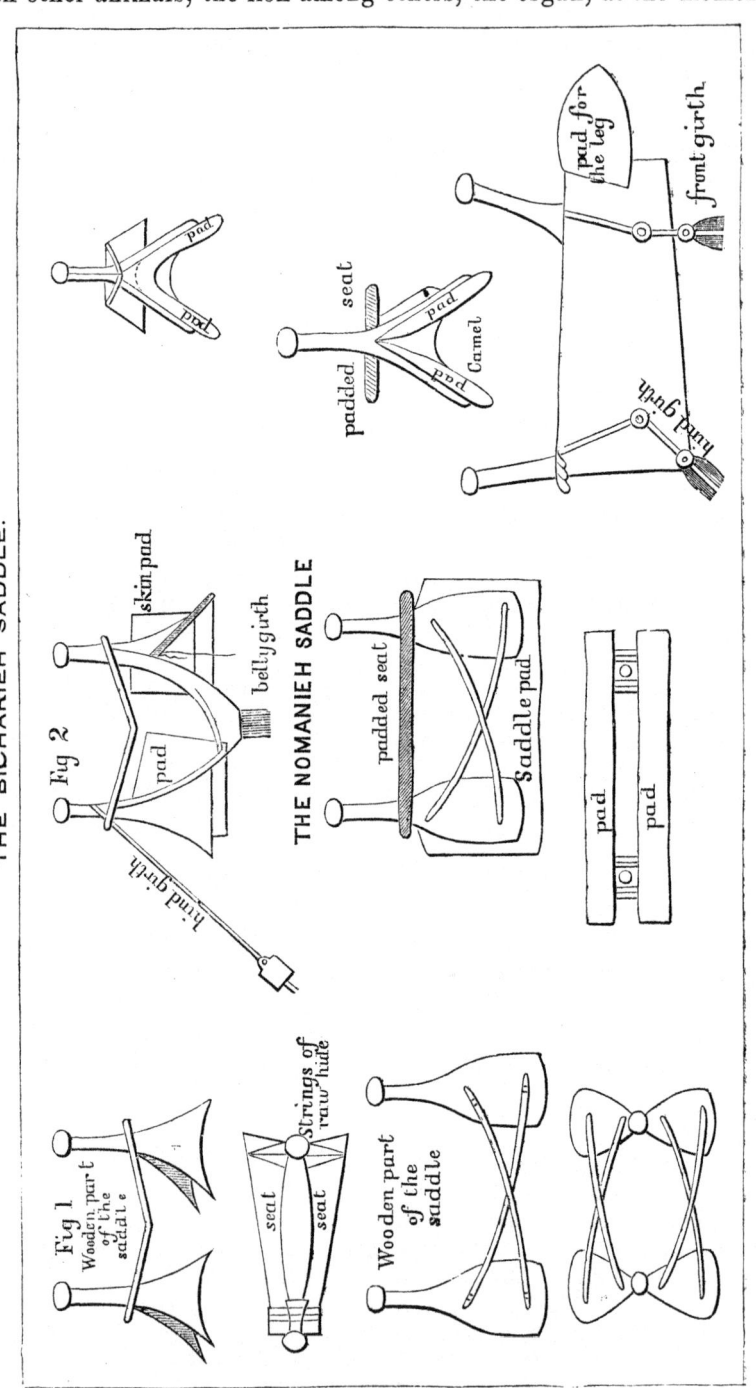

of copulation, turns to the front; the camel only differing in this, that the female lies down, as when receiving a load, and in this position the male covers her.

It is very certain that the camel does not require the assistance of man in copulating.

After twelve days it is known whether or not the female has conceived. If she has, at the moment of stepping out when started off she raises her tail, and does not cry.

The gestation of the dromedary is twelve lunar months. They can be ridden up to the last moment, and it often happens that females bring forth upon a journey, when, if a halt of some days cannot be made, the little one is placed upon its mother's back, and the journey is continued.

It is a great mistake to say that dromedaries do not lie down naturally, and that it is only by training that they are made to execute that motion. Dromedaries of a few hours old only will lie down near their mothers.

Dromedaries suckle their young for six months, at the least, and for a year at the most; at this age the young will eat grass, tender plants, and grain.

The rations per day of large dromedaries is equivalent to that of a horse, and is either of beans, dourha, (a small grain, farinaceous, and much used for food in Egypt, among other purposes in making bread, H. C. W.,) or wheat. The beans should be broken, the wheat also, which should, moreover, be slightly moistened. The dourha is given whole. The best food for a journey is wheat, the next dourha, and the next beans.

When in a town, a little chopped straw is given, in addition to the ration, and in the desert the dromedaries are permitted to eat certain plants. When pasture is found the ration is saved.

A dromedary should generally not drink oftener than every other day in the heat of summer, and every fourth day in winter. Often in travelling it goes eight and ten days without drinking, particularly if in winter, and when it can pasture.

Dromedaries are not broken to riding until they are between two or three years old, and to put it off longer would be to risk their being restiff.

The training of a young dromedary is first begun by saddling him for several days without mounting him. When accustomed to the saddle, he is then mounted and ridden only at the pace, being constantly kept up to it and restrained from exceeding it. Afterwards he is taught to run, and is urged and excited to pass other dromedaries that may run with him.

In the first stages of training the dromedary should not be made to lie down for the rider to mount or dismount, but should be mounted standing. Without this precaution the young dromedary will acquire the habit of lying down without orders whenever a little fatigued.

Consulate General of the U. S. A., in Egypt,
Alexandria, January 5, 1856.

Dear Sir: As the best and shortest way of answering your queries addressed to me, I enclose the replies of Mr. Ayrtoun, which were submitted to you on your arrival in Egypt, with the comments which I will now put in writing.

Mr. Ayrtoun is an Englishman, who has enjoyed rare facilities for obtaining such information—having been long resident in the country, speaking the language, and filling the post of agent for the estates of Ilhami Pasha, son of the late viceroy.

He informs me that his information was obtained from Arabs, whose chief companions have been camels and dromedaries.

Having myself paid much attention to the subject for the last three years, I can testify to the correctness of most, if not all, of the answers, which also coincide with the statements contained in the admirable essay of M. Linant Bey, forwarded to the department by my predecessor, Mr. McCauley, five years since, to which it is difficult to add anything.

The kind offices of this gentleman had been requested in your behalf, in advance of your arrival; but, unfortunately, he is now engaged with the Scientific European Commission in making the exploratory survey for the Suez canal, which occupies all his time and attention.

Regarding this simply as the initiative step in an enterprise, which it will require more than one trial to complete, I take the liberty of making a few practical suggestions connected with it—the fruits of my own investigations and eastern experience.

As respects the camel for burden, I think you have good reason for the opinion you have expressed, that the climate of Smyrna, approximating more nearly to that of Texas than that of other places in the Levant, renders the selection of those animals there most judicious; although I believe the Egyptian camel would also thrive, if proper care to acclimate the animal were taken at first.

As to the second and more important point—the selection of the fleet dromedary—the post and courier of the desert—the matter is a little more difficult.

These animals can be obtained in Egypt, but are rare, and command high prices; and the viceroy will not allow their exportation except in an extraordinary case like the present, as a matter of international courtesy. But the place whence they are brought into Egypt, and where the best are to be found, is the Hedjas in Arabia, a journey which will require more time than you can probably spare on this excursion.

The route to the Hedjas is either by way of Suez, by water, or across the desert from Cairo. Taking the former route, leaving Alexandria, you can reach Suez, via Cairo, in twenty-four hours, whence a steamer will carry you to Jedda, on the Red Sea, in fifteen or twenty days. At Jedda, the dromedaries can be purchased at moderate prices by sending into the interior, which may consume a week or two more. The dromedaries purchased can be sent across the desert to Cairo by the Bedouins, to be paid for on their arrival, in thirty days' slow time, or as much faster as may be required. The government agent can either return with the caravan, or by the same way he came; or the dromedaries can be sent to Cairo, without his making the voyage, by giving the order to the British consul at Jedda, (we have none there,) who is an intelligent Englishman, well acquainted with the people and the country.

In my recent interview with the viceroy, when he gave the permission to export ten dromedaries which I asked of him, (although he has refused similar requests from several of my colleagues,) and who has liberally proffered six of his own dromedaries as a gift, in addition, he suggested the Hedjas as the proper place; and volunteered, in the event of the return of the expedition next year, to furnish such firmans (on my application) as would ensure the respectful treatment of its members, and the free passage of the animals through his dominions to the place of embarkation here.

I need scarcely add how pleased I shall be to greet the return of the expedition, and give it all the aid in my power; and, with the expression of the hope that the results of the enterprise may be commensurate with its importance, take this occasion to express my own decided judgment both of its utility and practicability, if a fair trial only be given it.

You will be kind enough to communicate to the Secretary of War the suggestions and proffers of the viceroy, as I deem it his due that his courtesy should be known; and accept my warmest wishes for the successful issue of the important enterprise in which you are engaged.

I remain, dear sir, very truly yours,

EDWIN DE LEON.

Major H. C. WAYNE, U. S. A.,
  U. S. Ship Supply, Alexandria Harbor, Egypt.

CAIRO, *December* 3, 1855.

MY DEAR SIR: I mentioned the subject of your note of the 15th November to H. H. Ilthamy Pacha, who has, he says, no camels to dispose of, which, however, will not be of much importance to your purpose, if I rightly understand its object, since camels of almost every kind may be procured in Egypt at moderate rates. Those proper to Egypt are bred in the country, and are known in lower Egypt as "kufury," or village camels, and in upper Egypt as "saidy." There are, also, camels in upper Egypt of the tribes frequenting the adjacent deserts, such as "Bisharyeh," and the "ababdeh," and other tribes, which may readily be known by a reference to the great French work on Egypt, or to Buckhardt and other travellers well known.

Of the two tribes above mentioned, the "Bisharyeh" camels are the most esteemed, but they are not reckoned equal in powers of endurance to the Arabian camel in the estimation of the Arabs of Arabia, who may possibly have some prejudice in favor of their own stock.

Of the Arabian breeds, the Namanyeh are the most prized. They are, I believe, from the neighborhood of Muscat. After them come the camels of the Beni Jakkar, near Mesopotamia, and of the Arabs of Gilbet Thanimar, although each tribe may be able to boast of one or more dromedaries, (in Arabic, heigin; in the singular, hegin;) of extraordinary swiftness and powers of endurance. With respect to pace, the usual rate upon a journey is about five miles an hour for a "hegin," and I should say not more than two and three-quarters for a loaded camel.

Loads tell upon camels as upon other animals. A "hegin" usually carries her rider or owner and a slave or other attendant who sits behind his master on the croup of the camel holding on by the hinder peg of the "shedad" or saddle; and in purchasing camels for exportation to America, it would certainly be desirable to send samples of the different kinds of saddles in use as well for loading as for riding.

On an emergency a good hegin can increase his pace to a much higher rate than that mentioned as his usual pace. I should say to from twelve to fourteen miles an hour, which he might keep up for two or three miles. I have certainly seen hegins run at that rate when following hawks in hawking, and when running under fire, as often happened when I was at Aden in 1840, endeavoring to pick them off with light artillery in position on the land side of the isthmus.

Buckhardt, in his notes on the Bedouins, mentions an extraordinary feat of an "Abadeh hegin;" but that feat was surpassed by the performance of a "Nomany" hegin, which, if I am rightly informed, went, upon the occasion of the late Ibrahim Pashaw's decease, to announce the tidings to Abbas Pacha, from Cairo to Mecca, in nine days. At Mecca the animal is said to have knocked up, and the messenger there to have procured a fresh hegin to continue his journey to Tayf, where Abbas Pacha was.

The distance between Cairo and Mecca cannot, according to Scoresby's chart of the Red Sea, be less than nine hundred statute miles, which is tremendous going.

The weight usually carried by an ordinary carrying camel is five kantar, or 495 lbs., English net, and the packsaddle must weigh at least fifty more. Some camels may be able to carry more, and for short distances 700 and 800 lbs. are not an uncommon load for a camel, or even 1,000 lbs. I will now proceed to answer your questions as succinctly as I can, and in the order given.

Query. At what price could ten or twelve dromedaries be purchased? Answer. Nomany dromedaries will cost from $100 to $1,000 each; others, of Arabian breed, may be procured for from $50 to $100.

Query. How many miles per diem can they travel, and how many hours in each twenty-four? Answer. On an emergency 100 miles, and all day; the mail is carried regularly twice a month between Cairo and Suez, distant eighty-four miles, without a halt, in about eighteen hours, and the weight of each camel load cannot be less than 300 lbs., if so little. It is, in short, four mail boxes. The ordinary rate of travelling on a hegin does not exceed forty miles in about eight hours per day; when pressed, their daily distance may be increased to sixty, and even seventy miles for many consecutive days.

Query. At what price could ten or twelve camels for burden be purchased? Answer. The best camels for burden are the "kufury" or village camels, of lower Egypt, which are worth from 500 to 1,000 piasters ($25 to $50) each; but, perhaps, for general purposes, the most likely camels to thrive in a foreign country, according to the opinion of an Arab to whom I mentioned the subject, would be the "shemalieh," or northern camels, found with the "Aneze" Arabs; of these, the "khouauri and gudieh breeds in Arak" (Mesopotamia) would be the best; they could be purchased for from $50 to $75 each. After them come the sherarieh. This Arab also informed me that wherever a species of shrub, called in Arabic "hand," and the botanic name of which I do not know, grows, the northern camel will thrive; and it was doubtful whether the Nomany camel, or those from the south of Egypt, would thrive in a colder climate, or in a moist climate.

Query. What weight would they (the camels for burden) carry? Answer. Habitually, 500 lbs., net; and for short distances as much as 1,000 lbs.

Query. How many miles per diem, and how many hours in each twenty-four? Answer: The usual rate of loaded camels is from twenty-five to thirty miles a day, which they perform in from nine to twelve hours.

Query. Can the dromedary or camel travel over stony or mountainous country? Answer. Stony ground is apt to injure their feet, and they are awkward in surmounting obstacles in mountainous parts, still a moderate extent of hills will not interrupt their progress.

Query. Over snow? Answer. Certainly not; the Egyptian or Arabian camel is unaccustomed to snow; the camels of Asia, however, must be inured to snow.

Query. Could they swim, if necessary, with a burden? Answer. The camel can swim, but requires to be guided by a man swimming with it in the water. With burdens, unless of cork, they certainly would make little way above the surface of the water.

Query. What species of dromedary or camel is it that they have in use in Egypt? This has already been answered.

Query. How long can they go without water? Answer. In winter, five days; in summer, three days.

Query. Without food? Answer. The camel always finds food in the scanty herbage of the desert. God has left no part of the earth so bare as not to sustain the life it produces.

Query. Is their exportation forbidden? Answer. This depends upon the existing treaties, and the interpretation of them.

Query. What would be the proper season to send them by sea to a foreign country? Answer. About the end of May.

Query. Could five or six Arabs be hired to accompany them? Answer. Not easily; but slaves, accustomed to camels, and brought up with the Arabs, might be obtained for hire or otherwise; or perhaps some of the Arabs bordering Egypt might be induced to go; or even Egyptians, versed in the habits and treatment of camels, might be procured.

Query. If so, at what rate of wages? Answer. The rate of wages, compared to American rates, would be of no importance.

Yours, truly,

FREDERICK AYRTOUN.

Edwin De Leon, Esq.,
  U. S. Consul General for Egypt, &c.

YENI KAPOO, CONSTANTINOPLE,
November 7, 1855.

DEAR SIR: After my interview with you on board your ship, I prepared several copies of a circular, based upon the letter of inquiry* you handed me respecting camels, and sent them in different directions to our missionaries in every part of the Turkish empire and in Persia.

I hope to hear from all these persons in due time, and if you have the purpose of leaving here, I shall be glad to know how I am to get the replies into your hands.

Mr. Powers, of Trebizond, has already written to me, and he says: "We have no camels here. No camels, storks, magpies, or buffaloes, inhabit this region. Once or twice I have seen, in Trebizond, a few camels, but *only* once or twice. The last time, I think, was in the fall of 1849, when some half a dozen were seen here, and the next summer I passed their bones, by the road side in the mountains, the second day from here, when I was on my way to Erzroun. They undertook to cross the mountains when it was rather late, suffered from cold and want of food, and perished."

I presume I shall have much more satisfactory answers to your questions from other parts, though, in one view, the above intelligence must also be satisfactory, as it must be as desirable to you to know where camels are not to be found as where they are.

Since I had the pleasure of seeing you, I have been to Nicomedia, and I could not but regret that you were not with me there. I saw large numbers of camels there, and some of them were really splendid fellows. They are now bringing grain to Nicomedia in large quantities from various parts of the interior, and large caravans of camels are constantly coming in.

A steamer leaves this place every Saturday morning for Nicomedia, and returns early on Sunday. You could easily go there with your ship if you were so disposed, as vessels of the largest class go up the Nicomedia gulf. I saw an Egyptian two-decker lying there three weeks ago; and the Turkish government has a navy yard there, at which the largest sized ships-of-war are built.

I am sorry we have not had the pleasure of seeing you at our house.

I remain, very truly, yours,

H. G. O. DWIGHT.

Captain D. PORTER,
United States Ship Supply.

MARSOVAN, *November* 15, 1855.

MY DEAR BROTHER DWIGHT: Your circular of October 27 reached me two weeks ago. I took note of the request not to detain, but of necessity kept it over one post (one week,) as must be done wherever it

---

*The circular letter of inquiry, of which a copy was enclosed to the department in my communication of the 5th October, 1855.   H. C. W.

stops. But to facilitate the business I made another copy, and sent it direct to Sivas, to go thence to Ceserea, while the original went to Tocat, to go thence direct to Kharsish, thus making a gain of "one half" in time.

Camels are not raised in Marsovan, but in a region called Bozouk, sixty or eighty miles south of us, of which Yorgat may be regarded as a centre. They pass, however, in great numbers here, on their way to and from Samsoum. Their owners are Turcomen. I have proposed your questions to various breeders and drivers of camels amongst these Turcomen, whom I have found here, and have received the following statements, which I give as I received, having no personal acquaintance with the matter: Answer to question 1. The varieties of camels furnished here are "first" male camels with "two humps," called Bouhoun; single camels of this variety are brought to Bozouk from Erzroun and the regions beyond, and also from the Crimea, but solely for the purpose of breeding. They are never used for burden. The "two-humped" female is not found here. "Second variety" single-humped camels of both sexes, coming originally from Arabia, but raised to some extent in Bozouk; the males are called "Lok," the females "Arvana."

Then, by a cross between the "Bouhoun," or two-humped male, and the "Arvana," or one-humped female, we have a third variety, single-humped, as useless as mules for breeding, but, like them, of great value as burden bearers.

The females of this cross breed are, then, of course, natives of Bozouk, and are called "Maya." The males are almost always castrated, or rather their stones are destroyed by twisting or crushing, and then they are called "Khadin" or eunuchs. A camel driver, however, usually leaves one of his cross-breed males intact, and makes of him a leader for his company of camels. This leader must himself be led by the halter to keep him out of mischief; the rest will follow him whether they are led or not.

Answer to question 2. Bouhouns are never loaded; are kept only for breeding, as above; loks are sometimes loaded, but are principally used for breeding, particularly to procure "Arvanas" in order to cross with the Bouhouns. The camels almost universally used for loads are these "Arvanas," and the cross-breed Mayas, and the Khadins. A common load for an "Arvana" is 400 to 500 pounds; for a cross-breed (a Maya or Khadin) 600 pounds. There is no limit to the number of consecutive days these camels will travel with their burdens, provided they are driven no more than their usual distance of 18 miles a day, and are allowed eight to ten hours to make these 18 miles. During this eight to ten hours, which should commence early enough in the morning to terminate soon after noon, camels are "never eased of their burdens." After unloading, it is customary to take off the pack-saddle for a little to rub the camel with the hand, and to examine the state of the back.

Answer to question 3. Camels descend from the table-lands of central Asia Minor (6,000 feet above the sea) to the shores of the Black and Mediterranean seas, and return, through every variety of climate, crossing mountains and plains, over roads rocky and sandy, without injury; nor do I learn, in answer to question 4, of any particular effect upon their feet from their long journeys, even over rocky ground; but am told, in answer to question 6, that camel drivers are in the habit of carrying with them wooden shovels to make stepping places for their animals in mud or snow, when passing up or down steep hills. They also carry axes to break or roughen ice to enable the camels to pass without slipping.

Answer to question 5. When there is no snow on the ground, the camels are turned out, after their day's journey is finished, to find their own food from grass, leaves, tender twigs, &c. If there is not a sufficiency of this kind of food, cut straw is given in addition; and when snow covers the ground they are fed entirely with straw and barley meal wet with water, of which wet meal or dough two or three pounds are given to each camel at evening. Camels are watered once or twice a day if convenient, but can do without water two or three days if necessary. They are never stabled on their journeys; but are at home put under a roof (open at the sides) in the winter. When journeying through snow their camping ground is cleared with a shovel.

Answer to question 6. I hear of no precautions to be taken in loading or unloading a camel, except to confine the amount of the load to the strength of the animal. Camels, as is well known, are taught to kneel to receive and deposit their loads. This is done when young, by raising one of the fore feet, and, binding the leg in a bent position, the halter is jerked down; this brings the animal on his knees, when the other leg is bound, and he is thus compelled to sit. The driver accompanies this jerking, or bearing down of the halter, with a peculiar sound of "khrr," "khrr," "khrr," and, after a few lessons, the camel learns always to kneel when he hears the "khrr" or feels the jerk.

Answer to question 7. Camels rut in January. In preparation for this time, the Bouhoun, two months before, say early in November, is fed for fifteen or twenty days with wheat at the rate of one peck a day, and for the remainder of the two months with barley, at the rate of half a peck per day. In January he is brought to the "Arvanas," (four or five each day,) who receive him sitting. Sterility is not common among the "Arvanas" (one in one thousand.) The Mayas or cross breed camels are always sterile, or, if they have progeny, it is useless. The "Arvana" carries her young twelve months or a little more, and should not be heavily loaded for eight to nine months before or for the month after time of giving birth.

Answer to question 8. Calves, after birth, are bolstered up on both sides, to teach them to sit camel-fashion. They are fed for one or two days with a little butter, and for three days must be put to the mother's teats and be taught to suckle. After this, no further care is needed. They run by their mothers sides for ten to eleven months and then wean themselves. When two to three years old they begin to carry light loads, and will do service for twenty-five to thirty years. (For remainder of answer to question 8, see under question 6.)

Answer to question 9. I do not hear of any plants or food as hurtful to camels, nor of any diseases to which they are particularly subject. After taking cold black rings appear on their tongues. Upon these rings blue vitriol should be sprinkled. In the summer time the camel sheds his hair. He should then be smeared with tar, to keep off the flies, and sent to pasture in the mountains for a few weeks.

Answer to question 10. The price of a Bouhoun may be put down at $120; of the cross breed Khadin and Mayas $80 each; of Arabian camels, *id est* "Loks" and "Arvanas," at $40; of females with their calves running by their side, at $50 to $60. These I suppose to be the minimum prices. Arabian camels would be cheaper in Syria.

Question 11 answered in effect in No. 2.

Question 12 and 13. No dromedaries, no fighting camels, found here.

Question 14 and 15. Camels in great numbers, in the ordinary course of trade, pass this place to Sansoum on the Black Sea. They might be found there (extraordinaries excepted) at any time between October and April. I have passed, seemingly, interminable strings of them on the road to Sansoum (laden with wheat and barley) in February. Bouhouns would not be found there, not being used for burden. For the same reason few Loks would be found there. These would need to be obtained from Yoggat or other Turcoman place, or, better still, from their native lands; the one is the Crimea, the other is Syria.

Should anything of importance in addition to the above, or connexion of it, come to my knowledge I will write you again. Meanwhile, I remain, as ever, most truly yours,

EDWIN E. BLISS.

Rev. H. G. O. Dwight, D. D.,
    Constantinople.

Mosul, *November* 17, 1855.

Dear Sir: Your camel circular came at a most unpropitious time: Mr. March still an invalid, and I in the midst of lettering eight grave stones, and the stonecutters pressing me for "copy." If I keep the circular (which I have not time to copy) over to the next mail, and each of the other stations do the same, it will be three and half or four months before the replies get in. So I have done the best I could: called in two principal cameliers of my acquaintance and put to them the questions in their order. The replies, taken down from their mouths, you have here just as I scratched them off, for really I am unable to copy or digest them from want of time. I hope they will be found legible and intelligible, but I fear somewhat. The measurement I took myself. As to weighing, a camel was never weighed in these parts. Mr. March is now nearly well.

Truly yours,

W. F. WILLIAMS.

Rev. H. G. O. Dwight, D. D.,
    Constantinople.

P. S. I enclose for examination a specimen of a kind of herb whic is used here instead of soap, and which the camelier says is the best food in the world for camels; if this is found on the desert plains the camels there will become the finest in the world. (This specimen did not reach me. It would have been desirable to have compared it with the soap plant of the North American continent. H. C. W.)

Question 1. "Indee," from the Arâk *id est*, the plains of the Tigris and Euphrates, from Bagdad to the Persian Gulf, and the Khoo-wâr, from upper Mesopotamia, (that is Mesopotamia north of fifty miles above Bagdad, called El Tezereh.)

The "Indee" has a long thin nose and is usually a trifle larger than the Khoo-wâr, but the chief and probably only difference is that the latter will die from the effects of marsh grasses and insects, which have no injurious influence on the former, which are nourished and brought up in a marshy region, while those of El Tezereh in an intensely dry district; briefly, the "Indee" are "raised" in El Arâk, and the Khoo-wâr are raised in El Tezereh, and really this is the whole of the difference.

Question 2. As to burdens they are equal, say 400 to 600 pounds, average load 500 pounds, which they will carry year in and year out, daily, if well protected from cold, and well fed; six to eight hours a day's journey.

A caravan of camels once came in 13 days from Aleppo via Orfa and the desert, but ordinarily caravans are 25 to 45 days "en route." Ordinarily the loads are loosed every night, but on "emergency" the camels will travel three or four days without unloading or resting except to eat, provided he has all the food he needs; this without killing him. Pack saddles are removed only when the camels are turned out to grass in the spring.

Question 3. Climate most intensely hot and dry. Journeys are made to Aleppo, Scanderoon, Mecca, Egypt, and with the "Indee" to Busrah. The flies and marsh gnats about and below Bagdad kill the Khoo-wâr. They of course travel best in a level country, but can and do at times pass through rocky and mountainous localities.

Question 4. None, but difficult, and occasionally or frequently one will get lame, but rarely so as to disable it.

Question 5. Nine months of the year do not feed them; they browse on what they can pick up on the plains as they travel, and when turned out at night. The Bedaween never feed their camels. Caravan camels are fed three months, (winter) once a day. Seven pounds of ground barley or "backuly," (a large bean) kneaded into cakes, and cut dry straw always before them. When for three months in spring they are out at grass they do not drink at all, the rest of the year they are watered morning and evening. Are never stabled here; but if the country is cold and snowy they need open sheds or stables.

Question 6. None. When the road is very slippery they sometimes with an adze cut out the road, track it so as to make it rough.

Question 7. From the middle of December to the middle or end of January. For the three winter months the sexes are kept separate, except when it is desired to breed. Rest of the year the sexes travel together or not, as convenient. As to copulation, the cameliers put a male to 10, 15, or even 30 females; though it is known of one male attending to 120 females in the course of the rutting season. For the most part the breeding male is not worked, so that he may be strong and in good condition for breeding. But few females are barren, say "one per centum." No males impotent. The camels of the Bedaween do little but breed. The pregnant camel is rarely loaded, and then but lightly. Pregnancy is 14 months; not worked until the calf is 10 months old, when she is also ready for the male again.

Question 8. The mothers care for them. At 10 months the nose of the calf is adorned with a nail, so as to prevent suckling, or this is delayed till 12 months. He begins to bear burdens at 3 to 4 years. They begin by catching them and binding some light thing about them, as a carpet or two, and turning them loose with it. Some camels attain to the age of 25 years, bearing burdens, but a camel of 15 years is called old.

Question 9. Chiefly from marsh grass in spring and summer, rest of the year no harm. No remedy. Heavy burdens in spring and summer also disease them. Remedy, cautery in chest. For boils and irruptions in the skin the camel is dressed with a coat of tar. If the shoulder is sprained by a fall, the remedy is the "actual cautery;" if a bone is broken, "no remedy," let them die; if the neck becomes awry, apply the cautery to the side of the neck freely, thus, | | | | and cut a gash in the top of the head, and sew it up with thread of wool; abrasions from the pack saddle, apply pounded alum dry. If a wounded camel smells any spice or drug, he dies, unless the wound be cut semi-circularly around with a knife. The "Indee" can with impunity eat all grasses, and endure all insects; but for six months, spring or summer, these are deadly to the Khoo-wâr, as before mentioned.

Question 10. 300 to 700 piastres; from 300 to 700 francs; but if the calf is a year and a half old it is worth 100 to 150 francs.

Question 11. The "Indee" is preferred for the reasons above given, and there is also a fancy value from color, &c., &c., but as to actual worth no difference,

Question 12. Called "Delool." The only difference is in the training. A she "Delool" is no longer a "Delool" after she has become pregnant, but her calf stands a better chance than an ordinary calf. A first rate "Delool" will go to Aleppo via Orfa in 6 or 7 days, eating what she picks by the way, unless in early winter before the grass starts, when there is nothing to eat. If emergency requires, she will go three days without drink.

Question 13. Unless the "Delool," not known.

Question 14. Scanderoon (Alexandretta) any time, but better avoid the wet winter months.

Question 15. Frequently caravans from here visit Scanderoon and Busrah

Note to question 1. The average size here is about "one yard high;" when lying down, 5 feet 4 inches, to 5 feet 8 inches long from tail to root of neck; 3 feet from shoulder to head and from 3 feet 4 inches, to 3 feet 7½ inches in leg; height measured to the callosity on which they rest when lying.

Note to question 7. The two-humped camel found at Thaiserea, &c.,

is another animal. All here are "one-humped," and the size of this hump depends on the fatness of the animal; when very fat it is four or five times as large as when lean, indeed, at times it almost disappears. The "two-humped" is sometimes bought here (a male) at a great price (2,500 francs or so) for breeding purposes; but the result is a mule impotent of progeny.

Note to question 12. The "Delool" is trained from three years old. First caught and fastened to a stake three days, no food, only water; then some light thing is put on her, feeding her with grass, or so, and leave her with this some five days more; then increase the weight; then after ten days more loose her and mount her, and teach her to travel fast.

NOTES UPON THE CAMEL,

COLLECTED FROM

REPORTS UPON THE USE OF THE CAMEL IN ALGIERS

BY

GENERAL J. L. CARBUCCIA, OF THE FRENCH ARMY,

AND FROM

The letter of General E. Daumas, directeur des affaires de l'Algerie, &c., upon the acclimation of the camel in France: by Albert Ray, late pack-mule train and wagon master in the United States army, and attached to the camel expedition under Major Henry C. Wayne, United States army. U. S. ship Supply, September, 1855.

PROPAGATION.

Stud camels are never employed as beasts of burden. They should be, as much as possible of a uniform color, either exclusively black, white, bay, &c., with eyes large and black. They should be high statured, well limbed, with hump large, neck long, and chest wide and deep, this last quality is indispensable. Before the stud camel is used for propagation, he must have given proof in several journeys of his strength and vigor, and especially of his powers of abstinence.

GESTATION AND PARTURITION.

The female camel goes with young twelve months, and gives birth about the end of winter. They are at this period treated with great care and attention, the poor only loading and using them as usual, and even then ceasing to do so, at least, one month prior to delivery. The young born in the first month of spring will live, those born after this period, or in summer or autumn, will most likely die. The principal imperfections of the camel consist in the malconformation of the humps and of the sternum; irregularity of gait is caused by the same defects in the shoulders and the hind legs. The Arabs say that one year after the female has received the stud, day for day, she is delivered. When "enciente" the female is called "legaa;" sometimes the female is lightly loaded to the day of her delivery.

TREATMENT AFTER PARTURITION.

As soon as the camel has dropped her young, she is curried with care from the hump to the tail. The young is entirely covered with the exception of its hump, which protrudes through an aperture cut for it in the cover. The mother does not go to pasture for seven or eight days, when the young one can go with her. The young camel is taught to suck in the following manner:

A man greases his finger with warm butter and places it in his mouth, the little one sucks upon it, and then is introduced to its mother's teat. After a few such lessons it learns to suck of its own accord. At pasture it also soon learns to crop and graze.

The young camel sucks at all hours during the spring and summer, but in the autumn and winter following at night and morning only. To hinder the young from sucking the teats of the mother are secured by a bandage. When it is concluded to wean the young one it is placed in a separate pasture or troop, and in a few weeks it forgets its parent. If the female has been delivered towards the end of winter, she generally remains undisturbed until the next winter, when she again conceives so as to produce the winter after. In some instances females have been known to produce in two successive years. After delivery the mother calls her young in a hoarse and lugubrious cry; it is shown to her, and repeatedly presented to her, but she does not recognize it; until the calf has been shown and repeatedly presented to her, she will not allow it to approach her udder. The young suck after the first day, they do not walk until the seventh.

MISCARRIAGES.

Miscarriages are common, more so when the "legaa" is troubled by flies. A light load will not cause it. Abortions at two or three months are perfectly formed, even the hump being distinguishable.

BARRENNESS.

This is caused by over loading and is common. A protrusion of the vagina is also caused by the same carelessness, but is soon relieved by rest.

CASTRATION.

All camels intended for burden are to be castrated to avoid the trouble they cause when in heat, and also to increase their strength and hardihood. This is done early in the spring of the year, and in two modes, either by perforating the testicles with a red hot iron, or by opening the scrotum and detaching the testicles with a red hot knife, taking care to tie the suspensory cords. Up to twelve years old the operation may be performed. This operation, generally successful, is nevertheless not without danger.

SHEARING.

Towards the end of April the Arabs shear the camel. It is done as follows: the animal is made to lie down, and the herdsmen clip the hair with sharp knives, one of them following collecting the hair. It is a tedious operation. The shearing commences at two years old.

TARRING.

Every year after shearing the camel is covered with a mixture of oil and tar, thrice during the spring and twice during the summer. This is to preserve it from the itch.

PURGING.

This is generally done at the same time as the shearing and tarring. The Arabs make a purge by heating a pound of rancid butter and stirring therein two or three eggs.

DISEASES.

The itch, (or mange,) this is only mortal when the animal remains uncurried before the arrival of winter, as its body being then deprived of hair it cannot resist the cold. Every animal attacked with the itch must be at once separated from the rest, or in a few days he will have infected the whole troop. His saddle, harness, &c., must be carefully scrubbed prior to being again used. Tar must be applied to the parts affected, and if the weather is warm, the hair around them must be cut off. It is rare that one application is enough. On the fifteenth day, the skin being dry, it can be seen whether or not the disease is cured. If cured, the hair has commenced to grow again. The itch cannot be too carefully guarded against, nor can too much care be taken in separating the infected animals from the rest and from each other. A troop should be inspected every day, and tar kept always on hand to rub on suspected places. If the itch is old and inveterate, it is necessary to tar the animal not only on those parts of the body that seem to require it least, but even the mouth, teeth, and toe nails.

The slemma, (cholic,) this is not a serious malady. It is generally caused by the animal having drank stagnant water, and it soon disappears of itself.

The magout is a disease caused by the girth being placed in front of the sheath, instead of behind it. A tumor is formed, and the animal cannot urinate. The Arab method of curing it is to open the skin near the penis, which they lay hold of, and pull forward in such a manner as to relax the nerve. This operation proves sufficient.

The "moroos" is a cracking of the sole of the foot, which causes a bad lameness for a time, but it soon disappears, without requiring any application.

The "metla" is a disease peculiar to the female, and is caused by her being over loaded. It is a falling of the vagina. A few days' rest suffices for its cure.

The "dedab," a tormenting fly, peculiar to Arabia.

WOUNDS.

When a camel is lamed by a fall, the Arabs cauterize the wounded part. Wounds are generally cured by the application of tar mixed with the fat of fresh beef or mutton, or by the fat alone. The dressing is renewed every day. Tar, tobacco, ashes, the leaf of the tree or shrub *aria*, dried and powdered, is also used. Sulphate of copper is used as long as the wound contains worms or maggots, but must not be continued too long, as it has a tendency to burn the flesh, and instead of healing may retard the cure. The final cure must be affected by a compress, wet with brandy or alcohol, tincture of aloes, or powdered charcoal.

A judicious use of the above remedies will generally effect a cure, even of a bad wound, in about twenty days.

MEDICINES.

Tar, sulphate of copper, bi-sulphate of mercury, and the cautery are the only external remedies used by the Arabs. Oil, rancid butter, and garlic, the only internal medicines.

QUALITY OF THE TAR.

The health of the animal depending much on the quality of the tar, it must be carefully looked to in that respect, too free an application causing vertigo, and sometimes death. The French, in Algiers, in acquiring experience in the use of tar, have had to pay for it by loosing many of their camels in consequence of the ill-will and jealousy of the Arabs, who have always endeavored to disgust them on their attempts to use the camel for military or other purposes. Sometimes they have sold them pine-tree tar, which is of no effect against the itch; sometimes a compound of pitch, fish-oil, tallow, and oakum, that literally burnt the beasts, and caused the deaths of a great number. The Arabs have also sold them fir-tree tar, mixed with that produced by the trees called "arar" and "tagar," thus saving to themselves half the labor. The best tar is of a liquid aromatic resinous quality. The French, in Algiers, have tried to substitute sulphur ointment for tar. It appears, so far, to have succeeded, but as yet they have not had sufficient experience to decide positively on its merits. In places where sulphur ointment cannot be procured, workmen from the military laboratory have been employed in manufacturing the tar.

Abd-el-Kader has also a number of operatives engaged in the same business. A goat-skin full, containing twenty pints, costs three francs. Each animal requires forty pints per annum. This quantity is necessary not only to keep the animal in health, but to keep it free from the itch.

Camels should be tared no less than five times a year, especially if worked. It is well to remark that the itch often proceeds from uncleanness. The Arabs often change their bivouacs to hinder their animals from lying down in filthy places. They regard this sanitary precaution as very important.

In reference to the annual spring tarring of the camel, subsequent to its shearing, it is well to observe that it is better not to work the animal for one month after the operation.

The subsequent tarrings (in spring and summer) must be made lightly on the hair alone, without touching the parts covered by the pack-saddle. After these four last tarrings, the camel can be worked within twenty-four hours. Fine dry weather must be invariably chosen for the tarrings, or the animal is liable to die.

FOOD, &c.

The camel eats apparently whatever vegetation the earth produces. It loves to gather its own food, and will then eat almost anything. If its food is given to it ready cut, or gathered, it becomes then very fastidious, and cares only for thistles or other tender herbs. As a general rule, care must be taken that the camel is not sent out to pasture before the dew is off the grass. Ten at night is a good hour to return them from it. In autumn they are sent out after the rising, and returned home before the setting of the sun. In winter they are pastured as in autumn, but they are only allowed to drink when the water has been warmed by the sun.

Camels are in the habit of lying down and ruminating on their arrival at camp; they must be compelled to rise, and eat, as they sleep only four hours, they will have time enough to ruminate during the night. In reference to the dew the Arabs are not agreed as to its injurious effects. The French in Algiers, however, deem its effects hurtful. Barley and straw broken are fed to the camel when pasturage cannot be had. When on a march and on arrival at camp no herbage or long feed is to be obtained, the camel has then given to it a few balls of ground wheat, horse beans or barley, made into a thick paste or dough. Sustained by this, the traveller "Shaw" says he has seen a camel carry a load of seven hundred pounds ten or fifteen hours a day without stopping for several days. The Arabs say it is necessary to let camels have pasturage and young shrubs in summer, they give it then neither barley nor straw, and it subsists upon what it can get, preferring spinous plants, with the exception of the aloe, which it dislikes. To fatten the camel its pasturage should be occasionally changed. In a good pasturage it will eat enough in two hours to last it for twenty-four, after the spring of the year, or when the camel has not been allowed green food, it must be purged with wheat boiled in oil.

AGE AT WHICH THE CAMEL IS LOADED.

At four years the camel is loaded and used for all purposes; at five he is in full vigor and preserves it up to nine; from nine to thirteen he begins to lose his strength, and at seventeen he is old.

A CAMEL'S LOAD.

A strong vigorous animal can easily carry, on a level road, from seven hundred and fifty to eight hundred pounds. In a hilly country the load ought not to exceed five hundred pounds, saddle included. When necessity demands it they can be fully loaded, even in a mountainous region, but in that case there must be spare animals in the troop.

PACE OF THE CAMEL.

If not over driven the camel will march loaded from sunrise to sunset; stretching his neck from side to side of the road, he gathers the herbage within his reach, and in this manner makes his thirty to forty miles per day. It is well, or rather necessary, to rest him every sixth day. The camel must never be "pushed" but in cases of necessity During the march the pace is relaxed when the ground offers good pasturage, and accelerated when it does not.

SIGNS OF AGE BY THE TEETH.

At two years old the camel has no teeth; at four years, he has two incisors; at five, four teeth, (incisors;) at six, six incisors; at eight, eight incisors. It has also canine teeth and molars.

FLESH OF THE CAMEL.

If by accident a camel breaks a leg it must be killed. Its flesh so much resembles beef that it cannot readily be distinguished from it. It is much more tender than beef.

HUMP.

The condition of the camel can always be known by the size of the hump, which is formed from the superabundant nourishment. The re-absorption of this glandular like substance compensates in a manner for the scarcity of food. During a long march the hump is seen gradually to diminish. In case of famine it disappears first; then the fat of the belly; and lastly the flesh and fullness of the limbs. When the camel has arrived at the last of these stages, it must certainly die.

DRINK OF THE CAMEL, ITS RESERVOIRS FOR WATER.

The camel generally drinks once in three days, and the Arabs say the reason it drinks so seldom is that it secretes no bile. The quantity it drinks at one time varies from thirty to forty pints. It supports hunger and thirst with a patience that would be thought little short of miraculous were one ignorant of the construction of its stomach, which is not only capable of containing water in reserve but, according to Cuvier, of producing it. The camel has not only four stomachs like all ruminants, but has also in one of them a species of reservoir, formed by cavities, or cells, which may altogether contain twenty pints of water, which will remain in them without deterioration, and to such an extent, stated by a celebrated traveller, that he has seen a camel disemboweled that had been dead ten days, in whose reservoir was found three pints of water yet drinkable; compressing these cells or this reservoir, by the action of the appropriate muscles, the animal moistens its food. The Arabs say, (and the French in Algiers seem inclined to the same opinion,) that the water is produced by an alimentary secretion "per se."

A dromedary dying by accident, it was opened in the presence of several French officers. The reservoir presented the appearance and consistency of a melon and contained more than fifteen pints of a greenish water with no bad flavor. The Arabs present affirmed that if it were allowed to settle for three days it would become clear and drinkable. The French tried it, and the Arabs were found to be correct in their statements.

THE CAMEL IN BAD ROADS.

It often happens that in ascending an acclivity or muddy road, the camel falls upon his knees, his fore feet slipping. He does not then try to rise but goes on in that position, nor does he try to right himself until he is out of the bad part of the road. He easily slips on clay soil, especially after rain. He should in such case be brought to a halt, as he is liable to break his legs, especially the hinder ones. There is not the same amount of danger in rocky ground, although the Arabs in the latter case cover their feet with a sort of moccasin or shoe of bullock hide to protect them from being cut when they slip.

CHARACTER OF THE CAMEL.

The camel is the most gentle and submissive of all animals. It is somewhat stubborn, it is true, but not so much so as the mule, and it is easily and quickly corrected. It is so patient that it will proceed with its load until completely exhausted, and then it falls never again to rise. In the military expedition of the French in Algiers, in the month of April, 1844, it was astonishing to see their camels, although reduced to skeletons, making forced marches with their loads. Mules in their condition could not have carried even their saddles.

PACK-SADDLE.

The pack-saddle for the camel is composed of three parts: the cylindrical pack, or pad of woolen or hair cloth, the wooden frame, and the ropes. When the wool or hair cloth has been cut into the form of a cylinder, it is stuffed with straw or other light substance. The cloth must not be woven too close. The wooden part of the saddle is of various forms, differing according to the country in which the camel is used. It is made of two cross bars of hard wood, formed into the shape of the letter V reversed, and joined near the top by two horizontal transverse pieces of wood. It is placed over the pack, one of the cross bars being in front of the hump, the other in the rear of it. The saddle is attached to the body of the camel by a girth fastened to the middle of the right side of the cross bar, the first half of the girth in front of the saddle passing over the sternum. The second half of the girth behind the saddle is placed according to the sex of the animal, either in front of the udder or behind the sheath. This portion of the girth is apt to wound the animal in its most sensitive part, and requires to be carefully looked to on the road and in saddling. It must be often cleaned and covered with sheep skin with the wool on. The girth is of leather, four or five inches wide, and should also be lined with sheep skin where it takes over the breast. The lashings or ropes for the cargo should be of soft texture also, as the camel easily chafes.

HALTER.

The halter should be used, as it familiarizes the animal to man; perhaps the halter can be advantageously substituted by a ring passed through the nose, as is the custom in Eygpt. The camel is then as much the slave of man as the horse.

MANNER OF CONDUCTING AND MANAGEMENT.

Camels in their management require much care, judgment and attention. When the males are sent to pasture, they must be separated from the females as much as possible. It is also necessary to guard against the camels eating what horses may have left from their feed of the previous night. In summer and in autumn the camel should be watered once in three days. If in a bad road the animal falls, especially if caused by fatigue, he must be well attended to. To make him rise, slap him on the flanks now and then, cheering him as is the custom. If it becomes necessary to use blows, strike sharply, but only on the thighs, never on the head or belly. When harshness fails, give him some of his favorite food, a few thistles, or other plant of his liking, after which whistle sharply, when he will rise and continue his march. Previous to setting out on a long march, when forage is expected to be scarce, (or known to be so,) the fattest and most vigorous camels should be selected. Care should be taken to relax the pace when the train is passing through a country containing good feed, as the conductor can regain the lost distance so as to encamp at a reasonable hour. It is not true that the camel's load can be left on it all night with impunity, for the animal likes to roll and lie on its side as do other animals. The camel cannot be habitually used in a mountainous country, and if in case of necessity he is so used it must be in the dry season. He can ascend acclivities to the grade of "forty five degrees" even when loaded.

GENERAL REMARKS.

A train or troop of camels consists ordinarily of one hundred, thirty-five to forty of which are females. Two of the finest males are reserved to be used as stallions, the others are castrated. Every spring the animal sheds his coat.

It is thought by some that the animal's rutting season is marked by the sweating at the back of the head, and by the ejection from the mouth of the palate or skin. This phenomenon, however, takes place at any time when the animal is strongly excited or in anger; the sweat can be seen also standing between his ears. During the summer a wounded camel ought to be at once unloaded and attended to, if not worms will appear in the wound and be very apt to cause the animal to die. To prevent such losses, when circumstances require that the animals be worked the second month of summer, (in Algiers,) it is advisable to have one sixth of them spare animals. The annual loss of camels when at work averages twelve per cent.

THE ANATOMY OF THE DROMEDARY.

TRANSLATED

From the official report of General J. L. Carbuccia, by Dr. S. A. Engles, United States Navy.

NECESSITY FOR A SPECIAL EXAMINATION BY A SCIENTIFIC PERSON.

The anatomy of the dromedary would deserve to be seriously studied by a skillful veterinary surgeon. A report made by a competent person would be of great interest to science.

We will confine ourselves here to recording the observations which we have been able to make during several autopsies.

COMPARISON OF THE DROMEDARY WITH THE HORSE AND OX.

In order to give an exact idea of the anatomical organization of the dromedary, we will compare it sometimes to the horse, sometimes to the ox, and even now and then to both those animals at the same time, for it resembles both of them very much.

SKIN OF THE DROMEDARY.

The skin of the dromedary is one third thicker than that of the ox.

LIPS.

Its upper lip is swollen and splits for 34 millemetres, (about 1.3 inches, H. C. W.,) an arrangement necessary for its feeding.

LARYNX.

Its larynx contains usually some white worms two centimetres in length and five millimetres in thickness, (about .7 of an inch long by .1 of an inch thick, H. C. W.)

BRAIN.

Its brain is larger than that of the ox, but smaller than that of the horse.

BUCCAL MUCOUS MEMBRANE.

The buccal mucous membrane of the dromedary hangs in the pharynx; when the animal is rutting, or when it is greatly agitated, that mucous membrane is expelled from the mouth with a loud noise, produced by the air; it presents wrinkles and folds sufficiently large to form a pouch where the food remains during the act of rumination; on its surface that pouch is covered with papillae larger than those of the ox. The mucous membrane of the tongue also contains nervous papillae of remarkably irregular forms.

NECK.

The neck of the dromedary has on each side two veins and one artery, as is the case with all the ruminating animals; it is of a deformed length.

TRACHEA.

The trachea is formed by a tube, longer but not so large as those of all the other animals; the nostrils being also very narrow, it follows that the air has a small passage by which to arrive at the lungs, the main organ of respiration.

SUBSTANCE OF THE HUMP.

The substance of the hump is greasy, and can be compared to that of the udder of the cow.

ANTERIOR WALL OF THE ABDOMEN.

The anterior wall of the abdomen of the dromedary is much stronger than that of other animals; the white line which divides it into two parts in the middle is very prominent. The muscles of that region cross each other in the most solid manner.

COMPARTMENTS OF THE STOMACH.

The ox has his stomachic apparatus composed of four stomachs; it is the same case with the dromedary; those of this last, although having different and better defined forms, can receive the same names. We will content ourselves, nevertheless, with designating them by their numbers of order.

PAUNCH, OR FIRST STOMACH.

In the cases of all the dromedaries which had died the evening before, we have remarked that the paunch, the first stomach of the ruminants, contained 50 or 60 pounds of grass drowned in a more or less considerable quantity of greenish water; that paunch contains a great number of pockets, closed by some fibres or longitudinal bridles, which do not communicate with each other; these pockets or troughs, which give to the interior of that part of the paunch the appearance of a melon with very prominent slices, were, we repeat it, designedly filled with water and food, and more developed in the paunch of the dromedary than in that of the ox.

SECOND STOMACH.

The second stomach of the dromedary is composed of a number of tendinous bridles forming a great many small cells divided among themselves by the membrane of the stomach; the passage from the second to the third stomach is an opening of 30 millimetres (about 1.1 inches, H. C. W.) in diameter, formed in a very strong muscular bridle.

THIRD AND FOURTH STOMACHS.

These two stomachs present membranous partitions forming very numerous compartments in the third stomach, these partitions are held by strong bridles of a muscular character, the walls of which are furnished with thin laminæ close together or parallel; whilst in the fourth stomach, the interlacing of the blood vessels takes place through simple membranes.

DOUBTS ON THE EXISTENCE OF THE FIFTH STOMACH.

The appendix to the paunch, designated by naturalists under the name of reservoir of water, and which occupies the position of the "bonnet" in the ox, to which, however, it offers a different interior structure, has long been considered by some of them as forming the fifth stomach. This distinction, established wrongfully, between the two parts composing the first stomach has been abandoned. Other naturalists, renouncing the design of making a special stomach of the appendix to the first stomach, but pre-occupied also with the thought that there ought to be five stomachs in the dromedary, have counted as a stomach a dilatation of the digestive canal placed at the beginning of the duodenum. We believe this to be equally incorrect. To sum up, by an attentive comparison between the stomachic apparatus of the ox and that of the dromedary, it appears that the fifth stomach cannot be admitted to exist.

LUNGS OF THE DROMEDARY.

The lungs of the dromedary have a form similar to those of the horse; they are more voluminous than those of the latter; they are a little stronger than those of the ox. That spongy viscus can, then, only contain a small quantity of air in comparison to the mass of the body; from which fact it is necessary to conclude that the dromedary is an animal intended to support a continuous, but not violent, fatigue; that it can, for example, draw a carriage only with difficulty, and, in short, that it is not organized to work in hilly countries.

RIBS.

The ribs of the dromedary are twelve in number, like those of the ox.

KIDNEYS.

The two kidneys, composed, if it may be expressed thus, of a multitude of little kidneys, are more bulky than those of the horse; however, they do not offer the same conformation as those of that animal and the ox; they resemble a large, round, enclosed ear-ring. They are composed of three different substances. Each kidney weighs one and a half pounds; one is generally larger than the other.

HEART.

The heart of the dromedary resembles that of the horse; the auricles are twice as large as those of the heart of the latter.

LIVER.

The liver is composed of a large number of lobules, of a lozenge shape, which can be lifted up separately and which are more prominent on one side than on the other. The substance of it is firmer and more granular than that of other animals. The liver of the dromedary is divided into two, as that of the horse, whilst that of the ox is composed of one piece alone.

DOUBTS RESPECTING THE EXISTENCE OF THE BILIARY FLUID.

All the researches made in order to find the yellowish fluid which is called bile in the viscus of the abdomen, called the liver, which is composed of different glands fitted to separate that liquid from the mass of the blood, (Lavoisier's Dictionary of Medicine,) have been fruitless. It is generally known that the gall bladder, which always exists in the carnivorous animals, is wanting sometimes, even often, in the herbivorous; so it is not astonishing to find that bladder absent in the dromedary. But what is surprising is, that in the case of the animals who have died even after a long abstinence, no trace of bile is presented in the ducts of the liver.

OF THE GENITAL PARTS OF THE DROMEDARY.

The formation of the genital organs of the male dromedary is in all respects similar to that of those of the bull, excepting that the sheath, being directed backwards, draws with it the end of the yard, which changes in direction for the act of coupling.

The vagina of the female is the same as that of the cow; the urinary duct into the vagina is, however, more narrow in the first. The paps are placed between the thighs, as in all the ruminants.

CALLOSITIES.

The callosity of the sternum, the asseous portion of the front of the chest, is formed of a soft horn, or tumour without hair, in all respects similar to the ergot of the horse; this is natural, since it, as well as the hump, are found in the abortions.

Under the sternum is found a fatty tissue of fifteen millemitres (about .5 of an inch, H. C. W.) in thickness. As to the six other callosities, they are only the results of the thickening of the skin produced by the friction of those parts, for underneath them the flesh exists.

SOLE OF THE FEET.

The sole of the feet is a true, polished horn, only slightly hard. Underneath it is also a fatty cushion, denser and more bulky than that which exists in other animals; that sole connects, nearly to their extremities, the two toes. It is especially in consequence of the disproportion between its legs and its feet that the dromedary appears so deformed.

Note.—The reductions from centimetres and millemetres are, throughout, to inches and tenths of inches, English. H. C. W.

POWDER HORN,
Three miles below Indianola, May 1, 1856.

Sir: I have the honor to report my arrival off this bar, with the camels, on the afternoon of the 29th, at $4\frac{1}{2}$ p. m., and the anchoring of the Supply about 8 miles from the bar. Yesterday the sea was too rough to communicate with the shore, but this morning the Fashion came off to us. On account of the swell no lightering could be done to-day, so I am ashore to see what arrangements have been made and what more were necessary for the safe landing of the animals. Everything is now complete, if the sea, which is said to be unusually heavy for this season of the year, will permit the transfer of the animals from the Supply to the Fashion, or other lighters. I am happy to inform you that we have arrived, after an unusually rough passage, with one more camel than we started with. Further particulars by succeeding mails. I write in a hurry, in the post-office, as the Fashion is waiting to return to the ship.

Very repectfully, your obedient servant,
HENRY C. WAYNE,
Major U. S. Army.

Hon. JEFFERSON DAVIS,
Secretary of War, Washington.

UNITED STATES SHIP SUPPLY,
At Sea, May 5, 1856.

Sir: On the 1st instant I wrote you a few lines hastily, in the post office, at Powder Horn, to inform you of our arrival off the bar; and on the 2d I wrote to Col. Tompkins, at New Orleans, to telegraph you that Lieutenant Porter and Captain Baker thinking it unsafe, under existing circumstances, to attempt to lighter the camels off Indianola, (in which opinion I fully concurred,) I had determined to affect the transfer of them from the Supply to the Fashion inside of the Balize, this being the nearest smooth water for effectually accomplishing it, and also for making any arrangements that might be necessary for the trip thence in the Fashion to Indianola. I have now the honor to resume in detail the narrative of our proceedings from its discontinuance to date.

On the 8th and 11th of February last I wrote you from Smyrna that we should sail about the 15th of that month for the Canary islands, to examine the breed of camels used in them, and thence, after a delay of about a week, continue on our way to Indianola. In conformity with this arrangement, we left Smyrna early on the morning of the 15th of February. A rather stormy passage through the Mediterranean brought us to the straits of Gibraltar on the morning of the 5th of March, and running through them we entered upon the Atlantic on the afternoon of the same day. The next morning our course was shaped for the Canaries, but after several days of unsuccessful effort to reach them, during which we encountered variable and head winds, and a southwest gale, the attempt to make them was abandoned on the 15th of March, and the course of the vessel directed towards America. On the 13th of April, Lieutenant Porter put into Kingston, Jamaica, where we remained until the morning of the 19th, when we sailed for Indianola. At 4½ p. m., on the 29th of April, we made Pass Cavallo, and anchored about eight miles from the bar. The next day, the 30th, we had no communication from shore, owing, as we were told afterwards, to the unusual swell of the sea. The next day, May 1st, the Fashion, Captain Baker, came out to us early in the morning; but Lieutenant Porter and Captain Baker were both of the opinion that, on account of the heavy swell and the rolling of the Supply, it would be unsafe for the Fashion to lie alongside of the ship, the guards being in the way. They thought, however, that the lightering of the camels might be effected into schooners on the next day, as the sea then would apparently be smoother. Going on board the Fashion, I proceeded to Indianola, to see what schooners could be obtained, and also to examine the wharf at which the animals were to be disembarked, that any difficulties there might be obviated, and to see what arrangements had been made for their reception and care at Indianola. Returning to the Supply in the Fashion, with the only two suitable schooners that could be procured, early in the morning of the 2d instant, one of the schooners was brought alongside the vessel, and an attempt to transfer a camel was commenced. No sooner, however, was the car with a camel raised from the hold and held suspended in mid air, than it became, unfortunately, evident that its violent swinging and turning, caused by the rolling of the Supply, would endanger the safety of the animals too much to warrant the attempt of lightering them from the ship in a swell of any kind, and that the transfer could only be made without risk in smooth water. Lieutenant Porter and Captain Baker decided against any further attempts there, in which decision, as far as my judgment in such matters permitted, I heartily concurred, and I therefore requested Lieutenant Porter to run for the Balize, as the nearest best point for my purpose, and wrote to Captain Van Bokkelen, assistant quartermaster at Indianola, to direct Captain Baker to follow me there. My reason for preferring the Balize to the inside of Ship island, the nearest smooth water, was to secure a sufficiency of coal for the Fashion to run back to Powder Horn, and any other supplies that she might require for the trip, none of which could be obtained, as I was informed, at Ship island. We are now, to-day at 12 m., within one hundred and forty-five miles of the Balize, and I hope to find the Fashion there, and to be able soon after to report to you the safe landing of the camels on the shore of Texas.

The passage out from Smyrna was an uncommonly rough one, and much of it boisterous. Three gales, two of them severe ones, and the ceaseless rolling of the vessel, except for the short time that she was "on a wind," have amply demonstrated, not only the feasibility of transporting camels in numbers across the sea, but the fact that they are more easily carried and bear transportation better than horses or mules. I do not think the same number of horses or mules could have been brought across as safely and with such little trouble. This comparison is made from an observation of the transportation of the latter animals during the war with Mexico.

On the 15th February, a male camel was born on board, and on the 19th, a female. Both of these calves died on the 25th of the same month from the want of nourishment; their dams refusing, during a gale which lasted for three days, to rise and suckle them. They had apparently lost, through fear, all solicitude for their young. Every effort was made to get them up on their feet without injuring them, but in vain; and resort was had to thin gruel, preserved milk, and such other aliments as Lieutenant Porter's stores supplied, to keep the little ones alive. Nothing that could be had on board though, furnished the sustenance necessary to maintain life.

On the 27th February, another female calf was born, which is alive and thriving.

On the 19th March, another male camel was born, which died on the 26th of April, from fits, produced, it was thought, by teething.

On the 30th March, one of the original stock, an "Arvana," taken in at Smyrna, died in calving, from a ruptured vagina. On the same day, another male calf was born, which is alive and well.

On the 1st April, another male calf was born, which died on the 5th of the same month, from being laid upon and crushed by one of the large camels.

To recapitulate our gains and losses. Sailed from Smyrna with thirty-three camels, of which one died in calving. Six calves born on the passage, of which four died. Number of camels now on hand, thirty-four; being one more than we started with.

This successful transportation of the animals is due to the excellent and ingenious arrangements of Lieutenant Porter for securing them in rough weather, and to his indefatigable personal supervision and attention to them. In this connexion I cannot omit to mention the name of seaman Edward Fitzsimmons, who was especially charged by Lieutenant Porter with the care of the animals, and who, to a faithful discharge of the trust confided to him, added such zealous solicitude for their safety, that much of the favorable issue of the experiment, so far, is undoubtedly to be attributed to his watchfulness.

To the rest of the officers and crew of the ship the thanks of the department are also due, for the interest they have manifested in the object of the expedition and for the earnestness with which they at all times contributed to its success.

Will you permit me to call your attention again to my request of the 8th of February, for the work on climatology mentioned in my letter of that date; and to ask you to send me also a good work on the diseases of the ox tribe, the camel resembling very closely that class of ruminants. These, as well as any instructions you may have for me, will reach me at Indianola, where the condition of the animals will necessarily detain me a month or six weeks before I can think of proceeding with them into the interior.

Very respectfully, your obedient servant,
HENRY C. WAYNE,
Major, United States Army.

Hon. JEFFERSON DAVIS,
Secretary of War, Washington.

MAY 8, 11 *a. m.*

P. S. The "Supply" has just anchored inside of the Southwest Pass. The Fashion passed up on Tuesday, and is to be down again to-morrow.

H. C. W.

INDIANOLA, TEXAS, *May* 14, 1856.

SIR: I have the honor to report my arrival here with "the camels." The animals were safely landed, all, by 11½ a. m., at Powder Horn. They are in good condition, considering their long confinement on shipboard, and the tossing upon the sea that they have been subjected to, and with the exception of a few boils and swelled legs, are apparently in health. On being landed, and feeling once again the "solid earth" beneath them, they became excited to an almost uncontrollable degree, rearing, kicking, crying out, breaking halters, tearing up pickets, and by other fantastic tricks demonstrating their enjoyment of "the liberty of the soil." Some of the males, becoming even pugnacious in their excitement, were with difficulty restrained from attacking each other.

Saddling them as soon as it could be done, they were gently led to this place, arranged in the stable put up for them by Captain Van Bokkelen, and secured. This occupied us until about 8 p. m. My attention for two or three days must be given exclusively to the animals, which will prevent me, for that time, from writing to you fully, either in regard to them, or to the suggestion conveyed to me by General Jesup of again visiting the east.

With much respect, I am, sir, (in haste for the mail,) your obedient servant,
HENRY C. WAYNE,
Major United States Army.

Hon. JEFFERSON DAVIS,
Secretary of War, Washington.

P. S. I have requested Colonel Tompkins to telegraph to you my arrival here.
H. C. W.

INDIANOLA, TEXAS, *May* 17, 1856.

GENERAL: I have the honor to acknowledge the receipt of your letter of the 22d ultimo, in which you inform me that the Secretary of the Navy has stated that it will be in his power to send the "Supply" again to the Mediterranean, and wishing to be informed whether, in the event of the vessel being sent back, I desire to continue on the duty on which I am engaged, and to go again to the Mediterranean.

Appreciating the kindness that makes a return to the Mediterranean optional with myself, I will frankly say, that I prefer to continue with the camels already landed, and to carry out the remaining points of the experiment yet to be demonstrated, viz: acclimation and breeding. In thus stating my own wishes, I beg, however, to be understood as doing so with submission to the judgment of the Secretary of War and of yourself, and as being in readiness to return to the East, should my services be considered more necessary there than here.

The object of this second expedition I suppose to be simply to increase the number of the animals in the United States, and to do so as speedily as possible; which can be accomplished by sending some one who has a knowledge of animals in the vessel to Smyrna, or other points determined upon, to purchase them; or better by sending him ahead of the vessel to the given point, that his purchases may be ready for shipment upon her arrival at it. In twenty-three days from New York an agent can be in the Levant, and in five, six months, at furthest, from the present time, with proper energy and expedition, thirty or forty more camels can be landed upon our shores. Meanwhile, I can be determining the place for conducting the processes of acclimation and breeding and for testing their usefulness.

I should be loth to leave the camels already imported in the charge of persons unacquainted with details of their habits and management, and who have not systematised a plan for their employment, which would fulfill early the national purposes that induced their importation.

Very respectfully, your obedient servant,
HENRY C. WAYNE,
U. S. Army, Brevet Major, Acting Quartermaster.

Major General THOMAS S. JESUP,
U. S. Army, Quartermaster General, Washington, D. C.

INDIANOLA, TEXAS, *May* 17, 1856.

MY DEAR SIR: Enclosed is a letter to me from Mr. G. H. Heap, who accompanied us on our recent expedition for camels, on the purchase of dromedaries and burden camels, and their exportation through Syria. It has been prepared from information gathered by Mr. Heap during our journeys, and is well worth attentive consideration, should an extensive importation of the animals be contemplated.

It meets with my approval, with the exception of exporting dromedaries through Scanderoon (Alexandretta) in the north of Syria, instead of through Beirout, a nearer and as good a port. By going to the latter place, much land travelling and time would be saved. Neither, however, are good winter ports. Scanderoon would answer as a shipping port for animals purchased in Mesopotamia, but for purchases made in any part of Asia Minor, I should unhesitatingly recommend shipment through Smyrna, as more direct, cheaper, and offering greater facilities for embarking and fitting out the vessel or the animals, besides saving distance, risk and time on the voyage out and in.

In forwarding Mr. Heap's letter, it gives me great pleasure to recommend him as a suitable agent should a civilian be employed. His knowledge of the east, its customs and languages, and the information and experience of Asia Minor and Egypt, and of the purposes of our government, acquired by him during our recent expedition, peculiarly fit him for the duty.

The camels, so far, have done well, seem to enjoy good health, and to be rapidly recovering from the effects of their sea trip. The males are rather fierce and troublesome, but as soon as I can get their packs fitted to them, sometime next week, perhaps, I shall see what effect a little gentle work between this and the Powder Horn will have upon their tempers.

Very respectfully, your obedient servant,
HENRY C. WAYNE,
Major United States Army.

Hon. JEFFERSON DAVIS,
  Secretary of War, Washington City, D. C.

UNITED STATES SHIP SUPPLY,
At Sea, April 25, 1856.

SIR: The agent appointed to purchase dromedaries and camels should leave the United States the first of September, so as to be in Cairo about the beginning of October. He will start up the Nile as soon as possible, and go by boat as far as Assouan on the left bank from the mouth, situated just below the first cataract, stopping at Minich, Syoot, Gergeh, Esneh, and Edfou, all on the right bank going up, where markets are held and dromedaries brought for sale from Bosnou, Kordofan, and Darfoor. Syoot and Esneh are the two principal markets, for countries in the interior, west of the Nile.

At Assouan is a market for dromedaries from Ababdeh and Beshareh, countries situated between the Nile and Red Sea. The Beshareh and Ababdeeah breeds are considered by many quite equal to the dromedaries from Oman and Muscat. A few might be purchased at Assouan, or, if none found to suit, a sufficient number can be hired to go into the Ababdeh and Beshareh countries, where ten or fifteen of the best can be procured, and with these return to Cairo. This will occupy about three months, so that a departure from Cairo can be made about the middle of January.

The course will then be to Suez, travelling on the animals purchased in Upper Egypt, which will also carry all the baggage, distributed in light loads so as to move rapidly.

From Cairo to Suez, then to Tor, on the Red Sea, Mount Sinai, Akaba, Petra; then by the eastern or western shore of the Dead Sea, according to circumstances, to Damascus, Aleppo, and Scanderoon.

At Akaba, situated at the head of the Gulf of Akaba, to penetrate into the Hedjaz, as far as circumstances and the native tribes will permit.

Along the whole of this route good dromedaries of various breeds are found, and a careful selection of the best can be made, so that thirty or thirty-six will be procured by the time we reach Scanderoon, which will be about the first of May. The vessel will be in waiting to ship them as soon as they arrive, and will sail at once for the United States.

Scanderoon (Alexandretta) is a good port, and much the best on the coast of Syria.

While the ship is on her way to the United States and back to the Mediterranean, the agent will have ample time to purchase the number of burden camels required for a load.

There are two routes, by either of which burden camels of a superior quality will be found. The first route is as follows, and will occupy about six months: To Aleppo, Mardin, Mossoul, Ourmiah, in Persia, Van, Erzeroom, and Trebizonde or Samsoon.

Should the war in the east or other causes render this route impracticable, there is another one, viz: Aleppo, Anitab, Casarieh, Koniah, Kutaya, to Smyrna. This will occupy about three months; and by either route those provinces will be visited which produce the largest, strongest, and hardiest animals for burden; and they offer also every variety of soil and climate, as, by either, numerous ranges of mountains are crossed, which, in winter, are covered with snow, so that there will be a certainty of getting animals inured to a cold climate and rough country.

It is seen that, according to this plan, the winter will be spent in the south purchasing dromedaries, and the summer in the north purchasing burden camels, and that two shiploads will be landed in the United States by the same ship in less than twelve months.

Besides time, there will be found a saving of money by going into the countries where the animals are bred, instead of purchasing them in cities along the coast, where they are neither as abundant, as good, nor as cheap. Dromedaries, indeed, are scarce in the towns, more especially those of a finer quality. A wealthy citizen may keep a fine animal for his personal use, and will part with it when tempted by a large offer; but it is in the desert only that they are in common use by all classes. In Upper Egypt and Arabia, also to a great extent in Mesopotamia, the dromedary is almost the only riding animal in use. Every man has one or more. The Sheiks and wealthy men always have a number, and keep them for sale as well as for use. The same remarks apply to burden camels. Frequently the finest animals that come down to the seacoast with produce, belong to proprietors residing in Koniah, Caisarieh, Erzeroom, and other considerable inland towns, and they cannot be purchased at all without going or sending to the places where their owners reside.

I am, very respectfully, your obedient servant,

G. H. HEAP.

Major HENRY C. WAYNE,
    United States Army.

[Telegraph.]

WAR DEPARTMENT, *May* 2, 1856.

Inform Major Wayne, at Indianola, by first opportunity, that Lieutenant Porter, with storeship Supply, will make another trip for camels.

JEFF'N DAVIS.

Col. D. D. TOMPKINS,
    U. S. Quartermaster, New Orleans.

INDIANOLA, TEXAS, *May* 21, 1856.

SIR: On the 9th instant, while on board of the United States storeship "Supply," in the Southwest Pass, I received from Colonel Tompkins a copy of your telegrapic despatch of the 2d instant, informing me "that Lieutenant Porter, with the storeship 'Supply,' will make another trip for camels," and immediately communicated the information to Lieutenant Porter.

Permit me to suggest that all the animals brought over by this second trip, whether burden camels or dromedaries, be breeding cows, as we already have males enough for over three hundred females, according to the proportions established, and I have no doubt correctly, throughout the east. If burden camels are sought, it will be a saving, both of time and of money, to send the vessel for them direct to Smyrna; to return with them as soon as embarked to the United States. Thirty-five cows, at an average of $80 each, will require $2,800. Time to go out from New York, one month and a half; stay at Smyrna, one month; time to return to Southwest Pass, three months; total time required, five and a half months. If dromedaries are to be procured, from three to four months more will be necessary.

I would further suggest, with due deference to your judgment, that, as some years will be required to establish the animal permanently among us, the first and main object should be to cultivate the coarse and hardy stock, upon which the finer varieties may be engrafted, as experience shall hereafter direct. By so doing, moreover, our funds will go much further, and, instead of *fifty*, we can have at least *one hundred* animals landed in America within two years after the voting of the appropriation by Congress.

Very respectfully, your obedient servant,
HENRY C. WAYNE,
United States Army, Brevet Major.

Hon. JEFFERSON DAVIS,
Secretary of War, Washington city, D. C.

UNITED STATES SHIP "SUPPLY,"
New York, May 28, 1856.

SIR: I have the honor to report my arrival at this port, and to lay before you the report of my proceedings in connexion with the transportation of the camels, also a journal of events kept on the camel deck; and some correspondence in relation to the six dromedaries presented by the viceroy of Egypt; in connexion with this report there are some drawings of the different animals purchased, with their accoutrements, &c., and they will give you a faithful idea of the stock purchased. I will either send them on to you by express, or, if you deem it desirable to see me in Washington, and order me to report to you there, I will bring them with me.

Awaiting your further orders.

I have the honor to remain, sir, your obedient servant,
DAVID. D. PORTER,
Lieutenant Commanding.

Hon. JEFFERSON DAVIS,
Secretary of War, Washington city.

UNITED STATES SHIP "SUPPLY,"
New York, May 28, 1856.

SIR: I have the honor to inform you that your instructions relative to the importation of a lot of camels and dromedaries, for the purpose of trying whether they were suitable to the climate of Texas, have been carried out as far as practicable, and thirty-four camels and dromedaries were safely transferred to steamer "Fashion" in the southwest pass of the Mississippi river, on the 10th instant, and in better condition than they were when they came on board.

The present report professes to be nothing more than an account of the incidents of the voyage, and the treatment of camels at sea.

Many books have been written about their treatment and habits on shore; this report, then, will have the merit of novelty, if nothing more, for I doubt if so many camels were ever placed together on board ship, for so long a time, or ever performed so long a journey at sea, the majority of them have been transported over seven thousand miles, and one of them in particular, (a Tunisian camel,) has been on board nine months without landing, has sailed over ten thousand miles in that time, and has never been sick an hour since he came on board.

As my particular duty has been the transportation of the camels, and the care of them while on board ship, I will confine myself as much as possible to an account of their treatment and the means adopted for their comfort. If the precautions I have taken are strictly followed by persons who may hereafter undertake to import camels, I do not think there will be any doubt of success, as they are the result of careful watchfulness and tried experience.

I arrived in "Spezzia" in thirty-eight days after leaving New York, and finding that Major Wayne was just about leaving Paris to join me, and would not likely arrive for some days, I concluded to go to Florence and examine the camels of Tuscany, (as you expressed some desire to be informed on the subject,) the original stock of which was brought from Egypt and Barbary about two hundred years since, and they have increased and multiplied to some hundreds. If the number is limited, it is not because they do not breed as freely in Tuscany as in Egypt, but because the demand for them is small, the grand duke only requiring a certain number for his own use, and not permitting them to be bred by any one but himself. He has now on hand a number sufficient to do the work of one thousand horses. On my arrival at Florence I found that the cholera was raging violently, and as most of the public functionaries had left the city, I could not, without delay, obtain any documentary information relating to the camels of Tuscany. I found, indeed, that the animals had all been sent to Pisa to work on a farm belonging to the Grand duke, and I immediately started for that place. I cannot say that I derived any useful or important information from my visit, although I witnessed the practical illustration of the fitness of the camel for a climate more variable than the one to which it is intended to transport them in the United States. I found the Pisa camels not in the best condition, owing to their having been very much overlooked and badly cared for, being supplied with no food whatever beyond what they could glean from among the pine barrens, and not always being housed in winter, in latitude 43° 30', where they experience severe cold, and encounter a much more trying climate than that of Texas; besides this, they were losing their hair at the time I saw them, which renders the appearance of the camel anything but prepossessing. The burdens they are made to carry are, I think, beyond their strength, being equal to thirteen hundred English pounds, a weight only put upon the strongest camels in Turkey, and for short distances. The camels at Pisa work from sunrise till sunset, carrying this weight with but few intervals of rest. Notwithstanding all the bad treatment they are subjected to, and the little intelligence shown in the management of them, they are still in fair order, have not deteriorated, and would, with ordinary care, be kept in much better condition than the camels of the East. Taking their treatment into consideration, it is wonderful to me that the Tuscans have succeeded in propagating the species at all. I attribute their success more to the wonderful endurance of the camel than to any management on their part. I anticipate much better results from our experiment, for the intelligence of our people, and their keen perception of what is for their own interest, will, I am convinced, bring the breeding of camels to a high state of perfection; and we may hereafter be exporting the improved breed back to the shores from whence they originally come. I regret that I have nothing more interesting to communicate on this subject.

I sailed from Spezzia the day after the arrival of Major Wayne, and Tunis being directly in our route, I stopped there, with the intention of taking on board a camel of that country, to keep during the cruise, and try experiments with it; ascertain the best mode of management at sea, and the amount of time the camel will endure confinement on board ship, in reference to future shipments. An ordinary camel was accordingly purchased, which we afterwards regretted, as the Bey of Tunis presented the United States government with two good specimens through Mr. Chandler, our consul general. One of the camels was a remarkable fine one, has performed the whole voyage through the Mediterranean in the ship, without having been landed; has never been sick a day, or "off his feed," and is now, after a confinement of nine months, in better condition than any camel on board. So well satisfied am I with my experience with the Tunisian camel, that I would not hesitate to procure stock from that regency, being well satisfied that they will suit the climate of Texas. The climate of Tunis is much more variable than that of Texas, being colder in winter and hotter in summer, neither of which is exactly suitable for the camel, which delights in temperate weather, and thrives best in an equable clime; it suffers most the changes from heat to cold and from cold to heat, although from my own observations, I should conclude that they were indifferent to heat, cold, hunger, or thirst, and seem to be a machine only, capable of enduring every kind of hardship. I have seen them in Europe, Asia, and Africa, exposed to all kinds of temperature, and subjected to very bad treatment.

I invariably found them the same enduring, obedient, and uncomplaining animals; they labor on from day to day, under the care of brutal drivers, and kneel down at night, after a hard day's work (the picture of meekness) to chew their small allowance of food; always ready to start again at a moment's notice, and scarcely ever exhibit anything like fatigue.

The camels of Tunis are not generally so robust in appearance as those of Asia Minor, although the female is a larger and handsomer animal; neither can they carry such heavy burdens. The camel of Asia Minor has become more hardy by the change to a colder climate, and its frame and limbs are much larger than those of the more southern latitudes, but the Tunisian camel is more rapid in its movements, will carry easily five hundred pounds on a long journey, and is much more graceful in its appearance, approaching nearer to the form of the dromedary. They will suit the climate of Texas, and as appears from experiment, will endure a sea voyage of great length. Our opportunity of seeing camels in the regency of Tunis were small, and my impressions have been formed by seeing those to be found in and about the city of Tunis. In the interior and along the coast they are to be found in a much better condition, and I was told that the Pehlevan, or wrestling camel, (which is kept for a breeder,) is finer even than those of Smyrna or other parts of Asia Minor. "Susa," Sfax, and Gabes on the coast are the best markets where they are to be found.

I remained at Tunis eight days, and sailed the 9th of August, with three camels on board. I immediately put in operation the plan I had fixed upon for their future treatment.

Previous to my leaving the United States, I had the ship fitted with a view to carrying camels, and as the plan adopted has succeeded in every respect, without any change whatever, I beg leave to give you a minute description of it; it would be dangerous to attempt to transport any number of camels without some arrangement of the kind adopted on board the "Supply," although it might be possible to carry five or six on board an ordinary merchant vessel, with a little addition to her usual fittings.

In the first place, a trunk 60 feet long was raised upon the spar-deck of the "Supply," extending from abaft the foremast aft to the quarter-deck; this trunk was 12 feet wide, with a large hatch, 11 feet 3 inches by 6 feet 8 inches amid-ships, to let the camels down on to the lower deck by; there was also a hatch at the fore and after end to put windsails down. Along the sides of the trunk were placed port-holes, 2 feet long and 1 foot wide; 20 of these port-holes were cut on each side of the trunk; inside they were fitted with glass and frames to let down in cold weather, and outside they were fitted with wooden shutters to keep out the sea in bad weather. The main hatch being so high above the deck could be kept open in the heaviest gale, enabling the camels at all times to get a plentiful supply of fresh air, without which they would soon die between decks in a ship. In an ordinary vessel, without such trunk as I speak of, the hatches would have to be battened down on the least appearance of bad weather, and the result would be the death of every camel. I have never, on any occasion, known the "between decks" of the "Supply" to be uncomfortably warm; on the contrary, there was frequently more air thrown down there from the mainsail than was required.

To get the camels on board safely, I had a boat made expressly for the purpose, and a camel car (to fit inside the boat) in which the camels were placed when hoisted in or out; the boat was made "scow fashion," and flat-bottomed, to draw but little water, and enable it to run upon a beach. It was $7\frac{4}{12}$ feet wide, $20\frac{1}{2}$ feet long, and capable of bearing a weight of 6,000 pounds. The camel car was made of heavy oak, upright pieces and solid bottom, bolted strongly together and fitted with six small trucks (so as to roll it in and out of the scow if necessary,) and at each end it had a sliding door to ship and unship, and allow the camel to go in and out; notwithstanding the great strength of the car, it was not any too strong for the purpose; although, with the wood and iron on it, it weighed one thousand pounds; at times, the camels were so troublesome to get in and so strong and refractory when they were in, that they started the frame of the car in one or two places; consequently, the car should be made very strong. The one I had made was 8 feet 6 inches long, $4\frac{2}{12}$ feet wide, and $3\frac{6}{12}$ feet high, with light board sides on the inside extending half way up. I am thus minute in mentioning the boat and camel car, as the shipping of the camels is a very troublesome business, and without the above mentioned arrangements it would be almost impossible to get them safely on board. It would never do to hoist a camel on board with a pair of slings like those used in shipping horses. In the first place, their weight is too great, some of them weighing as much as two thousand pounds, the average weight being about fourteen hundred; in the second place, they would certainly injure themselves in their struggling to get free; by driving and coaxing them into the car, or putting them in by means they could not resist, (which I will explain,) and then making them lie down quietly, they would be transferred from the shore to the ship without being aware of the change. Out of thirty-three camels shipped in this way, not one received a scratch of any kind, and they were put on board at the rate of one in every thirty minutes. I consider our success in safely transporting so many is owing, in a great measure, to the fact that they all came on board without any bruises. The accompanying drawing of the boat and car will, I trust, be easily understood, and will render any further description unnecessary.

I also had fitted in the United States a set of harness for each camel; this harness is made of strong canvas, thrumbed on the inside to prevent chafes, and so arranged on the body of the animal that when the vessel rolls the camel is kept perfectly steady; two strong ropes, one on each side of the camel are passed through strong grommets in the side-pieces of the harness, and are set up taut to the ship's side and amidships; finally, a canvas strap is passed over the camel's neck and down around both knees, which effectually prevents its rising or moving in any direction during a gale; it is not an uncomfortable position for a camel to be in, as it is their natural one when they lie down. Where there are a number of camels, it was found necessary to have a strong breast rope (defended by strong gutta-percha air bags) running (or stretched) fore and aft the camel deck in front of them; this rope, with its fenders, rests against their breasts, the side ropes of the harness are fastened to it, and the ship may be thrown on her beam ends without a camel moving. To prevent any chafe to their knees (which are well protected by callosities,) I always kept under them a thick bed of hay, and large, well filled bags of hay between their rumps and the ship's side; these are all the precautions necessary to keep them from getting hurt; a drawing of a camel secured for a gale will accompany this report.

When I first took the Tunisian camels on board, of course the mode of treating them was new to me, and required some consideration; I adopted a plan, however, and have carried it out with all the camels on board with complete success. I do not hesitate to say they were transferred in finer order than when they came on board. I had been told a great deal about the difficulty of transporting them, how they were subject to a variety of intricate diseases, and how impossible it would be to take them unless they were under the charge of the natives of the countries where they were to be shipped from. No doubt the camels in Barbary, Asia Minor, and Egypt are subject to diseases of various kinds, owing to the ignorance and brutality of their keepers, and I only wonder that they are fit for anything at all, after passing through the hands of such people, who, although their main support frequently depends on this faithful beast, they treat it with the greatest inhumanity; and when it is sick are guilty of the grossest folly in the application of remedies for its cure.

My plan was to give them good food, and plenty of it; rub them thoroughly every day with currycomb and brush; keep every part of their deck clean by scrubbing and whitewashing, and wash parts of their bodies every day with soap and water; under this simple treatment I found the Tunisian camels improved greatly. Having been provided with the best of food before leaving New York, (good oats and hay,) I was enabled to supply them liberally, and although it is entirely different from the food to which the camel is accustomed, they thrive much better on it, and will eat nothing else when they once get used to it.

After leaving Tunis, and stopping a day at Malta, I proceeded to Smyrna to enable Major Wayne to look at the camels there, and having satisfied ourselves that they were good in quality and would suit our purposes provided we could get no better, I sailed for Saloniki, where I was told they had even finer camels than in Smyrna. I would not recommend any one to go there in pursuit of camels, as there are few to be found. The war in the East has drained that part of the country of all its good animals, and we left there without even seeing a camel.

My next course was towards Constantinople, and we arrived there, after some delay in the Dardanelles, on the fourth day of October.

Your instructions to Major Wayne and myself were to proceed into Persia for the purpose of looking at the dromedaries of that country, &c. I presume that Major Wayne has informed you fully of the reasons which prevented our doing so. It was thought to be impracticable at that late season, and no more could be made in that direction, if we both went, without abandoning the main object of the expedition. In the meantime, while inquiries were being made about the possibility of getting to Persia, Major Wayne, Mr. Heap, and myself, started for the Crimea to look at the camels there, particularly the Bactrian camel, supposing, at the time, that it was the only place where we would have an opportunity of seeing them, and not having an idea then that we should be so fortunate as to procure two males from Asia Minor. We saw but few Bactrians in the Crimea, and those were of an inferior quality, having been hardly treated, and left exposed throughout the winter to get their living as best they could. They were very little used—horses, mules, and the Arabian camel being preferred. The Bactrian is a very slow animal in its movements, does not offer the same facilities for loading, and would not suit at all the purposes for which camels are wanted in the United States. There would be some difficulty, also, in procuring any great number, for the Bactrian, being a native of the northern part of Persia, is not found in great numbers to the south, where the males (Bohoor) are only brought and sold as breeders. They produce a cross which is much esteemed by the people of Asia Minor, &c., and is of great strength and size. The cross, however, is a hybrid and does not propagate, or, if it does, the produce is a very small and inferior animal, not larger than a small horse; it is called a "kokurt" and will only carry very small burdens, besides being extremely delicate. The Arabian camel was used in the Crimea to some extent, particularly in the beginning of the war, when horses could not be procured. They were found at that time to be very serviceable in carrying up the heavy weights which horses could not move. If any doubt exists about the camel being able to endure the coldest kind of weather, a reference to the weather and winter of 1855-6, in the Crimea, will convince the most skeptical that cold is not the greatest inconvenience they have to apprehend. With good stabling and proper food, reasonable treatment when sick, and the absence of all Bedouin or Turkish doctoring, they will go through very severe cold.

I believe that camels have always been used in the "Crimea," particularly the Bactrian. I do not think any of the persons engaged in the transportation service were fair judges of their utility, neither did they seem to know much about their habits or the mode of using them, being naturally accustomed to the use of horses their prejudices likely led them to prefer the latter; nevertheless, the English government have bought up a good many in Asia Minor, (for the ensuing campaign,) which were on their way to the Crimea at last accounts. In an active war like that carried on before Sebastopol, horses, no doubt, are much preferable to camels, moving only for short distances and with rapidity. Camels have their advantages, but more particularly in making long journeys and passing over wide tracts of desert where there is a scarcity of food and water. We spent four days on shore in the Crimea; too short a time to learn much about the camel operations. We heard reports about large numbers being bought up by the French for future operations. I do not think there was any foundation for these reports, as the French have, apparently, discontinued the use of camels altogether, being more accustomed to the management of mules, of which they had a magnificent lot.

On our return to Constantinople, we found, from inquiries made by our dragoman (Mr. Brown), and from information given at the Persian embassy, that it was not advisable to go into Persia so late in the season, on account of snow; but more particularly for fear of meeting with delay on the return trip in the spring, when the snows begin to thaw and render the mountain roads impassable. If Major Wayne had gone, I should have been unable to have accompanied him, as it was necessary for me to remain and purchase the camels to allow us to make an early start for home. Taking all things into consideration, I think our wisest plan was to give the trip up and turn our attention to Egypt, which we accordingly did.

Our dragoman (Mr. Brown) informed me that the Turkish government had presented the United States, through our minister (Mr. Spence), with four camels, that were to be of the best breed; and as orders had been sent into Asia Minor to procure them, he requested me to remain in Constantinople eight or ten days longer to enable the government to carry out its intentions. As this time could be very profitably spent in examining the camels in Turkey in Europe, and in and about Nicomedia, I acquiesced in the proposal to remain, thinking there would be no delay. At the end of the ten days, the camels not arriving, I called on the prime minister and inquired at what time I might expect them. He assured me that they would soon be in Constantinople, and issued new instructions to expedite the matter. This brought the detention to ten days more, and I made preparations to sail. In the meantime, Mr. Brown received authority to order four of the finest camels to be found in European Turkey, and accordingly went to work to get them. My reasons for not taking the camels have been stated to you in a despatch from Constantinople, which I presume you have received; therefore it will not be necessary to repeat them here. In his communication to me, Mr. Brown seems to attach a great deal of importance to the transaction; more than I supposed it merited at the time. He also informed me that a report of the matter had gone home to the government, and seemed to think I might be censured for not keeping the ship there a longer time, though I know he was aware of my desire to take the camels on board, especially after he had gone to so much trouble to get them. Mr. Brown may attach more importance to the matter than it deserves. I have written to him to say that the kind intentions of the Turkish government can be carried out on some future occasion, if it is the intention of our government to proceed with the experiment. In these little matters of courtesy the Turkish authorities are very tenacious, and I should be very sorry to place either our minister or dragoman in a position where they might be called upon to make awkward explanations, and I think both of those gentlemen will acquit me of any responsibility in the matter.

In anticipation of receiving the four camels from the Turkish government, I landed two of the Tunisians, the one we purchased and one of those (the smaller one) presented by "His Highness the Bey;" both these camels had the itch slightly, and I was anxious to get rid of them for fear of innoculating those that were to come; with the one we purchased I had made every kind of experiment, and the other was not exactly the class of camel to take so far as the United States. It came on board sick, the Tunisians having injured it in getting it into their boat, which was not at all adapted for shipping camels. Both the above mentioned camels had been on board one hundred and five days, and I felt perfectly satisfied that any we might undertake to transport would stand the voyage to the United States, provided they were sound at starting and we could have moderately fair weather. They were exposed to two rough gales (one of which lasted three days) and neither of them suffered in the least; they both grew fat under the lazy life they were leading, and improved so much that I would have kept them but for their having the itch, which is a troublesome complaint to cure, and it is one which all city camels are liable to have; the good condition of these two camels recommended them to a butcher in Constantinople, who bought them for purposes known only to himself.

I sailed from Constantinople on the 22d of November, and after a pleasant run of seven days anchored in the harbor of Alexandria, in Egypt. Commodore Breeze, commanding the Mediterranean squadron, came in port a day or two after us, and our consul Mr. DeLeon (whose co-operation I was in hopes we would secure,) was called away by his duties to Cairo, whither he went to accompany thec ommodore. It was not possible to do much without the consul's assistance, and we lost two weeks waiting for the "Congress" to sail, when Mr. DeLeon would have leisure to attend us.

Major Wayne proceeded at once to Cairo, but met with difficulties there he did not anticipate, of which, no doubt, he has kept you informed; the consul returning to Alexandria with the commodore, his services for the moment were not available.

.I received a message from Major Wayne, informing me that he had been able to get a permit to take only four dromedaries out of the country; "the viceroy refused to allow any more than that number to be exported." His highness returning to Alexandria about that time, I called on him, in company with Mr. DeLeon, hoping to be able to remove his objections. I found him very averse to rescinding any of his regulations on the subject of the exportation of animals of every kind, but after Mr. DeLeon had explained to him the object of the expedition, and expressed the disappointment that would be felt by our government at such poor results from our visit to Egypt, he consented to let us have ten dromedaries besides the four he had already granted permission for. It was too late then to take advantage of his courtesy. Major Wayne had been in Cairo a month and returned the same day the permit was granted. To return to Cairo to purchase ten dromedaries would require another month to be lost; it was getting late in the season, and we had to purchase our Smyrna camels; so we concluded to let the matter lie over for another year, in hopes of meeting with better success another time.

Dromedaries are not animals that can be bought in a day to advantage; the finest kind are scarce in Cairo, and the ordinary ones are not, in my opinion, worth the trouble of importing; a well trained dromedary, like a fine horse, has a strong hold on the affections of his master, and it requires days and sometimes weeks, before a bargain can be struck on anything like reasonable terms. Major Wayne had the assistance of Mr. Heap, who has been indefatigable in the duties he undertook to perform; and although the two were constantly on the look out, they found but two very fine dromedaries for sale.

These details are uninteresting, but they are necessary to account for the time we have spent in carrying out your instructions, particularly as you impressed upon us "that time was an important element, and you wished us to be as prompt in the execution of this duty as the security of the experiment would permit." In an undertaking of this kind, and in carrying out an experiment all the details of which were new to me, I should not consider myself justifiable in hurrying over the matter. It is not an experiment that can be fully tested in a day or a year with success; it is necessary to feel our way, especially in the transportation and in the choice of animals, otherwise we should meet with a mortifying failure, and those persons who have ridiculed the project as impracticable would rejoice over our want of success, and attribute it both to our unfitness for the duty and the unsuitableness of the camels for what they are intended to do in Texas.

In the selection of camels and dromedaries, my idea has been to procure those suitable for breeding rather than purchase those that were only fit to be used as burden camels; on the same principle that I would buy the best stock of cattle, sheep, or horses, if I wanted to introduce them into a new country. It is a very foolish idea to purchase the ordinary stock to carry out such an experiment; is opposed to common sense, and is not, in my opinion, what was anticipated by the government. I do not suppose it is the intention to set the present lot of animals immediately to work, for it would most likely frustrate all the objects originally intended; the small number of camels would at present render it unadvisable to pursue that course. What, by breeding with those on hand, and a more rapid system of importation, the government would, in three years, have a stock of three or four hundred to commence operations with, and in the meantime they could be trained either as dromedaries or burden camels. Taking these things into consideration, I have not been anxious to hurry the matter through unnecessarily, though I believe I have always been ready to sail when there was no further necessity for remaining in port.

On the ——, the four dromedaries from Cairo arrived, and I obtained a permit from the government of Alexandria to ship them; in presenting the permit at the custom-house the dromedaries were stopped, and I was treated with so much disrespect that I complained to the consul, Mr. De Leon, and requested him to lodge a complaint against the custom-house authorities, which he promptly did; the "amende honorable" was as promptly made, and at the same time I received a notification from Mr. De Leon that his highness the viceroy of Egypt intended presenting the United States government with six of his finest dromedaries; he has many fine ones belonging to himself, and was at that time engaged in drilling a dromedary corps on the Persian system, each dromedary to carry two men armed with carbines. I was all ready for sea when I heard this news, but was requested by Mr. De Leon to wait three or four days until the dromedaries could be brought down from the interior, which I did. In the meantime Mr. Heap had been despatched to Smyrna to purchase what camels he required, so that we might lose no time on our arrival there, and be ready to sail by the 1st of March.

It was very gratifying to me to hear that we were to receive six dromedaries from his highness the viceroy's own stock. Of course I expected nothing but the very best blood of Oman or Nubia, knowing that the eastern potentates take a pride in making presents of the choicest kind. I felt that you would be very much disappointed in our bringing home so few dromedaries, and I was very glad to get the six that were promised. The selection of the animals was placed in the hands of the governor of Alexandria; he passed the matter on to the next in office, and he in turn passed it on still to a "cavass," or under officer, who went to work to make a handsome profit out of the business. After more than a week's delay, and many inquiries on my part as to when we might expect them, I was at last informed that the dromedaries were ready to be delivered over to any one I might send for them. I sent an officer to receive them, who returned in a few minutes and informed me that the animals were so wretched in appearance, and so rotten with disease, that he would not take the responsibility of accepting them without further orders. To avoid all mistakes, I went and inspected them myself, and found them infinitely worse than they had been represented; they were not dromedaries at all, but the common street camel of Alexandria, the most ill used and wretched looking beast in the world. What made the matter worse, two of them had been purchased by Major Wayne, in Cairo, and rejected, on their arrival in Alexandria, because they turned out to be diseased, and they were about the best of the lot presented.

The whole affair, at first, looked like a studied insult, for the purpose of turning the expedition into ridicule. I promptly refused to receive the present, and the accompanying correspondence took place, which will explain the whole affair to you.

I felt that there was some improper course pursued by the subordinates of the pacha, and I thought it my duty to expose it. Mr. De Leon approved of my course, and warmly seconded my remonstrances. These letters will tend to show how many impediments are thrown in the way of strangers in the prosecution of any purpose in Egypt. The well intended liberality of his highness the viceroy is often turned aside by his subordinates, who thereby reap some small advantage themselves, at the risk even of meeting with severe punishment. This piece of trickery caused another delay of a week; but when it was brought to the notice of his highness the viceroy, he put the matter in proper hands, and in seven days a fair lot of dromedaries were brought down from the interior, and six were selected out of fifteen, two males and four females.

The dromedaries presented by his highness were not such as I would have bought; they are not the far-famed and swift dromedaries of the desert, but the ordinary "Mount Sinai breed" used in the transportation of goods and passengers across the Isthmus of Suez, and for two or three days' journey about the country they are good strong animals, and will make their fifty miles a day for seven or eight days in succession, perhaps longer. We had no opportunity of trying their paces, and had to trust to luck about their being in a sound healthy condition; fortunately they proved to be fine animals, and stood the transportation better, if anything, than the burden camels of Asia Minor. The viceroy expressed great doubt about our ever reaching America with any of them alive, much less in good condition, as he said it had been found they would not stand a sea voyage. It appears that he was mistaken. If it is the intention of government to import any more dromedaries from Egypt, it will be necessary to make some arrangements through our consul general, Mr. De Leon, so that he may obtain concessions from the viceroy. To avoid having all his fine stock of horses and other cattle sent out of the country to supply the wants of the eastern war, he passed a law "that no animal of any kind should be permitted to go out of his territory." The law was a general one, and not made with any allusion to camels or dromedaries, and I think it can be set aside with a little management on the part of our consul. If objections are made, we can still get them, by having them shipped from some port outside of the Egyptian boundaries—Acre, Jaffa, or Beirout, for instance; and by going to Iskenderoon, in the territory of Aleppo, a person would be within six days' journey of "Haleb," or city of Aleppo, where dromedaries of as good a breed as those of Egypt are to be found. Fine dromedaries can also be purchased in upper Egypt, at moderate prices, and driven down, or sent down in Nile boats, as far as Cairo, from thence, in a short time, they can be sent to "Palestine," which is outside of the viceroy's dominions, and shipped at one of the above mentioned ports.

If the importation of camels or dromedaries into the United States is to be continued, the plan adopted on this occasion (of having the ship to wait while the animals are sought for) is a bad one, as far as expense is concerned, and I will take this occasion to make a recommendation, which I think will expedite the business and save the expense of the ship lying idle, besides doing away with the risk of having sickness among the crew while lying in a sickly port.

I would propose that some person of experience be employed to purchase the camels or dromedaries, while the ship is on her way home with those already purchased. If the animals are to be bought in Egypt, the purchaser should be in Cairo about the first of October, to start up the Nile as soon as possible and go by boat as far as the first cataract, stopping at "Minich," "Syout," "Gergeh," and other places on the route where markets are held. Dromedaries are brought from "Kordofan" and Dorfoor; "Syout" and "Esneh" are the two principle markets for countries in the interior west of the Nile. At Assuan there is a market for dromedaries from "Ababdeh" and "Beshareh," which lie between the Nile and Red sea. The Ababdeh and Beshareh are considered by many persons to be superior to the dromedaries of Oman, I think they will suit our climate better.

To procure a number of animals would require about three months, the course will then be to Suez (travelling on the purchased dromedaries) across Palestine, and stopping at such port as is designated for the ship to go to; if the viceroy of Egypt consents to let the animals go out through his territory, (which he has promised to do,) then Alexandria will be the port to embark from; if he does not consent, then "Jappa," "Acre" or "Beirout" will be the places. The ship should be at the point designated on the first of May. A moment's reflection will show you that this plan is not only cheaper, but more expeditious than any other, to say nothing of the opportunities thus offered of picking up the best kind of stock in the interior of Egypt, Syria, &c., where they are to be found in quantities. I got Mr. Heap to make inquiries while in Egypt, and the above is the result which I have quoted. The limits of this communication will not permit me to go into all the details of this proposed plan, but I shall be happy to extend my observations on the subject if you desire it.

After getting all the dromedaries on board, I sailed on the 22d January for Smyrna. Previous to our leaving Egypt, Major Wayne secured the services of three natives of the country (one of them a Bedouin Arab, and two of them spoke a little English) to go to the United States and help take care of the animals; I also shipped three extra men (sailors) for the same purpose. I don't know how the former may answer when they get on shore, but I would not recommend to any one in future to procure this kind of help, for in heavy weather (the very time when the animals require the most assistance and attention) the natives are perfectly helpless, and in good weather they are not of much use; under proper directions the sailors are the best hands to take care of camels on board of ship, and there will always be found some handy person who has a taste for a knowledge of stabling. A Bedouin or Egyptian cannot be taught much beyond what they already know, and I am of opinion that an intelligent American will in a short time know more about the treatment of camels than they do; if they are only required to clean up the camel decks, &c , that duty could be better performed by sailors. To suppose that any one at all acquainted with the management of camels would allow them to be treated by Arabs as if they were in the desert, would be absurd, and to place the animals under their sole control and management after landing them would not, in my opinion, be contributing much to the success of the enterprise. It might be advisable to obtain the services of one good and experienced man who has had the care of camels; one of the men (the Bedouin) I found servicable in good weather in taking care of the young ones born on board, and while the females were bringing forth, as that is a branch of the business not likely to be understood by those who have not seen it. It might do to have a portion of the camel tenders natives, provided they were accustomed to the business, but I would advise those who take them to be very strict, though at the same time to treat them kindly, and to give them no other indulgences besides those given to the crew, otherwise they will prove troublesome. This kind of help can be procured in Egypt for ten dollars a month, or less, with an outfit of some good stout clothes to do their work in. I would, however, in all cases prefer sailors to take care of animals at sea, and it is remarkable that during this voyage not an accident of any kind had happened to a camel under charge of the sailors; while the Egyptians were so careless and so treacherous that something was wrong with their animals all the time; I attribute the deaths of young ones to their want of attention altogether; it is better not to have one of them on board at all.

I was much pleased with the dromedaries when I got them all on board and cleaned up; they had just come from a long journey when they were selected, were dirty and travel-worn, and did not appear to advantage; but when I saw them all standing side by side, their backs just clearing our deck, (which is seven feet four inches high,) and their fine muscular proportions showing to such advantage, I regretted very much that we were unable to procure more of the same kind, particularly the females, which are much larger and finer looking animals in every way than the female camels of Asia Minor, consequently they would produce a better breed. It is thought by many who profess to know a great deal about the Egyptian dromedary that will not suit the climate of Texas at all, and under the existence of these doubts it is, perhaps, well that we only procured a limited number; fortunately we have enough to decide the question with, although my mind is fully made up that there will be no difficulty at all in the acclimation. We have only to look into the history of the Tuscan camels (which came from Barbary and Egypt) to convince ourselves that the chance of succeeding with them in Texas is very great. It is probable for the first winter or two they will require a little extra care in stabling, which they are at all times as much entitled to as a horse or a cow, and who is there in the United States who does not give his horse and cow good shelter at all seasons? This is what camels do not get in Egypt, and not very good shelter in Turkey. Gentlemen who keep fine and expensive dromedaries to ride, take good care of their beasts, but the majority are very badly housed. In Egypt, the climate in winter is very equable, perhaps the most so of any climate in the world, but I have seen one or two days when the weather was extremely cold, more so than it would ever be in Texas. The only covering the dromedary has in cold weather is a very light open blanket. Those that I took on board at Alexandria were, in six days after leaving port, transported from 31 degrees north latitude to nearly 40 degrees north, changing the climate nearly ten degrees. And encountering at Smyrna a longer and colder spell of bad weather than had been known there for some years, I think it pretty conclusive evidence that the dromedary is not so tender an animal as it is represented to be.

From what I have seen in Egypt and Asia Minor, I have come to the conclusion that camels contract most of their diseases, to which they are said to be subject, to want of attention to their comfort, and to a total absence of cleanliness. Nothing can exceed the filth of a Turkish or Egyptian "khan" (or stable) where camels are stowed away, closely packed for the night; the filth of ages seems to have accumulated there, and the smell of ammonia is so strong that it is painful to the olfactories. On board ship, on the camel deck there was scarcely any odor perceptible, because the deck was kept constantly scrubbed, and the white-wash brush kept going. It might naturally be expected that some smell would be perceptible in a close ship, but there is no excuse for it on shore. How can it be expected that animals will keep healthy under such treatment? I am convinced that the itch (a complaint to which camels are more subject than any other) is caused by the filth and ammonia in which they lie down. It is a very uncommon thing in the city of Alexandria to see a camel without the itch, (many of them are a mass of sores,) and out of the fifteen dromedaries sent down from the villages for us to select from, eight had the itch badly, and two were doubtful. I took the latter, which I thought were slightly affected, otherwise we could not have made up our number. I cured them, however, in three days, by applications of sulphur externally and internally. The Egyptians seem to have no hesitation in offering dromedaries as a present or for sale when they have the itch, as they do not seem to think the complaint interferes at all with their efficiency; their remedy for the itch is to smear the animal all over with tar, which is said to cure it, but as far as I could see, not until the skin was almost taken off the body, and in that condition they are the most pitiable looking animals it is possible to imagine. It only goes to show that people in Egypt who have the care of camels are extremely ignorant, and cause the complaints to assume a worse character by their treatment of them. I had two cases of violent itch occur with the Egyptian dromedaries on board ship, caused by their lying on the same bed of hay for three days during a gale. I cured them both effectually in five days by giving them each a handful of the flour of sulphur in their oats, and rubbing the parts of the body attacked with sulphur, mixed with olive oil. At the end of five days the bodies of the animals were washed with castile soap and tepid water.

It is quite amusing to listen to one of the native doctors, (camel doctors,) and hear him give an account of the medicines used in the treatment of camels. I heard of one person in Cairo, who had a valuable dromedary who was sick with some ordinary complaint. He boiled down a young sheep in molasses and made the dromedary swallow it half scalding hot. Another who had been practising his art without success, made a requisition for a "chameleon's tail" to tickle the camel's nose, without which he said he could not effect a cure. Another, to my knowledge, asked for a piece of cheese to cure an animal of a slight cold, and the same person recommended to me to administer an ounce of tea mixed with five grains of gunpowder, to cure a camel with swollen legs. Cauterizing with a hot iron is a favorite remedy for many diseases, and there is scarcely an animal that has not somewhere about it the marks of a hot iron. In purchasing camels, it is very necessary to examine carefully if they have been cauterized, and in what places about the body, for in some spots it denotes an incurable disease. For directions to persons who are going to purchase, I would recommend them to a pamphlet written by "Linant Bey," a French engineer, who has resided many years in Egypt, and who gives the most sensible directions about all matters connected with the dromedary. It is the best and only good account I have met with anywhere. Among the animals I received on board were two remarkably handsome ones, one a "Nomanieh" or supposed to be, from Oman, the other a "Sennai," from Nubia; the former is supposed to be the swiftest, easiest, and most enduring; the easy motion of this animal is owing to its moving hind leg and fore leg on opposite sides at the same time, or I should say rather, that every leg is moved in very rapid succession; this gait is natural to a thorough bred Oman, but has to be taught to the cross-breeds. The "Becharieh" dromedary and those of Mount Sinai, and other parts of Egypt, move both legs on one side together, which gives them a rolling motion and not quite so easy as the other. To acquire the Nomanieh gait, it is necessary to commence with the dromedary at the age of one year; a noose is first placed around his nose with a small rope, and an Arab runs ahead of him, pulling him along, while another runs at his side, striking him lightly on the head or neck, to make him keep his head near the ground; the harder the Arab in advance pulls the tighter the noose becomes, and the dromedary finally falls into the "Nomanieh" pace; whenever he gets out of it the noose is tightened. After a good deal of training he learns what is required of him. When he is pretty well broken in, in this way, a saddle is placed upon his back, with which alone he is drilled for some time longer, and finally, when he is strong enough, he is made to kneel and rise with a rider, who carries on the same system until the dromedary is willing to go without a man in advance of him; this they soon do, as they are an intelligent animal and learn fast, as I have seen them easily taught several things while on the voyage.

The "Becharieh" gait is more universal in Egypt than that of the Nomanieh," and is natural to the dromedary, though not quite so pleasant a motion as the other; it makes the breaking in of a dromedary a more simple business. The "Becharieh" is taught to carry its head very high by reining it up, which gives them a very handsome appearance. The dromedary of "Oman" is not common in and about "Cairo" or Alexandria, they are sometimes brought from Mecca by the returning pilgrims, who purchase them from other pilgrims from "Oman;" but they command high prices, and would not, in my opinion, suit our climate as well as the "Becharieh." I have found the "Nomanieh" female to be the most delicate of those obtained in Egypt, while the "Sennaar" proved to be the most hardy animals on board. I would, therefore, recommend the "Becharieh" as best adapted for our climate. I think they will thrive there, and stand the transportation well.

All the dromedaries taken on board were rutting at the time, and the females that required it were covered by the males on board ship before leaving Alexandria, and every day after we sailed until we reached Smyrna. So that it is likely all the females, except the "Nomanieh," will have young ones next February; sterility is scarcely known amongst the females, and the males being very vigorous and not allowed to run to excesses, the result of a connexion is almost sure to be a young one at the end of the year.

The same system was put in operation with the dromedaries that I had used with the Tunisian camel so successfully; in the first place, I had them thoroughly cleaned with soap and water, gave them a wine glass of powdered sulphur in their drink for three days to purify them; and had every suspicious looking spot on their bodies rubbed with sulphur and olive oil mixed together; if they had any itch about them, it was perfectly eradicated.

The system I adopted for feeding them was to commence at three o'clock every day, and give each one a gallon of oats, or oats and peas mixed; their hay racks were always kept filled, and each animal ate on an average ten pounds of hay a day in good weather.

They were watered every day before feeding them, and were allowed one ship's bucket full of water, or three gallons, each time; those that had young were watered twice every day and fed with a gallon of oats in the morning, besides their evening feed; this amount of water I found was quite enough for them, except in very warm weather, when I had their allowance increased; great care must be taken not to give them more water than the above allowance, which is *ample;* if permitted, they would drink twenty gallons, and that would do them great harm. As the plan I adopted has succeeded, I would not recommend any other, and do not think it necessary to make any further recommendation about the manner of feeding them.

At 9 o'clock in the morning, after the deck was scrubbed up, the men who attended them commenced currying them, combing their long hair with wooden combs, and rubbing their legs, joints, and feet, with hard brushes; this latter I found prevented their limbs from swelling, and whenever any were swollen (which happened with two or three) they were immediately rubbed with "British oil," which effectually cured them. After the animals were thoroughly cleaned an inspection of each one was carefully made, to see if there were any signs of itch, or if they had any hurts; once or twice it was found that a camel could not get upon its legs. On the first occasion I consulted one of the natives, who immediately recommended "cauterizing" the back, as he said the animal had received a strain in that part, or, what he said would be quite as effectual, was to pour boiling hot pitch over her loins, and he was sure it would make her get up. I had no doubt of the efficacy of the application as regarded the camel's getting up quickly, but I tried a more simple remedy and found it to answer very well: I had the camel turned over on its side, rubbed the legs well with hard brushes and made it kick out, after which a cut with a small rope made it rise instantly. Camels are liable to this stiffness from lying all night in a confined position, without being able to turn over on their sides as they are accustomed to do when on shore. I mention it as it might be mistaken for sickness; it is a good rule to make them get up on their legs during the night and not to let them lie down too much in the day time. An observance of these little details will tend greatly to the success of transportation.

Of the burden camel we did not procure any in Egypt, our attention being directed to Smyrna; but from the manner in which the dromedaries have borne the voyage, I think favorably of importing the former from Egypt. These camels are generally of great size, and many that I have seen would not be able to stand up under the deck of the "Supply" by two or three inches. It is calculated that they will carry 600 English pounds on a journey, not including the saddle, which weighs at least 60 pounds more; for short distances they will carry one thousand pounds. The best camels are the "Kufury," or village camels of lower Egypt, which are worth from thirty to seventy-five dollars, though it is likely we would have to pay more for them, to say nothing of the pay of dragoman, presents, &c , which runs the price up almost to double the original cost. The "Shemalieh" or northern camels, found with the Anese Arabs, would be the most likely to thrive, (so says a gentleman writing to Mr. De Leon,) and the "Khowahir" and "Gudieh" breeds would be the best. I do not think, however, that it is so safe an experiment as importing those from Asia Minor or Tunis.

On the 29th of January I anchored in Smyrna, and found that Mr. Heap had purchased all the animals required, with the exception of one or two which were afterwards added to the number; he was employed when we arrived in having them all completely equipped with saddles, bridles, coverings, &c., and had them comfortably lodged in a good "khan," that had been well cleansed, and presented quite a different appearance to the Turkish khans in the neighborhood. On the 10th February they were all equipped, and I commenced taking them on board. As this is a process on which much depends, I will here give a short description of the manner of getting them in; having described the boat and camel car, it will be unnecessary to do so a second time.

In the first place, the ship is anchored as close as possible to the place of embarkation, to save time; the camel boat, with the car in it, is towed on shore, and a force of about ten men sent to get the camels in; there is also sent on shore, in the boat, a good tackle, (not very large,) a camel harness complete, spare plank, hammer and nails, and about fifty fathoms of two-inch rope, all of which will be of use. It is requisite to select a place for the boat, where she will lie with her bow on a level with the wharf; if this cannot be done, and it is necessary to "beach" her, then a strong bridge made of stout plank, and about eight feet wide, will have to be constructed, strong enough to bear not only the camels' weight, but to stand their struggling; this I was obliged to do. The bow of the boat being secured firmly to the wharf or bridge, the harness is placed on the camel, and it is led up as close as it will go; if it will walk right into the car, one end of which is placed on the gunwale of the bow, so much the better, (in no instance did we find them willing to go in without force;) but if it will not go in, then hook on the tackle to the breast strap of the harness on the camel, let the men keep a steady pull upon it, and the camel will go in without a hurt, no matter how much he may resist; four men guide the camel and keep it in the centre of the planks, and one man leads it by the halter into the car, through which the tackle is led, one block hooked to the other end of the boat. After it is in, it is made to lie down, the knees tied around with ropes, a rope across the neck and made fast to the *knees*, and two or three ropes across the back to *keep* it down, it is then hoisted on to the camel deck without fright or excitement of any kind; all this will be intelligible to a seaman, who necessarily will have charge of the business.

Having taken in all the camels, two days were occupied in fitting to each one its proper harness, (for almost every one of them differed in size and form,) marking their numbers on the harness, and fitting out each one with brush and curry-comb, all of which is necessary to be done before going to sea. Hay racks, made of large open net-work, were fitted amid-ships, extending the whole length of camel deck; large bags, filled with hay, were placed against the ship's side for their haunches to rest against, and two ropes fitted for securing to the harness on each camel. Four large lanterns with reflectors were put up and lighted every evening at sunset; two large water tubs kept filled, in case of fire; and the fire apparatus, that was fitted up before leaving New York, kept ready for immediate use. The following regulations were hung up on the camel deck, and as they may serve as a guide hereafter, I herewith insert them:

Rules and Regulations for camel deck.

1. No open light to be allowed; lamp to be lighted at sunset.
2. One person is always to be on watch on the camel deck, even at meal time.
3. Nothing of any kind is to be kept unlashed, and no tools of any kind, by which the animals can be hurt, to be allowed on the deck.
4. The camels are to be fed and watered every day at three o'clock precisely; the females having young ones to be fed and watered at seven o'clock in the morning besides.
5. The camels are always to have their covers on in cold weather; harness kept on at all times, and harness ropes rove at sunset.
6. The deck is never to be wet, unless by order.
7. The hay racks must be filled every two days, and the amount of feed expended kept account of.
8. The least thing the matter with an animal must be reported to me at once by the person in charge, and no change whatever in the management of them to be made without my orders.
9. The camels must never be struck with anything but the flat of the hand; their beds to be littered down before sunset.
10. Each camel is to be curried and brushed half an hour every day, and their legs and feet well rubbed.
11. The "argols" are never to be left lying on the deck, but the men on watch are to keep them cleaned up and thrown overboard; the camels' feet are to be cleaned with soap and water twice a week, and salt to be given them once a week.
12. When the camels lie down at sea, particular care must be observed in putting hay under their knees and haunches.
13. In warm weather the ventilating windows must be kept open, and the wind sails kept trimmed.
14. The men in charge of camels to sleep on the camel deck.
15. The "callosities" on the camels' knees are to be oiled once a week.

The above regulations were well observed, and I believe they embrace almost everything relating to the treatment of camels at sea.

The treatment of the camel and dromedary is about the same. At first some of the former refused to eat the oats and peas, when four pounds of dough-ball (or barley flour mixed with water) was given them, of which they ate heartily. In a day or two, however, they will take to the oats if deprived of their dough-ball, and the oats is much better food for them at sea.

Mr. Heap procured a lot of very good camels at Smyrna; the males were remarkably fine, but the females were not so handsome (though young and strong) as he would have obtained had more time been allowed him. The mistake we made was in not sending him through "Asia Minor" to hunt up choice animals while the ship was visiting other places. We were fortunate in procuring all sound camels; not one of them turned out badly.

Smyrna is, without doubt, the best port in Asia Minor to ship camels from; but although there are immense numbers in Smyrna, it does not follow that the best can be bought there.

Mr. Heap had to send some distance into the country for those he purchased. His duties would not permit him to leave Smyrna, as he had to expedite matters so as to be ready for the ship, and he had to employ trusty persons to hunt up camels in the country.

I would suggest that if any more camels are to be purchased, that a competent person be sent into the interior of "Asia Minor;" starting from Smyrna and going even as far as "Karamania," he can select the animals on the route, and on his return by the same way he can purchase them and add them to the train. "Konieh," in "Karamania," is one of the most famous camel stations, and is the great stopping place for caravans between Smyrna and Persia, and other parts of "Anadolia." It is about seven hundred miles from Smyrna in a straight line, and about twenty-five days' travel at camel pace. In this way the very choicest stock can be procured. I do not think myself that an experiment of this kind can be carried out successfully by the introduction of inferior stock. If it is not considered desirable to undertake so long a journey, there are places nearer to Smyrna where good purchases can be made. Among those known are "Allah Shir," "Ishkel," "Degnish," &c., and many other places on the route to "Karamania."

There is always a doubt about purchasing a camel in or about a city, no matter how fine looking it may be, particularly if it has been used in a "caravan," for although it may not have the itch at the time it is bought, there is no knowing how soon it may break out. If the camel is bought from a private gentleman, (who has merely used it for his amusement or about his grounds,) and has been kept in a private stable, there is no danger of disease, for it is only in the filthy khans where they contract it. All those bought by Mr. Heap were either from the country or brought from private stables, consequently they were all good healthy camels.

Mr. Heap was fortunate enough to be able to purchase two very fine Bactrian males for breeding purposes; he heard of their being about six days' journey from Smyrna, and had them brought in; one of them had been brought from Persia, being marked with a Persian mark or brand, and the other was picked up at "Gheuzel," near Samos. This powerful animal, although a native of northern Asia, is found on the confines of Persia, in the "Kurdistan" country, and is brought in yearly to the southwestern part of Asia Minor to cross with the female Arabian camel, (or Arvanas,) passing through a large extent of country in the rutting season, and returning again in the spring to the northeast, where the weather is temperate and the pasturage abundant. The connexion between the Bactrian male and the Arvana, or female Arabian, produces a cross called "Tulu," generally known as the "Turcoman" camel, large numbers of which are to be found throughout Asia Minor, and large caravans of them go annually from Smyrna to Persia and the northeast countries of Asia Minor, carrying immense loads. This cross or "Tulu" is a hybrid, and if it does produce at all, the issue is very small and very inferior; it is called a "Kokurt;" they are not worth five dollars. We procured only one "Tulu" as a specimen, and though he is a huge and powerful animal, he is not to compare with many of the same kind to be met with in Asia Minor. We had to consult the height of our decks, which were only seven feet five inches between the planks. The "Tulu" purchased was rutting at the time, and was in consequence very thin; he measured, however, seven feet four inches in height, ten feet two inches in length, with head erect, and eight feet ten inches around the body; when in fair order he will weigh over two thousand pounds. The weight carried by a "Tulu" on a journey is twelve hundred English pounds, and he will make eighteen miles a day with this load for many consecutive days. Their food is one dough-ball of four pounds while travelling, with the herbage they can pick up at resting times. The "Maya," or female issue of the Bactrian and Arabian female, is also a very powerful animal, but cannot carry such heavy weights as the "Tulu." Most novices who went to purchase camels would be much struck with the "Tulu" and "Maya," and, if they had no experience, would likely purchase all of that kind; but that course would not have answered in our case, for if it should so happen that this was to be the last attempt to import camels, we will, at all events, be provided with the means of raising a number hereafter from the limited stock on hand, although it will take some years to produce any great results from so small a number. If the experiment is only to ascertain whether they will carry heavy loads and suit the climate of Texas, that could have been found out at Smyrna without the trouble of bringing any over, for it is well known that the "Kurdistan" mountains, "Akabzik," "Mount Ararat," and the mountains from Erzroun to "Tabrees" are all covered with deep snow until late in the spring, and large caravans of these are passing constantly over them. To import the "Tulu" and "Maya" would be a slow process of accumulating them. They take up a great deal of room on board ship, (as much as two ordinary camels,) and I think it altogether more advisable to import the male Bactrian camel and breed them in the United States.

The only difficulty now is to find out whether the "Bactrian" will stand the heat of Texas. Having passed through the heat of the tropics, I think I can safely predict that he will survive the heat of Texas. They are a very hardy animal and give very little trouble on board ship, provided they are kindly treated, but they wont bear harsh treatment, and will fret under it. In getting the Bactrian on board great care must be observed not to let his humps touch anywhere, as the animal is very tender about those parts; the best plan is to keep his knees tied around securely with ropes, and let him walk on them (which he can easily do) to the place he is to stand in between the beams. I was obliged to cut away part of the deck for one of the Bactrians; he could not stand under it without rubbing the top of his humps; he was seven feet five inches high, ten feet long, and nine feet nine inches around the body, including his fore hump.

The Bactrian "Bohoor," or male, can always be procured in "Anadolia" and "Karamania," although they are not numerous, and cost from three to four hundred dollars; if the eastern war was over they could be purchased in the Crimea at low prices; but the trouble of going there would be great. If they are wanted in the United States hereafter, to any extent, Arnour or Seghalien river in Russia is the best place to get them; the distance from there to California is nothing like as great as a voyage from Smyrna to the United States, to say nothing of the difference in time, and the suitableness of the climates through which they pass. As an animal of burden, I do not think they would answer as well as the Arabian camel or the "Tulu;" they are a clumsy, lumbering beast, and are not at all trained in Asia Minor to carry weights. Although I should judge from their powerful make that they could carry more than either the "Arabian" or "Tulu," their speed on a journey would not be more than a mile and a half an hour, which they could likely keep up for ten hours without resting, and carry all that time about one thousand pounds. While in the "Crimea" I saw two of them attached to a small cart, which they were drawing no doubt with very great ease, but the pace at which they were travelling was very slow, (not more than two miles an hour,) and one good horse would have done twice as much, with the same cart, in the same time. I do not think they are at all suited to wagons, although for moving heavy weights, for a short distance on wheels, they would do very well. The female Bactrian is not known to the south of "Tartary, the Black Sea: and the Caspian Sea;" and if it is wanted to raise that breed in the United States, it will be necessary to import them from the Amour river or thereabouts.

It is customary to cover up the Bactrian in the rutting season (humps and all) with a thick blanket, in consequence of which his hair becomes closely matted together, and a thick felt forms all over his body. When it comes off in the spring it leaves the body in flakes of a yard square, very much resembling thick cloth. Nature has made a very wise provision for the Bactrian, and indeed, for all camels, for the moment the warm weather commences, their thick pea jacket of fur or wool comes off entirely, leaving the body perfectly bare, but before winter comes again the coat is out full and luxuriant, and seems sufficient to protect them against the severest cold. On board ship the Bactrians seemed to suffer with heat while their thick coverings were on, and I had them removed; a short time after which their hair all came off and they seemed to be less restive, and improved rapidly in appearance. When rutting they grow thin, and will not eat much; they nibble the whitewash off the beams and sides of th ship, which seems to do them good; when they do so it is because they require salt, which must be furnished to them twice a week. I found it necessary to keep them ironed on the fore legs the first day or two, but after that time they became very tractable; the most violent camels become very quiet the moment the ship is in motion, and remain so ever afterwards.

Among the camels bought at Smyrna were four fine Loks; these have all been trained as "Pehlevans," or wrestlers. Wresting matches between camels being an amusement in which Turks take great delight, although they sometimes get a fine animal maimed in the sport. Many gentlemen keep them for no other purpose, and one person in Smyrna kept twenty at one time, for the amusement of his wife, who had a fondness for the sport. The camels are trained to wrestling when quite young; they exhibit great dexterity in throwing their antagonists, and seem to take much pleasure in the fray.

We had a young one on board, only a month old, and having been born under the flag, he was christened "Uncle Sam." One of the Turks amused himself on the voyage making a "Pehlevan" of him, and when six weeks old he was more than a match for his teacher, using *his legs*, neck and mouth with such dexterity, and exhibiting such wonderful strength in so young a thing, that he became a very rough playmate, and frequently hurt the men on the deck by throwing himself on *them suddenly* and knocking them down. This feature seems to be natural to the camel, for when two strange ones meet together where they are any females, they immediately have a wrestling match for the supremacy, and the conquered one ever afterwards acknowledges his inferiority by not so much as daring to look at a female. Unlike the amusement of "bull-baiting," this wrestling is a harmless pastime, though the animals do sometimes get their legs broken, or are stiff for some time after with their bruises; well trained animals seldom injure each other, being taught to throw their antagonist by getting his neck under their fore leg (the right) and then throwing the whole weight of their body on him, and bringing him to the ground. Perhaps the love of amusement (as our countrymen are fond of novelties,) may render the importation of camels in Texas popular, if their utility does not recommend them. I have no fear but that they will soon find out their value in other respects. A Turk who was told that we had no camels in America expressed much surprise, and said that we must be many years behind the age.

In considering the future transportation of camels, my idea is that it would be much easier to carry over young ones, from one to two years of age. Among the number of those I brought over was one a year old, purchased with its mother. It was the heartiest of the whole lot, and required very little looking after. A ship fitted like the "Supply" could carry at least ninety of this size, or forty with their mothers only. Thirty-four of the full-grown camel is as many as she could possibly accommodate. The one or two-year old camel is about the size of a year-old heifer, and would pack close, without fear of injury from their weight. These, when landed in Texas, could be trained either as burden or riding camels, and serve to form a corps of mounted dromedaries that would soon drive everything in the shape of an hostile Indian out of the country, for the Indian could not escape on the swiftest horse the steady enduring pace of the dromedary, which will carry him a hundred miles a day.

Any young camel can be trained as a dromedary, though they would not be so swift as the "Nomanieh" or "Becharieh" of the desert, yet they would exhibit an endurance of days and weeks unknown to any kind of horse, and when the latter would likely be "blown" after a journey of a hundred miles, which he would require three days to perform, the dromedary (the common stock even) would be travelling its sixty miles a day with ease, going through all kinds of weather, and over all kinds of roads, and wading through mud where a horse would be stalled. They require no shoeing nor any repairs to harness, which is of the most simple kind. They will carry, withal, two or three hundred pounds of baggage, besides their rider. If they come up with an enemy, they lie down and form a rampart with their bodies, and are not like horses, subject to "stampede."

If the camel of one year be introduced into Texas, in two years more it will be fit to use with light burdens, and certainly fit to be trained as a dromedary and carry a rider. To get them brought rapidly into use this is the only plan; breeding is a much slower process.

Among the female camels that were purchased ten were large with young, and were expected to give birth in from two to six weeks. Though a hazardous experiment in so long a voyage, it was determined to try if we could not raise the young on board; at all events, they would take up but little room, and if we lost them we considered that we would be no worse off than before; if we succeeded, there would be so many more added to our stock, and we would gain some experience in the matter by which others might be benefitted. Those that were not with young were covered by the Bactrians before leaving Smyrna, and may be expected to calve in February next.

The female is said to be very delicate when with young, and a slight thing, it is said, will cause a miscarriage. I do not think this can be so, for with all the tumbling and tossing they have experienced on this voyage, and the fright they exhibited while getting them on board, nothing of the kind has happened, and the report may be set down as one of the many fables told about camels by travellers, who, passing merely through the countries where camels abound, know little or nothing of the habits of the animal. A female camel with young is worked to the last moment, though lightly, and when travelling in a caravan where they cannot stop she is often obliged to carry the young one on her back, where it is slung in a blanket by the driver. We had one case, it is true, where we lost a fine camel in giving birth to her young, but that was owing to the great size of the calf, which had evidently been dead in the womb three or four weeks; the female, nevertheless, preserved her health all that time, and ate as heartily as the rest. Two or three times she gave indications of "prolapsus of the uterus," and was treated accordingly, until her complaint became so bad that half of her inside seemed to be coming from her. I exerted every bit of energy I had to save her, and felt quite as anxious as if I had a human being in the same situation. As I did not succeed in my endeavors to save her life, it will be unnecessary to go into the details. Suffice it to say, that with such information as I could obtain from medical books, and which I found applicable to the purpose, I succeeded in so far restoring her to shape that she was enabled to bring forth her young, assisted by ten men, who were hauling on it with ropes. The surprise was that any animal could stand so painful an operation; but the one I am mentioning seemed to suffer very little, and after she was bound up with proper appliances she looked as usual. That night she had a prolapsus of the uterus again, of which, unfortunately, I was not informed until next morning, though it is doubtful if I could have relieved such a case. It was very distressing to behold, and to relieve the poor animal, I had an end put to her life. I looked upon the loss of this female as quite a serious calamity; but in two or three hours she was replaced by a fine young one from another female, and the next day by another.

The loss of such a camel to a poor Turk would have been a great misfortune; to a poor man a female camel is the greatest blessing; there is no end to their endurance; their usefulness is beyond comparison. She supplies his family with milk far richer than that of the cow; he clothes his children with the wool which she yields in abundance, and which is as fine and as warm as that of the sheep; she carries his produce to market, and is satisfied with nibbling the dried grass she can pick up on the roadside; it costs but little to feed her, and she continues her usefulness to an age which the cow or horse scarcely ever reach.

If (it will be asked) the camel is so useful an animal, why is it not left to private enterprise to introduce them and reap the benefits arising from them? I simply answer, because the subject is not fully understood and appreciated in the United States. People form their opinions of the camel from the diminutive and sickly looking specimens they give a shilling to see in a menagerie; as well might they form their opinions of the great monarch of beasts from the half starved and listless animal crouching meekly in his cage; if some of the specimens brought over in the "Supply" could be seen by those who have only seen a menagerie camel, or the ill drawn picture of them in "Buffon," they would be very much struck with the difference. Private individuals do not care to undertake an enterprise about the details of which they know so little, and about which heretofore there has been such a variety of opinions of the ultimate cost; it is one of those cases where government must take the lead—private individuals will follow the moment they see the experiment successful; besides, at present, government is the most interested party, and will, in the end, derive all the benefit. How invaluable would a "Tulu" be to a southern planter who could not get his cotton to market on account of bad roads or the absence of steamboats? whereas, if he was provided with a few of these powerful animals, that could carry their twelve hundred pounds each twenty miles a day, he would have a great advantage over his neighbors who were not so well off as himself. This is one of the many advantages to be derived from the importation of the camel into the United States, and it is an important one.

On the 14th of February I sailed direct for the United States, having made everything comfortable for the camels before weighing anchor. Before leaving New York I had been furnished with the best of oats and hay, and had tanks on board sufficient to hold thirty thousand gallons of water. It is best to lay in the food for the camels in the United States, as it is much cheaper and better than can be purchased in the East, particularly the hay; twenty pounds of hay and two gallons of oats should be calculated on as the daily average for each animal on the voyage; this will allow for any loss by waste or damage.

Before leaving Smyrna we took on board two Turkish saddle makers, the same who were employed in making saddles for our camels, one of them was also said to be a professed M. D. of camels, and understood all their diseases, the mode of providing for their young, &c. Mr. Heap recommended them, and thought they would be useful in Texas in fitting the camels, and no doubt they will be, for it requires some ingenuity and practice to make a good camel saddle. The Turks were not of as much use (at sea in bad weather) in taking care of the camels as sailors, but got along very well in fair weather; they seemed to accommodate themselves very easily to the Christian mode of life, and were good, honest men; they are much preferable to the Egyptian and are of a higher order of intellect. I would not object to taking Turks on a voyage to assist in the care of camels; this kind of help, if desirable, can be procured at ten to fifteen dollars a month.

The day we left Smyrna one of the female camels presented us with a fine young male, and it was turned over to the Turkish M. D., who superintended all the arrangements for its birth; as this is quite a delicate operation, and as a knowledge of the manner in which it is done may be useful to others hereafter, I will give my experience as far as practicable, having had more (in a short time) on this subject than most people. The first indication given by a female of bringing forth is a swelling of the udder and a sinking in of the rump near the tail on each side of the spine; she also becomes cross and snappish a few hours before the event takes place; her eye-balls, also, seem to protrude a little; she begins by lying first on one side and then on the other, when shortly after the young one makes its appearance, head and fore feet foremost; no doubt if they were left to themselves nature would bring about a safe delivery, but the Turks think it necessary to assist the mother, which they do by pulling the young one away from her by the head and feet, and pressing on her sides. This unnatural proceeding is, no doubt, an injury to the young, (as the neck is subjected to severe tension,) although the mother is speedily relieved during the process of parturition; the practitioner blows into the young one's nostrils, which is finally released, apparently in the last agonies of death; the navel string is then tied with a cord; the young one is cleansed and wrapped up in a blanket and presented to the female; (this is the Turkish mode of doing business;) the latter suffers very little from the operation, but quietly eats her hay as if nothing had happened, and takes but little notice of her progeny; it is probable that she does not recognize it so wrapped up in a bundle of colored rags, or, if she does, is so disappointed with its appearance that she does not care about owning it. In half an hour the young one begins to show signs of liveliness; the mother is then milked and a little is poured down its throat, and it is taught to suck at the finger, after which it is allowed to repose, if it can do so with such a mass of wrappings around, and its limbs painfully compressed; the mother passes the afterbirth in half an hour, and needs no further care. In the case alluded to, the young one was kept wrapped up for six days, during all which time the mother refused to let it suck, except by force; we had to resort finally to a bottle, from which it fed voraciously.

On the fifth day out another female brought forth young, and the same treatment was observed; as they both seemed to improve slowly,

I did not interfere in the matter, but neither of these were ever able to stand up, no doubt being cramped in their limbs by the wrappings. On the seventh or eight day a severe gale of wind commenced blowing, and lasted with some violence for forty-eight hours, at the end of that time the young ones both were dead, either through exhaustion or from the unnatural course of treatment they had gone through; they were thrown overboard, the mothers testifying no grief whatever, nor taking any notice of the absence of their young. Before throwing them overboard, I had them skinned and examined, and found their backs much bruised and discolored, with coagulated blood under the spot where the bandages were tied across; the cause of their deaths was no longer doubtful, nature had not been sufficiently consulted in the matter, I determined to pursue a different course with those to come.

Our voyage down the Mediterranean was a rough one, the first ten days we had nothing but head winds and heavy head seas, and in that time experienced two gales of wind, in which the ship rolled heavily; the camels stood it all beautifully, and not one of them received the slightest injury; they were kept tied down on their knees, with a thick bed of hay under them, and examined every half hour, night and day, to see that all was right. After the second gale we were favored with a good breeze that carried us out of the Mediterranean, and I was in hopes of reaching the trade winds in two or three days, when I felt the camels would be safe, but we unfortunately encountered westerly gales, which lasted six days, accompanied by a heavy swell that lasted many days afterwards. During most of this time the camels had to be kept secured on their knees, and were only permitted to rise, one at a time to remake their beds of hay, they bore the rolling admirably, and did not seem to have suffered in the least, although during ten days they obtained scarcely any repose. The elements indeed seemed to conspire against us, and I thought at one time that the animals would certainly suffer from so long a spell of bad weather, but they ate and drank heartily in their recumbent position, and when the gale was over, and they were permitted to rise, they looked as fresh as if they been on shore. If any doubt exists about camels being able to stand the transportation for so long a voyage, the experience we have gained during the heavy weather will put that doubt to rest; for I think they will stand any kind of weather, provided they are properly secured. All they want is good ventilation, good food and water, and to be allowed to rise now and then to relieve their limbs. Unlike a horse (that would be kicking himself and those around him) the camels kneel of their own accord when there is too much motion for them, and accommodate themselves to the rolling of the vessel; care must be taken to put *no sand* under them or about them, as it soon chafes the skin off.

I may, perhaps, have dwelt too long on this subject, but so many persons have laughed at the absurdity of endeavoring to import camels, that I wish to do away with their prejudices, if they still exist, and also to encourage those who would desire to embark in the enterprise.

When opposite to Tunis, another female gave symptoms of approaching maturity, and being desirous to secure at least one of those born on board, I undertook the direction of the affair myself, the Bedouin acting as practitioner. No force whatever was used, but nature allowed to have her way; the result was, that everything turned out well, and the young one stood on its legs one hour after it was born; it was then presented to the mother for recognition, and she testified much affection for it, not being shocked by the sight of the unsightly clothes by which the others had been so disguised, that the mothers did not recognize them as their own offspring; in two hours after birth, this young one was sucking heartily at its mother's teats; after a hearty meal it was rubbed in the joints, made to stand up every hour, and in four days was running about among the camels. In a week the young one was frisking about the deck as lively as a young lamb, generously permitting the young camel, "Uncle Sam," to draw from the same fount, that precocious animal, having discovered that the mother had a superabundance of milk, was frequently caught poaching, to which the female in no way objected. Suffice it to say that the above mentioned system was carried out with all the young ones, and never failed. Young camels are very little trouble on board after they are ten days old; having been born at sea they are perfectly steady on their legs, even in the heaviest weather, and when a sailor even has to hold on they can balance themselves and not fall. In gales they go about the deck without danger; at the age of one month they eat heartily of oats and dough-ball, and drink their water, it seems to agree with them, and they grow rapidly from that moment. On board ship they suck indiscriminately from each other's mother, (which I presume would not be allowed on shore,) and it was no uncommon thing to see three sucking at one female at the same time. The plan I adopted for introducing the young ones into the world seems the most natural one, notwithstanding Turkish precedents; it is, I believe, the Egyptian way of doing; at the least, the Bedouin approved of it, and he moreover told me that in the desert the young ones were put out in the rain without receiving any injury from it.

I have endeavored to get some reliable information relative to the diseases to which camels are liable, and which, I am told, are numerous. I cannot, however, find that they are liable to any disease not engendered by filth and negligent treatment; the most common complaint is the itch, with which the Turks and Egyptians take very little trouble beyond smearing the animal with tar, when it is nearly eaten up with sores, and which, perhaps, eventuates a cure when the camel is brought to a pretty low condition. The itch, as I have already mentioned, can be cured in four days, by rubbing sulphur and olive oil mixed together on the part affected, and giving the animal a handful of flour of sulphur every day, (for ten days,) in its oats. Both camels and dromedaries are subject to colds, particularly the latter. I had seven cases on hand at one time; the animals coughed painfully, and had a running at the nose, and also seemed to have a difficulty in swallowing hay. I gave to each one a half pint of olive oil for two days, (stopped the use of hay,) and gave them a wine glass of olive oil, night and morning, until they were cured, which was in six days. They took cold, I think, from having too thick covers on them while between decks, for they seemed to sweat profusely under them, and were never troubled with colds when I had them removed. Contusions and sores in camels require very simple treatment; "British oil" is a certain cure for all bruises, and washing sores with castile soap and tepid water will soon heal them up. Some of those I took charge of were saddle galled; but I found that the sore places healed up immediately on the application of castile soap and tepid water, and a small plaster of simple "cerate." I would caution persons about to buy camels to examine carefully under the saddle, to see if any saddle galls exist; the Turks are very great "jockies," and are very adroit in plastering the long hair down on the sores, so that they cannot be seen unless very closely examined; this cannot happen with the dromedary, which has the body covered with short hair, and every mark shows. The "Bactrian" camel, the "Tulu," and the "Luk," are said to be very delicate when rutting, and liable to take cold, from which they die. It is customary with the Turks to keep their heavy saddles on (each weighing nearly a hundred pounds) night and day; the Bactrian is kept covered with a thick blanket. As the rutting season commences in January and ends some time in April, the camels are liable to be severely galled with such a weight on them all this time; no doubt a covering is necessary, but I am sure that the plan of keeping the saddle on all the time is a bad one, as the humps of the camel dwindle away very much under this treatment.

I don't know, sir, that I can say any more on this subject, without being guilty of plagiarism. My desire has been, in making this report, to furnish as many practical hints as possible, and to enable others who may undertake the transportation of camels to benefit by my experience, and from facts that have come under my immediate observation; if the experiment is to be carried out on a grander scale, I am sure that a close adherence to the rules laid down will, in most cases, ensure success.

As Jamaica laid in my route, I stopped there three or four days to fill up with water, and obtain refreshments, which I afterwards regretted, though it could not very well be helped; the camels seemed to suffer very much from the heat, in the absence of the sea breeze, although I kept the ship swung broadside to the wind all the time; they were somewhat fretted also by the citizens of the place, who visited the ship in great numbers, as many as four thousand coming on board in one day. Camels were many years since used in Jamaica, but owing to the "chiqua's" getting into their feet they soon became useless. The chiqua is a very small insect, which oftentimes get into the feet of the negroes, and without great care their toes and feet are soon eaten off.

I met a gentleman in Jamaica, who had had charge of some camels, working the copper mines in "St. Jago de Cuba;" he informed me that they were very useful until the "chiqua" got into their feet, and after that they were given up. As the "chiqua," it is to be hoped, does not exist in Texas, there is no danger of their being afflicted by them. The same gentleman informed me that in every other respect they suited admirably, and stood the climate.

On the 29th of May I anchored off Indianola, but the sea being very rough we could not communicate with the shore. On the 1st the steamer "Fashion" came out to us, and finding that she could do nothing, Major Wayne went on shore, and returned with two schooners. I made the attempt to get the camels on board the lighters, but found it impossible to do so, and I weighed anchor and stood for the mouth of the Mississippi, where, on the 10th of May, all the camels were safely transferred to the charge of Major Wayne, on board the steamer "Fashion."

I have the honor to remain your obedient servant,

DAVID D. PORTER,
United States Navy.

Hon. JEFFERSON DAVIS,
Secretary of War, Washington city.

DAILY JOURNAL

KEPT ON

THE CAMEL DECK OF UNITED STATES SHIP SUPPLY,

D. D. PORTER, LIEUTENANT COMMANDING,

CONTAINING

Expenditures of feed and water, and incidents of the voyage while the camels were on board.

CAMEL JOURNAL.

Date.	Hay.	Water.	Oats.	Peas.	Meal.	Medicines.	Remarks.
1856.	Bales.	Galls.	Bags.	Galls.	Lbs.		
Jan. 21	280 lbs.	30	2	......	....	¼ lb. sulphur.	Received on board 6 camels, 2 of them males; washed them and secured them in their stalls; put sulphur in their water.
22	220 lbs.	40	1	......	....	....	Fitted the harness where required, and rubbed the camels well with currycombs and brushes; named the camels, and lettered the harness; Mahomet, the Tunisian camel, was this day put to the Egyptian camel Adela.*
23	1	40	1	......	....	....	Refilled the netting with hay, as also the fenders for their behinds; went round the camels with sulphuric ointment, and applied it, well rubbed in, on all suspicious looking places; Mahomet again served Adela. This day Ibrim, an Egyptian camel, (stud,) served an Egyptian female named Massanda; ditto Gourmal to Preguada; ditto ceased to issue oats; littered with hay.
24	....	....	....	......	....	....	Ship's motion this day rather uneasy and camels not caring for their hay; issued 4 quarts of crushed beans and oats to each animal, of which they eat well; keep their harness on ready to use; curried and brushed as usual; littered with hay.
25	....	35	10 galls. oats and beans.	......	....	¼ lb. sulphur.	Issued 4 quarts of crushed beans and oats to each animal; put Ibrim to Massanda, Mahomet to Adela; watered camels and put sulphur in the water.
26	2	40	20 galls., half beans.	......	....	½ pint British oil.	This day put Ibrim to Massanda; rubbed Amisa on the legs with British oil for fear of a sprain; camels all well and do not seem very sea sick; clean and currycomb as usual; whitewashed where necessary.
27	1	40	20 galls, half beans.	......	....	....	Blowing fresh; secured the animals by their harness to the ropes, and liberated them as soon as the rolling motion ceased; clean and curry as usual.
28	....	40	20 galls., half beans.	......	....	....	Animals none the worse for their confinement yesterday; watered them without sulphur; clean as usual.
29	1	30	20	......	....	....	Animals well; cleaned as usual. Mem. "Use hay for litter as well as feed."
30	....	40	....	......	....	....	Detected signs of itch on Gourmal; used the sulphur ointment; fed as usual; animals in good health generally.
31	....	40	20	......	....	....	Animals continue the same; the animal supposed to be itchy shows no further signs; clean and curry as usual.
Feb. 1	1	30	20	......	....	....	Preparing for the reception of some new camels; nothing to remark.
2	....	30	20	......	....	....	Animals in good health; feed as usual; nothing to note.

* Some days prior to this received from Cairo 3 dromedaries, whose treatment was exactly similar.

CAMEL JOURNAL—Continued.

Date.	Hay.	Water.	Oats.	P ea	Meal.	Medicines.	Remarks.
1856.	Bales.	Galls.	Bags.	Galls.	Lbs.		
Feb. 3	1	30	20				Camels continue in good health; have them all blanketed, as the weather is none too warm; feed as usual.
4	2	50	30	8	2		Received from this place (Smyrna) this day seven camels, two of them very large male Bactrian camels, five females, and one of them with a calf by her side; secured them and disposed of them in their places; fed hay and oats, of which they eat lightly.
5	1	50	20	4	8		Tried to put Said to Ayesha, (both of them fast dromedaries,) but Said took no notice of the lady; camels all well, and mother and calf seem quite at home; this day employed in fitting harness, &c., preparatory for sea.
6	1	50	20	8	4		Received this day 33 sacks peas (crushed;) — sacks of crushed barley or meal, and three sacks ground oats, for use on the voyage home; Bactrian camel on the port side eats nothing; gave him salt; employed fitting gear, &c., for sea.
7	1	60	30	18	4		Bactrian camel still sick or sulky; gave him more salt and made him some balls of barley meal and water, of which he eat about one gallon; fitting gear this day; clean, &c., as usual; white-washed where necessary; rubbed sulphur ointment on Gourmal (for showing signs of itch;) weather cold, and animals blanketed.
8	1	60	30	30	4		This day receiving camels and securing them; nothing to note.
9	2	60	30	30	5		Received this day the last of our lot of Smyrna camels, making in all 31 full grown camels and two calves, one a year old, and the other 15 days; no further signs of itch on Gourmal; Bactrian camel eats better and seems to be more reconciled to his change of habitation.
10	2	60	30	30			Bactrian camel still seems out of sorts; the female dromedary, Ayesha, appears to have a delicate chest, coughs at night; Gourmal, a fine Alexandrian camel, seems out of sorts also.
11	1	60	30	30	20		One or two of the Smyrna camels do not seem to take to their feed as kindly as they might; no change in the camels mentioned on the 10th; fitted hobbles to each camel.
12	1	60	30	30			Gourmal this day sick; gave him a drench of sweet oil, and Arabs bled him a little; Bactrian remains the same; ditto, Ayesha; Said coughs at night also, but not so badly as his mate, Ayesha; continue to litter with hay.
13	2	60	20	20			Gourmal this day relieved a little; do not allow him any hay; found a female camel this day with a gathering over the left eye; applied blue-stone ointment after extracting the matter and core, and washing with castile soap; reduced the feed, and issue to sick camels, &c., barley meal balls.
14	1	60	15	15	25	Half pint sweet oil.	Bactrian camel still seems not to care for feed; one of the female camels, No. 22, from Smyrna, shows signs of her time for delivery approaching; sore on the eye of the camel improving; gave to the Bactrian half pint sweet oil; worked him very little; Gourmal better.
15	1	60	15	20	20		The evening of this day No. 22 gave birth to a young camel; the camel is delivered as the cow, with the exception that it is necessary after delivery to breathe immediately into the nostrils of young animals, and to swaddle it in warm wrappers, having also a man to watch by it day and night, who, the day after parturition, has to milk the mother himself, and dipping his fingers into the warm milk, puts one of them in the calf's mouth, and thus it is gradually learnt to recognize the odor of milk, the use of the teat, and its own requirements; the mother for a day or two hardly notices it; and perhaps were her udder not to become uneasy to her for want of milking, would not let it suck her; the calf lies constantly before her, and is fed as above men-

CAMEL JOURNAL—Continued.

Date.	Hay.	Water.	Oats.	Peas.	Meal.	Medicines.	Remarks.
1856.	Bales.	Galls.	Bags.	Galls.	Lbs.		
							tioned, until it gathers strength to stand on its legs and be introduced to its mother's teats; the feed of the animal is not changed by the Arabs in charge on board the ship; but when on shore the camel, after delivered, (as the cow,) has plenty of green food given it; nothing else to note.
Feb. 16	1	66	15	20	20	....	Mother and calf doing well; this night blowing fresh, had to secure the camels, (for which purpose the Arabs are more hindrance than use;) in the morning, moderating, released them; Gourmal much better; no change in the Bactrian; still refuses feed in any reasonable quantity; the eye of the camel before mentioned being washed every day with castile soap and warm water, is gradually healing; those camels who do not eat oats, peas, or mixed feed, have barley meal balls given them in about three to four pound balls; animals curried and cleaned each day.
17	1	70	15	15	25	1 pint oil.	Nothing in particular to note, save that one or two camels had sweet oil given to them to purge them; clean, &c., as usual.
18	1	70	10	15	25	1 pint oil.	Camels as usual; the Bactrian will not eat, and drinks little; the wound over the eye of aforementioned camel is now healed; cleaned, &c., as usual.
19	1	70	10	15	25¼	Half pint oil.	White-washed the stalls, and employed in making light covers for camels preparatory to the hot weather; Bactrian will not eat; at 4 p. m. No. 3 (Smyrnian) safely dropped a calf, (female;) noticed that the Arabs *made up* the humps prior to swaddling it, and that the legs of the young camel were also placed in the kneeling position, and the swaddling clothes then securely fastened, leaving the head and neck free for the mother to smell at and caress; the young one is placed directly in front of her, and she ought to be left, if possible, free in her movements.
20	1	70	10	15	30	Half pint British oil.	Blowing heavy; secured the camels in the night, the calves unable therefore to suck; camels uneasy, but do not seem to suffer much from the heavy rolling; Bactrian eats better; this evening gave to the calves some preserved milk, diluted with water, and sweetened a little; after a few trials they drank thereof.
21	1	70	10	15	30	....	Cleared up all the litter preparatory to bedding down afresh; changed the heavy blankets for lighter ones, and gave this morning one gallon of oats extra feed to each animal.
22	1	70	20	10	40	....	Ceased to bed the animals; heavy weather coming on again; prepared to secure animals; blew heavy in the night, and ship labored badly.
23	1	70	20	15	40	....	Ship rolling excessively; had to secure the camels with extra fastenings; some of the camels having a sort of heave or cold, give them, by order, sweet oil when they cough.
24	1	70	20	12	40	....	This day nothing to note but heavy weather.
25	1	70	15	20	35	1½ pt. British oil. 1 quart turpentine 1 quart sweet oil.	Ship this day easier, and sea moderating. Let the camels up; one or two rather stiff, but after chafing their legs, and bending them backward and forward, they soon got up. Rubbed in British oil and turpentine on all that required it. This day the two calves died, the mothers having dried up, and when they had milk refused to let them suck. (Sic *transit camellus*.) Examined the legs, &c., and find that in the knee of the camel there are four separate and distinct joints. The muscles of the leg are also more numerous than those of the ox, and much stronger, or ligamentous. The hind legs are double-jointed. The callosities on the apex of the breast-bone and other parts of the animal's body are not on it when born, (as is said,) but are produced by habitude. On examining the foot, found that it is so jointed that it can fold together, as a man can compress his forefinger together, and that underneath the horny outer covering

CAMEL JOURNAL—Continued.

Date.	Hay.	Water.	Oats.	Peas.	Meal.	Medicines	Remarks.
1856.	Bales.	Galls.	Bags.	Galls.	Lbs.		
							produced by nature, (and which in the young calf when born is one-fourth of an inch thick,) nature has provided a gristly, pulpy cushion, intervening between it and the bones of the foot, which are thus admirably protected. Employed constructing fresh gear to hinder the animals from sliding from one side of the deck to the other when the ship is rolling heavily.
Feb. 26	3	70	20	15	40	1 pint turpentine.	Cleaning, &c., as usual. Bactrian, on the port side, eats very little; has not eaten much since he came on board.
27	2	70	20	15	40	1 quart sweet oil.	This day No. 10 (Smyrnian) gave birth to a female calf, very strong and lively. As the Turks on board have hitherto had charge of the young ones, and with poor success, this one has been turned over to the Bedouin, Mahomet. He did not swaddle it as the Turks, but left it free in its movements. The consequence was, that the calf in a few hours was on its legs and trying to suck the mother. The labor in this instance was rather protracted. The mother, also, is "kinder" than the others were. The sand used under the camels' legs and callosities having, during the heavy rolling in the late gale, chafed and fretted off the outer covering of the callosities, this day ceased to use sand, and substituted hay.
28	2	70	20	15	40	¼ pint British oil.	Calf doing remarkably well, and the mother lets it suck; the Bedouin careful of it. Oiled the callosities of all the camels, some of them having cracked. Littered well with hay.
29	2	70	20	20	40	1 quart sweet oil.	Gourmal still in heat. Rubbed in, on camels with swelled legs, equal parts of sweet oil, British oil, and turpentine.
Mar. 1	....	17	2½ bags.	15	40	1 oz. bluestone. 1 quart sweet oil.	This day Ibrim accidentally covered No. —, a Smyrnian camel. Continue to give oil to camels that require it. A Smyrnian male camel in the late gale having chafed his hind leg on the hamstring, some of the tendon appears to puff out in the form of a ball with a stem to it. Applied bluestone ointment, and bandaged.
2	2	80	2	15	40	1 pt. sweet oil.	Camel's protuberance on the hind leg increases in size, but no suppuration or inflammation. Continue the same ointment. The young camel doing well. Nothing to note. Cleaned out well.
3	....	17	2	15	40	....	This day applied lunar caustic to the camel's leg; no inflammation. Nothing to note.
4	2	75	2	15	40	....	Removed all the stale and wet litter from the camel deck, and littered afresh. The ball of extraneous matter or muscle dropped off the leg of the camel during the night of this day, leaving a clean wound, devoid of suppuration or inflammation; to keep out dirt, applied strips of dyacholon plaster. This day removed the light blankets from the camels, but blanket those in the wake of the hatch at night. "Getting hot below." Cleaned this day with lime, to kill the odor of the urine.
5	....	80	20	15	40	1 quart sweet oil.	Oiled all the callosities of the camels this day, and had them well cleaned. The evening of this day, finding it too hot for the animals, opened a few of the windows forward and aft, and set two windsails in the main hatch. Nothing to note.
6	....	17	20	10	30	....	Cleansed out from behind the animals; curried and brushed them; oiled any hard places required to be served so. Ventilation, &c., received all necessary attention. Camels generally appear to be improving in appearance. Received orders from Capt. Porter to take charge of the camel deck.
7	2	70	2	10	30	1 quart sweet oil	Cleaned out and curried animals as usual. Rubbed Gourmal with sulphuric ointment on his sore spots. Dosed Said, Gourmal, and No. 10 Smyrna mare with oil.

CAMEL JOURNAL—Continued.

Date.	Hay.	Water.	Oats.	Peas.	Meal.	Medicines	Remarks.
1856.	Bales.	Galls.	Bags.	Galls.	Lbs.		
Mar. 8	....	17	2	10	30	....	Cleaned stalls, and brushed and curried animals as usual. Washed the hoofs of all the animals. Mare No. 7's hind legs swollen; applied British oil, as per order. Gourmal as yesterday. Set up breast-ropes, &c., preparing for heavy weather.
9	....	75	1	12	25	....	Cleansed and brushed and curried as usual. Gave Said, Gourmal, and No. 10 Smyrna mare doses of oil. This evening secured animals for heavy weather.
10	2	17	2¼	8	35	....	Cleansed animals as far as weather would admit. Kept the animals harnessed down, it still blowing very heavy, but relieved them as far as possible.
11	....	70	1	10	25	....	It still blowing heavy, and ship rolling badly, got the camels on their legs singly and well rubbed them, &c. Examined each closely for chafes; found none.
12	....	17	2	10	40	1 quart sweet oil.	Animals still in harness on account of heavy weather. Rubbed them as yesterday.
13	....	65	2	8	35	....	Weather moderate. Let up the camels, and well brushed and curried them. Scrubbed deck. Whitewashed in every place where required. Animals all in good condition. Gave Said, Gourmal, and mare No. 10 doses of oil.
14	....	17	2	6	30	....	Curried and brushed animals as usual; scrubbed behind them; repaired damages to harness. Ibrim having shown signs of itch, moved him alongside of Gourmal, and placed both under treatment. Secured them by a tarpaulin from the others. Using sulphur mixture, and giving them sulphur in their feed.
15	3	75	2	5	35	1 qt. oil.	Rove rolling gear; harnessed and stopped ends back, in preparation for heavy weather; curried, &c., as usual. Camels all well, with exception of Gourmal and Ibrim, who are improving. Gave all the animals a little sulphur with their feed.
16	....	17	2	7	30	....	Animals as yesterday; all well with exception of Gourmal and Ibrim, progressing favorably. Whitewashed the bags for fenders. Gave each animal a thorough currying.
17	....	80	2	5	35	....	Curried and brushed as yesterday. Examined each animal strictly for defects, &c. All well. Rubbing Gourmal and Ibrim with the sulphur ointment, and giving sulphur in their feed every day.
18	....	20	2	8	30	....	Curried and brushed animals as usual; cleaned out from behind them with lime and water; all well. The two on the list for itch progressing favorably, their treatment being the same. At 9.15 p. m., Smyrna mare No. 7 calved—a fine male. The mare seemed easier during her time, and seemed to take a great interest in her young one. She had plenty of milk. Gave the calf in charge of Mahomet, Bedouin, by order of commander. Both cow and calf appear to be as well as either cases seen yet. Salted animals this day.
19	....	84	3	5	30	....	Curried and brushed the animals as usual; mare No. 7 and calf in good health; Gourmal and Ibrim improving.
20	....	20	2	5	30	1 oz. sweet oil.	Brushed and curried the animals as usual; found a slight chafe on mare No. 7, applied simple ointment; washed animals' hoofs.
21	2	80	2	8	30	....	Brushed and curried as usual; scrubbed deck; No. 7 calf not over well; gave it rubbing, &c., as it appeared to have symptoms of colic. Gourmal and Ibrim progressing favorably.
22	....	17	2	5	30	20 drops. paragoric.	Curried and brushed the animals as usual. Deeming the sickness of No. 7 calf to proceed from its mother's milk souring, the commander administered twenty drops of paragoric, which relieved it.
2	....	80	2	4	.. ..	20 drops paragoric.	Brushed and curried as usual; animals all well; Gourmal and Ibrim still under treatment; gave No. 7 calf twenty more drops of paragoric, it having done it good; stopped giving the mother any dough-ball.

CAMEL JOURNAL—Continued.

Date.	Hay.	Water.	Oats.	Peas.	Meal.	Medicines.	Remarks.
1856.	Bales.	Galls.	Bags.	Galls.	Lbs.		
Mar. 24	....	78	3	6	....	....	Brushed and curried the animals as usual; kept litter under the camels; rove ropes and stopped ends back, to ease animals to motion of ship, she rolling heavily at times; rubbed the animals' callosities with oil; Ibrim and Gourmal still under treatment, and progressing favorably; mare No. 7 and calf much better.
25	....	18	3	5	....	....	Brushed and curried animals as usual; sponged animals' eyes; all well; the two sick with mare No. 7 improving.
26	1	80	2	2	7	....	Brushed and curried animals as usual; mare No. 7 and calf progressing favorably; gave the mare dough-balls; Ibrim and Gourmal better; salted all the animals; shook down bedding, &c.
27	2	17	3	2	15	....	Brushed and curried animals as usual; scrubbed out and cleaned from behind all the animals; discharged the two camels Ibrim and Gourmal off the sick list, well; mare No. 7 and calf much better; bedded down and rove gear; ship rolling heavily.
28	....	200	....	....	....	Half pint sweet oil.	Curried and brushed animals as usual; scrubbed deck behind animals; Smyrna mare No. 21, who has appeared to suffer from enlarged vagina, this forenoon showed symptoms of a falling of the womb, but, on the application of cold water by a sponge, it receded, and she seemed relieved; but in the afternoon it occurred in a far more severe and extended manner; reported to the commander, who directed the Turks, by application of oil, &c., to replace it and bandage it; at 8 p. m. the mare seemed easy and clear of suffering; dosed camels requiring oil for cough, &c.
29	....	....	1	....	10	....	Curried and brushed the animals as usual; scrubbed deck behind animals, and whitewashed where it required; mare No. 21 seemed to have passed an easy night, but early in the forenoon, as the parts around the vagina appeared swollen and inflamed, and to be very relaxed, eased and removed the bandages and injected a light solution of blue stone, and, to keep the internals from again forcing themselves out, placed a stopper with bandages, applying cold water to the parts frequently. Early in the afternoon discovered the various signs of premature labor, reported the same, and at 3.30 p. m. came up with all bandages, fastenings, &c., and the mare was delivered of a male calf, dead, and appeared to have been for many days so. Wrapped mare in blankets, syringed her with lukewarm water, bedded her down, and eased her so as to render her comfortable; the syringing to be continued every two hours.
30	2	80	2	6	10	¼ oz. blue stone.	During the night mare No. 21 attempted to pass her after birth, but up to seven in the morning it had not cleared from her; it then appeared that part of her entrails, with other parts connected with the vagina, were attached, and the animal seemed to suffer greatly by it. At 9 a. m. there being no signs of a reaction on the part of the nerves of the vagina, which emitted a most noxious effluvia, and the animal seeming to be in great torture, though sinking slowly, the commandant deemed it prudent and as an act of mercy to strangle her, which was done, and her carcase thrown overboard. Every thing was done by both the Arabs and Turks to try and alleviate the pains of the mare, but all was of no avail. Curried, brushed, and cleaned the animals as usual; whitewashed where required. At 6.30 p. m. Smyrna mare No. 13 showed signs of calving, reported same, and at 7.30 she was delivered of a male calf; mare seemed to suffer more, and was longer calving, it being her first calf.
31	....	25	2	8	10	....	Curried and brushed the animals as usual; removed mare No. 13 to nursery; herself and calf well; found a chafe on mare No. 6's hind leg; applied simple salve; animals all well.

CAMEL JOURNAL—Continued.

Date.	Hay.	Water.	Oats.	Peas.	Meal.	Medicines.	Remarks.
	Bales.	Galls.	Bags.	Galls.	Lbs.		
1856. April 1	2	100	1	8	20	....	Curried and brushed the animals as usual; washed hind quarters, legs, &c., with warm water and castile soap; white-washed bags at various places; At 2 p. m. Smyrna mare No. 6 calved, a fine male calf, the largest and strongest calf of any born as yet; animals and calves all well; applied ointment to mare No. 6's hind legs, (chafed.)
2	....	60	2	4	15	....	Curried and brushed animals as usual; holystoned and cleaned deck; all well; gave calf "Trades" rice water for looseness in the bowels.
	1	120	2	4	18		Curried and brushed animals as usual; white-washed where necessary; applied salve to mare No. 6's legs; salted animals and oiled their callosities; gave animals fresh bedding.
4	....	85	2	6	25	....	Brushed and curried animals as usual; mare No. 6 having lain on her calf, appears to have injured it internally, through the negligence of Arab on watch.
5	....	130	1	4	25	....	Curried and brushed animals as usual; scrubbed deck behind animals; calf No. 6 appearing to be still worse, gave her a dose of oil and two injections, but she grew worse and died about 10.45 a. m.
6	....	80	1	5	20	....	Curried and brushed animals as usual; scrubbed deck; found another itch symptom on Gourmal; applied sulphur ointment and gave him sulphur in his food; salted animals.
7	2	120	2	6	20	....	Curried and brushed animals as usual; oiled callosities; found a tumor-like swelling on near hind leg of Smyrna mare No. 10; applied British oil; continued treatment of Gourmal for itch.
8	....	70	2	7	10	....	Brushed and curried animals as usual; ventilated by taking out weather air ports; calf No. 13 had symptoms of a diarrhœa; gave her rice water three times a day.
9		120	2	5	15	....	Curried and brushed animals as usual; thoroughly white-washed every part of the deck; mare No. 6's chafe much better; mare No. 10 improving; applying British oil.
10	1	60	2	7	12	....	Curried and brushed animals as usual; holystoned and well cleansed the deck; mares Nos. 6 and 10 improving; rest of the animals all well.
11	....	130	1	10	20	....	Brushed and curried animals as usual; had a rigid examination of each animal for chafes, itch spots, &c.; found all well but those under treatment.
12	....	75	2	8	30	....	Brushed and curried the animals as usual; examined all the camels; oiled their callosities; Gourmal still under treatment, but improving.
13	2	140	1	10	25	....	Curried and brushed animals as usual; washed deck round stern of animals; poulticed mare No. 10's leg with bread and milk; salted animals; arrived at Jamaica.
14	....	70	2	8	20	....	Curried and brushed the animals as usual; scrubbed deck with lime and sand; mare No. 10 improving under same treatment; numbers of visitors to see the camels.
15	1	120	2	8	25	....	Brushed and curried animals; white-washed where required; commander permitted the Arabs and Turks to go on shore for a short absence; all returned in the evening; an immense quantity of persons (4,000) visited the ship this day to see the camels, &c.
16	....	70	1	10	25	....	Curried and brushed animals; white-washed and cleaned deck; calf No. 13 had another attack of diarrhœa; gave her rice water as per order; numbers of visitors this day.
17	....	115	3	6	20	....	Brushed and curried animals; cleansed, &c., where required; salted animals; ventilation, &c., receiving all attention; numbers of visitors on board.
18	1	75	2	5	25	....	Brushed and curried animals; animals under treatment improving; rest of camels all well, though shedding their hair.
19	....	120	3	8	15	....	Brushed and curried animals as usual; poulticed mare No. 10's tumor; continued rice water to calf No. 13; left Jamaica this day; secured animals for rolling, &c.

CAMEL JOURNAL—Continued.

Date.	Hay.	Water.	Oats.	Peas.	Meal.	Medicines	Remarks.
1856.	Bales.	Galls.	Bags.	Galls.	Lbs.		
April 20	....	75	2	10	15	....	Brushed and curried animals as usual; continued treatment of animals; calf No. 13 was troubled with convulsive affection this evening; applied cold water.
21	....	130	2	8	20	....	Curried and brushed animals; cleansed and whitewashed where necessary; oiled callossities and salted animals; invalids improving.
22	2	70	3	5	15	....	Brushed and curried animals; ventilation receiving all necessary attention; continued rice water to calf No. 13; calf Trades had a slight attack; treated him the same.
23	....	115	2	6	18	....	Brushed and curried animals as usual. Rigid examination for itch, chafes, &c. Rubbed Gourmal and Ibrim with sulphur, as per order.
24	1	75	3	8	15	....	Curried and brushed animals as usual. Calf No. 13 worse this day, through weakness. Continued same treatment.
25	....	120	1	6	20	....	Brushed and curried animals as usual. Removed poultice from mare No. 10's leg, and applied a sugar and soap poultice, which on removal brought away a quantity of fetid matter with the core. Continued treatment with washing part three times daily. Calf No. 13 still in a very low state. Rest of animals all well.
26	....	75	1	5	25	....	Curried and brushed animals as usual. Calf No. 13 had another fit; she appears to be suffering from cutting the teeth, which cause the convulsions; lanced his gums and gave an injection of warm water; gave it twenty drops of paragoric in water, which seemed to relieve it. At 7 p. m. the calf had another fit, which was reported, and it died about 7.20.
27	....	120	1	10	20	....	Curried and brushed animals as usual. Washed deck and examined animals. Animals under treatment improving. Found Egyptian mare Preguada's leg swollen; applied British oil, well rubbed in. At 5 p. m. secured animals for heavy weather.
28	....	80	1	20	10	....	Ship rolling heavily. Eased animals as much as possible, keeping hay under them. Heavy rain and gale. Battered down trunk shutters, and secured everything for a hard gale. Camels examined every half hour as to security of harness, &c.
29	2	120	1	15	10	....	Curried and brushed the animals. Well rubbed their legs. Removed all wet litter off the deck. Examined and found all the animals clear of chafes, &c. Gourmal and mare No. 10 improving. Anchored off Indianola bar this evening, but received no news from shore.
30	1	75	1	20	18	....	Curried and brushed animals as usual. The swelling in Preguada's leg entirely disappeared.
May 1	1	150	2	10	20	....	Curried and brushed animals as usual. Kept hay under the animals to keep them easy, as the vessel continued to roll heavily at times. The steamer Fashion, Capt. Baker, came off from shore, and returned with Major Wayne to make the necessary preparations and arrangements for disembarking and discharging camels, stores, &c., on transit for the shore.
2	2	70	....	15	10	....	Curried and brushed animals as usual. Making active preparations for discharging camels. Fashion arrived, with two schooners in tow, 7.30. Got a schooner alongside, and, after preparing to send Ibrim, the vessels rolled so that the commander deemed it advisable to leave for the Southwest Pass of the Mississippi, where it would be still water, and effect the discharging there. Left Indianola in tow of steamer for short distance.
3	....	130	1	12	20	....	Curried and brushed animals as usual. Well rubbed all the animals' legs; sponged their eyes, and washed their feet. Examined for chafes; found none. This evening, rove ropes, set up gear, and prepared for heavy weather.
4	....	130	1	15	15	....	Curried and brushed animals as usual. Salted animals all round. Poulticed mare No. 10's leg; rapidly improving. Animals all well. Rove gear, &c.

CAMEL JOURNAL—Continued.

Date.	Hay.	Water.	Oats.	Peas.	Meal.	Medicines	Remarks.
1856.	Bales.	Galls.	Bags.	Galls.	Lbs.		
May 5	....	130	....	20	20	....	Curried and brushed animals as usual. Whitewashed where necessary. Kept litter under animals, on account of motion of ship.
6	2	85	....	25	15	....	Curried and brushed animals as usual. Kept them well littered. Rove ropes, as per order.
7	....	200	....	20	20	....	Curried and brushed animals as usual. Well cleansed under the animals, and examined for chafes, &c.; found the hind legs of one or two slightly swollen; applied British oil.
8	3	95	....	25	18	1 pt. sweet oil.	Curried and brushed animals as usual. Cleansed all round animals. Arrived in the Southwest Pass. Prepared to send animals away as soon as steamer shall arrive.
9	2	210	....	20	25	....	Curried and brushed animals as usual. Cleansed animals, &c. Steamer Fashion came along side. Commenced discharging hay, oats, meal, &c.
10	....	150	....	10	10	....	Curried animals, and prepared to discharge them. 6.30, commenced to discharge camels. 12.30, finished discharging the whole of the camels, feed, stores, &c. 2.45, steamer Fashion cast off from alongside, and steamed down the river. Cleared off camel deck.

N. B.—Only four of the camels transferred out of order—one with a bile on the leg, three with swollen feet from long confinement.

UNITED STATES SHIP "SUPPLY,"
Alexandria, January 13, 1856.

SIR: Agreeably to a notification received from you this morning, "that the camels presented by his highness the viceroy of Egypt were ready to be delivered to me, and were waiting my pleasure in the palace yard," I sent an officer and some other persons to receive them.

The persons returned on board immediately, and reported to me that the dromedaries were so worthless and diseased that they would not take the responsibility of receiving them without further orders from me.

On the receipt of this intelligence, I went to the palace myself, and found the animals in really worse condition than they were represented to be; and two of them were those that had been bought by Major Wayne in Cairo, and rejected and sold again in Alexandria, because we did not consider them fit animals to take to the United States, (being diseased.)

I knew the two that formerly belonged to us at once, by private marks, although their identity was very certain without any very close examination. They were far superior to any of the dromedaries in company with them; therefore you can judge whether it would be proper in us to receive them on board.

Perhaps, for your own satisfaction, you would like to see them yourself, and I have directed them to be kept in their present location until other orders are received about them.

I regret to say that I cannot conscientiously receive on board the "five" dromedaries that were shown me as a present from his highness. At the same time, I do not wish his highness to suppose that I do not appreciate the compliment it was his intention to pay to the government of the United States; but I could not, nor would Major Wayne, consent to jeopardize an experiment so full of interest to our people by any false feelings of delicacy.

The dromedaries in question are not such as we would have accepted on any terms from any one, and I do not think that we are bound by any forms of etiquette to have anything to do with those now offered by the subordinates of the pacha.

I do not think for a moment his highness would pay us so poor a compliment as to suppose we were selected for th s duty without some knowledge of the matter in hand; and I do not think he would send a present to our government inferior to that he might reasonably give to his camel driver.

If he were to do so, it would no longer be an interchange of courtesy, but a direct insult; and if his highness is cognizant of the manner in which his promise to you has been carried out, it looks very much like turning the mission into ridicule; consequently it is a great want of courtesy on the part of the Egyptian authorities, both to you and to our government.

When this vessel came to this port it was for the purpose of purchasing the best dromedaries the country afforded; and, although it might be expected that a mission of this kind would very naturally enlist the liberality of the viceroy, and induce him to aid and show his appreciation of the enterprise, by a present from a good stock, (which act would not only have been gratifying to us, as an addition to our collection, but would have been so to you, as a proof of the friendly relations existing at this time between the two governments,) yet I do not think we are at all called upon to accept the present animals on any terms whatever, and I am certain that his highness would feel mortified if he was compromised by our doing so.

It is a delicate thing to refuse an official present from high authority. If it was one or two camels we might receive them, and get rid of them at some future time; but we have a certain amount of responsibility resting on us that prevents us from taking into consideration anything but the success of the task imposed on us. And I have less objection to decline receiving the dromedaries, feeling convinced, as I do, that his highness is not cognizant how his orders are carried out.

No doubt you will feel disappointed, as well as Major Wayne and myself, but as you have done all you could in the premises to forward this matter, you can rest satisfied with that, and can have the gratification of hereafter seeing the affair properly represented to his highness.

To us the only disappointment is in not being able to obtain the number of animals we came for; for we would much rather purchase any time than have presents made to us.

In the first place, we could get better stock; and in the second place, relieve ourselves from tedious formalities, and the government from resting under doubtful obligations.

You would confer a favor (if diplomatic etiquette does not forbid) by taking a look at the dromedaries in question. I do not want you to suppose for an instant that I am unreasonable, or have come to any other determination than you would come to yourself.

I think you will agree with me, that "we have touched pitch and been defiled."

One look at the dromedaries I saw this morning will convince you that a surer way of defeating our object could not be offered; and an acceptance on our part of his highness' present would be an ill performance of our duty, for which we could offer no reasonable excuse to our government.

I am thus particular in making to you this full and official communication, as I am sure that you would desire such detailed statements of facts as would enable you hereafter to show his highness the grounds on which we were obliged to decline his present.

Very respectfully, your obedient, &c.,
DAVID D. PORTER,
Lieutenant Commanding.

Edwin De Leon, Esq.,
Consul General, &c., &c., Alexandria..

United States Ship "Supply,"
Alexandria, January 13, 1856.

Dear Sir: I have taken a look at the last camels sent down to me; three of them are those I mentioned in my official letter to you this morning, and *one* of them was bought by Major Wayne, in Cairo, and rejected here because he was diseased. The three large ones are *street* camels, and have been picked up since ten o'clock this morning to replace the three miserable beasts first offered us.

I can but take the same view of the case as I did this morning. They have made the matter a little worse by endeavoring fraudulently to force a present on us unworthy of the acceptance of our government. If the government of the United States were to send his excellency a present of rusty muskets, or a rotten ship, I am sure he would not appreciate it.

We have too good a country, my dear sir, to allow any one to depreciate it by such offerings. Crowned heads and despots in their intercourse with each other omit no courtesies, and make no presents that they may blush to show. There is as much due to the intelligence of our country as to any crowned head in Europe, and we will not accept any gift unless made in a proper manner.

I am sure you will agree with me.

Very respectfully, your obedient servant,
DAVID D. PORTER,
Lieutenant Commanding.

Edwin De Leon, Esq.,
Consul General, &c.

Consulate General of the United States of America, in Egypt,
Alexandria, January 14, 1856.

Sir: I have the honor to acknowledge the receipt of your letter dated January 13, and to inform you that I also have received from the governor of Alexandria a letter, of which the enclosed, marked A, is a copy, accompanying *six* camels sent by order of the viceroy as a present to our government.

The statements contained in your letter, and the course adopted by you, (of which I cordially approve,) have induced me promptly to return the camels to the governor, with a letter, (a copy of which, marked B, is enclosed.)

I have also addressed to the viceroy, through Tulfeccan Pacha, a letter, (marked C, enclosed,) which I sent this morning by my dragoman, enclosing yours, with orders to translate both to him, and request their immediate transmission to the viceroy.

Tulfeccan Pacha expressed lively indignation on perusal of the letters, and declared that the viceroy would assuredly punish his servants for the shameful manner in which they had executed his orders.

He also added, that if the ship would only stay a little longer, a gift worthy of the parties should be made.

To this Mr. Chasseaud replied, (by my orders,) that the ship could not be detained longer, and that he was instructed so to say, but that the *intention*, and not the gift, was what our government appreciated.

He then promised to communicate the letters to the viceroy to-day; and as M. Chasseaud returned from the palace, he met the governor going in great haste towards it.

It is perfectly evident that the whole affair has been an attempt at speculation on the part of the employés, but the governor will suffer for the sins of his subordinates, and ample apologies be made to us by the viceroy, whose good intentions have been frustrated by the knavery of his servants.

Allow me, sir, in conclusion, to return you my thanks for the decided and dignified manner in which you met and repulsed this attempt at imposition on our government, and their own, by these faithless employés.

I remain, with sentiments of high consideration, yours, very respectfully,

EDWIN De LEON.

D. D. PORTER, Esq.,
  Lieut. Com'g U. S. Ship "Supply," Harbor of Alexandria.

Correspondence alluded to in the above official letter, (endorsed A, B, and C, respectively.)

A.

MONSIEUR LE CONSUL GÉNÉRAL : Sur l'ordre que nous avons reçu de Son Altesse, le Vice Roi, de vous faire envoi, M. le Consul, de six chameaux, connue present de sa parte au government des Etats Unis, nous en avons fait chercher trois males et trois femelles de la meilleure race qui se trouve, et nous nous empressons de vous les accompagner de la présente afin que nous en fassiez expedition connue présente. Vice Royal, telle est la volonté de Son Altesse.

Le 5 Gramad, 1272.

                MOHAMED SCIAKIR, [L. S.]
                  Le Gouv. d'Alexandrie.

B.

CONSULATE GENERAL OF THE U. S. OF AMERICA IN EGYPT,
Alexandria, January 14, 1856.

EXCELLENCY : The camels tendered to you through my government, which were sent yesterday, have not been accepted, and are therefore returned by the bearer of this.

His highness the viceroy shall be informed of the reasons why his polite proffer has been declined.

Accept the assurances of my high consideration,

EDWIN De LEON.

His Excellency MOHAMED SCIAKIR,
    Governor of Alexandria.

C.

CONSULATE GENERAL OF THE U. S. OF AMERICA IN EGYPT,
Alexandria, January 14, 1856.

EXCELLENCY: You will oblige me by promptly submitting to his highness the viceroy the enclosed letter from Captain Porter, commandant of the United States ship "Supply," which will show his highness how his kind intentions have been frustrated through the negligence of his servants.

I entirely approve of the refusal of Captain Porter to accept, on behalf of my government, a gift which his highness himself would have considered (had he seen it) unworthy for him to offer, or for it to accept.

With the expression of my regret for this awkward occurrence, accept the assurances of my high consideration,

EDWIN De LEON.

His Excellency HULFUKAR PACHA,
    Vekil of Foreign Affairs, Alexandria.

CONSULATE GENERAL OF THE U. S. OF AMERICA IN EGYPT,
Alexandria, January 16, 1856.

SIR: Mr. Koenig Bey, confidential secretary to the viceroy, has called upon me with a request that you will delay your departure a few days, until the intentions of the viceroy can be properly carried out by a gift worthy of our acceptance.

He requests me to tender, on behalf of the viceroy, the expression of his regret and annoyance at the conduct of his servants, and to assure you that there shall be no mistake and no unnecessary delay this time.

Enclosed you will find a copy of a note which he has addressed to me for your information on the subject.

Respectfully, your obedient servant,

EDWIN De LEON.

D. D. PORTER, Esq.,
    Lieut. Com'g U. S. ship "Supply," Harbor of Alexandia.

ALEXANDRIA, *January* 16, 1856.
MONCHER MONSIEUR DE LEON: Je viens de prendre connaissance de la copie de la lettre qui vous a été addressée par M. le Commandante Porter.

Je vais écrire a l'instant pour faire remplacer par des dromédaires les chameaux qu'on avait l'intention d'acheter de sorte qu'au lieu de deux dromédaires et quatre chameaux, il y aura six dromédaires, et je ferai en sorte qu'il y dit moitié femelles et males, si la chose est possible.

Dans tous le cas vous pouvez être certain que ce sera Animaux de chois, Quant au jour ou il sera possible de les offrir, je ne puis prendre sur moi de le fixer. Tout ce que je puis faire, cest de recommander que l'achat et l'expedition se fassent dans le plus bref délai possible.

Agréez Monsieur, &c., &c.,
KOENIG BEY.
M. E. DE LEON,
Consul General of the United States of America.

ALEXANDRIA, *January* 16, 1856.
DEAR CAPTAIN: Koenig Bey, the private secretary of the viceroy, has called to beg that you will delay a few days, to secure animals worthy of being carried to America, which have been sent for.

He is very anxious about it, and you will get good animals if you stay.

Yours, truly,
EDWIN DE LEON,
Consul General.

P. S. Koenig Bey will make you apologies in person, if you will wait.
E. DE L.

UNITED STATES SHIP "SUPPLY,"
Bay of Alexandria, January 16, 1856.
MY DEAR SIR: Although it will interfere with my arrangements, yet, not to be guilty of anything like a want of courtesy to the authorities, I will wait for the *dromedaries.*

I do not conceive that the viceroy would sanction anything like the rudeness that was practised on us, and, as I know it would afford him pleasure to do the thing handsomely, and as the honorable Secretary of War will be much disappointed at our having so few dromedaries, I will wait on those grounds, and hurry up somewhere else.

As to the apology, the presentation of six such animals as will be worthy the acceptance of our government, will be sufficient amends.

I would like him to name some definite time, that I may be ready to sail at a moment's notice.

Yours, very truly,
DAVID D. PORTER,
Lieut. Commanding.

Edwin De Leon, Esq.,
Consul General.

P. S. Allow me to remind you that "dromedaries," and not camels of burden, are the animals we are desirous to obtain.

D. D. P.

San Antonio, Texas, *June* 19, 1856.

Sir: I have the honor to report my arrival here yesterday with the camels in my charge. I left Indianola sooner than I had anticipated when I landed, as the animals appeared to be in good condition for the journey, and as the rainy season was daily expected to commence, which would have rendered the Hog Wallow prairie (forty miles of it) impracticable for them for six weeks or two months. The air, water, and grass, I thought, moreover, would be better in the interior than so immediately upon the seaboard.

Leaving Indianola, then, on the morning of the 4th of June, with light loads, I camped at 5 p. m. at Chocolate Bayou, twelve miles. The road was very bad, the camels frisky and unruly, and the pack saddles and loads requiring adjustment, gave trouble by slipping.

June 5. Left camp at $6\frac{3}{4}$ a. m. Road exceedingly rough and deep—much worse than that of yesterday. Some of the weaker animals showed signs of fatigue. Halted for two hours, from 12 m. to 2 p. m. Resumed the march, and arrived, at 5 p. m., at Alligator Pond, fifteen miles. Determined to halt a few days at the first good grazing ground I came to, and to relieve the weakest animals of their burdens.

June 6. Left camp at 6 a. m. Went five miles, when we struck a beautiful prairie, abounding in fine grass, and with *mottes* of timber for camps. Good water at hand. Camped, and turned the animals loose to graze.

June 7, 8, 9, 10, 11, in camp. Animals luxuriating in grass and improving in appearance.

June 12. Left camp at $6\frac{1}{2}$ a. m. Arrived at Victoria at $9\frac{1}{2}$ a. m. Remained there three hours. Resumed march, and camped at Wright's Water-Hole at 3 p. m., eleven miles.

June 13. Left camp at $8\frac{1}{2}$ a. m.; marched nine miles and halted for an hour and a half, then continued and camped at Pierpont's at 4 p. m., seventeen and a half miles.

June 14. Took the road at $5\frac{3}{4}$ a. m.; camped at Salt Creek at 2 p. m., twenty-one miles.

June 15. Left Salt Creek $5\frac{3}{4}$ a. m.; camped at the Big Ecleto at $12\frac{1}{2}$ p. m., seventeen and a half miles.

June 16. Left camp at 5½ a. m.; came to the Cibolo at 10¼ a. m.; halted until 11 a. m.; camped at the Sulphur Springs at 12½ p. m., sixteen miles. At 1½ p. m. one of the female camels, not purchased or marked as pregnant, nor exhibiting the least evidences of being in that condition, gave birth to a female calf, a *maya*, full sized but weakly. The calf never held up its head, but, breathing with difficulty, lingered until the next morning at 5 a. m., when it died. Upon examining the body the glands of the throat were found swollen to about three and a half to four inches in length by about two inches in diameter, pressing upon and closing the air passage; lungs a good deal conjested.

June 17. Left camp at 6½ a. m. and arrived at Grayson's at 1 p. m., seventeen miles. Camped. At 3 p. m., leaving the caravan in charge of my clerk and overseer, Mr. Ray, I rode into San Antonio (twelve miles) to make such arrangements as might be necessary. On arrival, found that Colonel Myers had selected a camping place at the headwaters of the San Pedro, about two miles from town, furnishing good grass and water. The ground is owned by the corporation of San Antonio, and, by permission, is occupied free of any charge.

June 18. The camels were brought in by Mr. Ray at 11½ a. m. and taken out to camp.

I have everything now arranged, and shall remain here, where the animals can have good grass and water, until I receive instructions as to their destination.

I moved slowly, both on account of their recent sea trip, and for the little ones that were unable to march long. My object was to bring the animals safely to this place, and not to show what they could do as carriers and travellers. The Bactrians I thought of making useful in a wagon, after the Tartar fashion, but I abandoned the idea for the march, as being too severe upon them so soon after their disembarkation. I tried them, however, for a short distance, and found that they travelled well together; so well that I am induced to think they have been harnessed up before. The weather was exceedingly hot and the roads dusty, unusually so, I am told; yet the animals travelled without suffering, and are in good condition. After acclimation, I think they will be capable of rendering good service.

Very respectfully, your obedient servant,

HENRY C. WAYNE,
Major United States Army.

Hon. JEFFERSON DAVIS,
Secretary of War, Washington City.

[Extract.]

SAN ANTONIO, TEXAS,
June 20, 1856.

GENERAL: I have the honor to acknowledge the receipt yesterday of your letter of the 3d instant, addressed to me at Indianola, requesting me to name a suitable agent for the purchase of additional camels, and to report my opinion of the relative advantages of Powderhorn and Indianola for a depot for the quartermaster's department.

If it is the intention of government to send out to the east an officer of the army to procure an additional supply of camels, I can specify no one for the duty, as, with the exception of Major Crosman, who declined the commission last year, I know of none especially qualified for it, by interest in the experiment, or by study of the animal and the localities in which it is to be found. If it is intended to send a civilian, I have already recommeded one, (Mr. Heap,) who accompanied me in my recent trip, to the favorable notice of the Secretary of War.

* * * * * * * * * * *

Very respectfully, your obedient servant,
HENRY C. WAYNE,
Brevet Major, Assistant Quartermaster.
Major General THOS. S. JESUP,
Quartermaster General, Washington City, D. C.

SAN ANTONIO, *June* 28, 1856.

SIR: On the 19th instant I reported to you my arrival here with the camels, and that they were camped about two miles from this at the headwaters of the San Pedro. Finding, however, that this proximity to town was not beneficial to my men or animals, I moved them out to the Medina, about twelve miles, to the ranch of Major Howard, of San Antonio, with whom I have made a temporary arrangement until their permanent disposition is determined.

From all that I have learned, the vicinity of this place appears to be as well adapted to the acclimation and breeding of the camel as any part of the country, and to offer more facilities for carrying out these experiments than any other of our posts in Texas. Wherever I may go in Texas, the necessary conveniences for both animals and men must, I find, be constructed, and here I understand that can be done more economically and readily than at other stations. The grazing and water are good, the climate as suitable as any between this and the Pacific, and there is no risk of injury by the Indians. It is, moreover, at convenient distance from the coast for the reception of any future importations that may be made.

In the selection of a permanent site, however, much will depend upon the views of government as to the purpose of the importation and the uses to which it is desired to put those imported. As to the comparative utility and economy of the animal as a means of transportation, there can be no doubt; and in other respects it is unquestionably a desirable addition to our stock of domestic animals. Shall those, then, introduced be mainly devoted to breeding and increasing the number, or shall they be put to hard labor with the risk of being worn out in the service?

In my view, the introduction of the animal has been the primary object, and to achieve this will require time, five years at least. To be successfully conducted, the animals, I think, should have a permanent home, where breeding can be carefully attended to, and to which use should be subordinate, their labor being applied to the necessary wants of the post or farm, and not extended to any great degree beyond it. In this way, and with the addition of more breeding cows, the climate proving favorable, I have little doubt but that in ten years the race can be well spread through Texas, whence it can be carried to any part of the continent.

As far as general use in the military service is concerned, the services of the few imported would, in our very widely spread operations, be inappreciable, and it seems to me better to sacrifice any such small immediate advantage to the prospective benefit to be derived from the successful introduction and general diffusion of the animal among us.

Land can readily be hired for a term of years, and a breeding farm established; or a ranch, with the necessary buildings, put up in a cheap manner, according to a given plan, can be rented by the month.

Requesting full information as to your views to guide me in my course, and at as early a day as your convenience will permit,

I am, very respectfully, your obedient servant,
        HENRY C. WAYNE,
         Major United States Army.

Hon. JEFFERSON DAVIS,
 Secretary of War, Washington.

         WAR DEPARTMENT,
        Washington, July 5, 1856.

SIR: I have received your letter of the 19th ultimo, announcing your arrival with the camels, in good order, at San Antonio, and your intention to remain there some time in camp.

It appears to me that, after so long a sea voyage, the animals should be allowed a considerable time to recruit before being put to work. Horses, under the same circumstances, would require many months to regain their full efficiency, and animals of a larger size would require a still longer period of rest.

   Very respectfully, your obedient servant,
         JEFF'N DAVIS,
          Secretary of War.

Major H. C. WAYNE,
 United States Army, San Antonio, Texas.

      QUARTERMASTER GENERAL'S OFFICE,
       Washington City, July 14, 1856.

SIR: The Secretary of War has referred to this office your letter of the 28th ultimo, with an endorsement, of which the following is a copy:

"The establishment of a breeding farm did not enter into the plans of the department. The object at present is to ascertain whether the animal is adapted to the military service, and can be economically and usefully employed therein. When this is satisfactorily established, arrangements can be made for importing or breeding camels to any extent that may be deemed desirable."

I am, sir, &c.,
TH. S. JESUP,
Quartermaster General.

Major H. C. WAYNE,
Assistant Quartermaster U. S. Army,
San Antonio, Texas.

QUARTERMASTER GENERAL'S OFFICE,
Washington City, July 30, 1856.

SIR: The Secretary of War has referred to this office your letter of the 21st instant, covering propositions for furnishing accommodations for camels and quarters for the men attending them. You will adopt such measures in regard to this matter as may, in your judgment, be best for the public interests.

In regard to the preparation and place for keeping the camels, the first and important point to be determined is their fitness for our military service, and until this be established it is needless to inquire whether they may be bred in the United States.

I am, sir, &c.,
TH. S. JESUP,
Quartermaster General.

Major H. C. WAYNE,
Assistant Quartermaster, San Antonio, Texas.

SAN ANTONIO, *July* 22, 1856.

SIR: It is with regret that I report the death of one of our best female camels from Smyrna. Through the neglect of the Arabs herding the females, this one strayed, and when hunted up was found about two miles off lying upon its side and evidently very ill. It was brought into camp carefully under the personal superintendence of Mr. Ray, and there, after lingering several hours, died. Its disease was supposed to be inflammation of the bowels, but after death an examination was made by Dr. A. Z. Herman, M. D., a physician living in the neighborhood, who discovered that the animal had been killed by one or more heavy blows. The Doctor's statement to me is, that the animal's death was occasioned by a heavy blow or blows inflicted on the neck of the animal, fracturing the clavicles in several places, and one dorsal and one side rib. The spiculæ of bone were driven into the cavity of the chest, causing a severe inflammation of the lungs, and under which the animal sunk. The lungs, he says, showed an intense degree of inflammation, being highly engorged with bloody and frothy serum. All the other internal organs were in a perfectly healthy and sound state.

Inquiry so far has failed to elicit anything to indicate the perpetrator of this brutal deed. The Arabs deny all knowledge of it, and persistently declare their own and each other's innocence of it. As the animal was gentle, I can hardly think the act one of self-defence. Besides, in such a case, the defender would be apt to report the fact himself and the necessity that induced it.

My visit to Fort Martin Scott has been unavoidably delayed until this week, but to-morrow I hope to get off for it.

Very respectfully, your obedient servant,
HENRY C. WAYNE,
Major U. S. Army.

Hon. JEFFERSON DAVIS,
Secretary of War, Washington City, D. C.

SAN ANTONIO, *July* 28, 1856.

SIR: I returned yesterday from an examination of Fort Martin Scott. This post is situated in a tract of barren sand and post oak. In the immediate vicinity of the fort there is no grazing worth anything, and within a range of two or three miles of it, it is at the best indifferent. The buildings, from positive injury and the want of care, are in bad condition, requiring a good deal of repair to be habitable; and there are no stables nor stabling suitable, though a large storehouse might be converted to that use. Altogether, the place is not such as I would select, but may be made to answer in the event of my failing to secure a better arrangement. The owner, Mr. Twohig, offers its use to government unreservedly, with the general right of grazing outside, on a lease of five or ten years, at $50 per month.

A post having been established at Green Valley, (Val Verde,) within sixty miles of this place, and in a country, according to representations made to me, suitable to our purposes, I shall take an opportunity in this or the next week to visit and examine it. If the troops are to be kept there for two or three years, and as everything for the accommodation of officers, men, and horses, has to be constructed, it may, perhaps, require but a slightly additional expense to make all necessary arrangements for the camels and the men attending them. As far as the intentions of the present department commander are concerned, I am at liberty to say that he considers Green Valley an important point, and that troops should be kept at it until the settlement there is strong enough to protect itself.

Any other arrangements that may occur to me, or that may be offered to me, shall be promptly reported to you for your consideration and instructions.

I have the honor, also, to acknowledge the receipt this morning of your letter of the 5th instant, in reply to my report of the 19th ultimo, and to express my gratification at finding your views in respect to recruiting the animals after their sea voyage coincident with my own. Their improvement during their short rest here has been very marked.

Again requesting to be fully informed of your views in relation to the permanent disposition of the camels, that I may conform to them in my arrangements and management, I am, with much respect, your obedient servant,

HENRY C. WAYNE,
Major U. S. Army.

Hon. JEFFERSON DAVIS,
Secretary of War, Washington City.

SAN ANTONIO, *August* 4, 1856.

SIR: It is with regret that I have again to report the death of one of the camels, one of the female dromedaries presented by the viceroy of Egypt. At daybreak this morning she was found lying dead in her place. Yesterday, and up to the time of her being put up for the night, she seemed well and lively. On the day before (Saturday) I pointed her out especially to two gentlemen as one of the most thriving, and she fully sustained then, by her appearance and liveliness, the hopes I expressed in regard to her.

There being no one at hand competent to make a scientific examination of the body, I am unable to state the probable cause of death.

There are no external causes apparent to account for it, and an autopsy by Mr. Ray developed no internal derangement or injury.

Very respectfully, your obedient servant,
HENRY C. WAYNE,
Major U. S. Army.

Hon. JEFFERSON DAVIS,
Secretary of War, Washington City, D. C.

SAN ANTONIO, *August* 12, 1856.

MY DEAR SIR: I have the honor to enclose herewith a pair of socks knit for the President by Mrs. Mary A. Shirkey, of Victoria, Texas, (lately of Virginia,) from the pile of one of our camels.

In her letter to me accompanying the socks, Mrs. Shirkey says: "I have been much longer preparing the socks than I thought I should be when you left my house. I knit one, and found it too coarse. I then spun some finer, and knit the pair I have sent you. If I had the machinery, I could have made you a better specimen of what the camel's wool could do in Texas. I have spun the first thread and made the first article of clothing out of the wool in this country. I think if it was carded in the factory it would do much better; all the long hair would drop out from the fine wool."

The fleece from which these socks were knit consisted of the loose dead hair of the past year that I had clipped off on the 9th of June, to relieve the animal from its weight and heat. The fact of its being dead (not living) hair may have, perhaps, some influence upon the softness of the fabric woven from it. The socks, at any rate, demonstrate the practical utility of the camel's pile, and convey an idea of its probable value should the animal live and thrive among us.

* * * * * * * *

Very respectfully, your obedient servant,
HENRY C. WAYNE,
Major U. S. Army.

Hon. JEFFERSON DAVIS,
Secretary of War, Washington.

SAN ANTONIO, *August* 12, 1856.

SIR: I returned yesterday from the examination of the camp at Green Valley, which I advised you on the 28th ultimo I intended making. The position is in every respect favorable for our animals, and for demonstrating their usefulness for burden, for expresses, and for scouting. An abundance of fine grass and good water, of lime to be had for the burning, of sand, stone, and timber, and of lumber and shingles, to be procured within a distance of five miles, gives me every facility for keeping and sheltering the animals at a comparatively moderate rate. With such aid as the commander of the troops in the camp says he can give me I shall be able to put up the shelters I require in a short time, and to make all arrangements for setting the animals to work whenever it may be deemed advisable to do so.

Situated three miles outside of the "Bandera Pass" and the settlements, at a distance of sixty miles from San Antonio, and in direct communication with all of the frontier posts, I can conceive of no more suitable point for demonstrating everything we desire to know in regard to the camel's adaptation to our climate, to the military service, and to commerce, and where its breeding can at the same time be overseen and carefully conducted. The burden animals can be used in transporting supplies from San Antonio to the camp and to other points. The dromedaries may be sent express anywhere along the frontier or within the settlements, as necessity may require, and may be used as pack animals to scouting parties instead of mules. In time men may be mounted upon them to accompany in scouting, and one or more may be mounted with a small gun throwing shrapnell, &c. These experiments may be so conducted as not only to show the absolute value of the animal for burden and for the saddle, but also its relative usefulness in comparison with the horse, the mule, and waggoning.

From the intelligence of Captain Palmer and of his officers, and from the interest they all manifested in the purposes of the experiment, I feel warranted in believing that they will second our views with judgment and zeal.

As to the continuance of the camp in its present position for some four or five years I have but little doubt, from all that I have heard, and from what I have myself seen of its military importance, so that the breeding of the animals can be systematically attended to, as suggested in my letter of the 28th June last.

Should the next mail bring me no instructions from yourself for the disposition of the animals, I shall commence preparations for their removal to Green Valley, where I shall await your orders, trusting, however, that you will approve, on this representation, of my establishing them there for the winter at least.

On my arrival at Green Valley in the event of the above mentioned contingency, I shall at once commence the arrangements for sheltering; as, even should the camels be ordered elsewhere, the work done will be of service to the troops remaining.

With much respect, I am your obedient servant,
HENRY C. WAYNE,
Major U. S. Army.

Hon. JEFFERSON DAVIS,
Secretary of War, Washington City, D. C.

CAMP VERDE, *August* 30, 1856.

SIR: I have the honor to acknowledge the receipt of your instructions through the quartermaster general, in his communication of the 17th and 30th of July last, and to report that, in accordance with them, and with the views expressed to you in my letter of the 12th ultimo, I have established the camels at this post. We arrived on the evenings of the 26th and 27th August, the camels preceding me by twenty-four hours, under my clerk, Mr. Ray, as I had to remain behind to complete some arrangements for putting up the shelters re-required here.

Preparations for the accommodation of the animals are already in progress, and with the assistance that Captain Palmer can give me from his company, I hope to have them under good cover in five or six weeks.

My address is "Camp Verde," care United States quartermaster at San Antonio, Texas. From San Antonio our communications are sent to us by express.

Very respectfully, your obedient servant,
HENRY C. WAYNE,
Major United States Army.

Hon. JEFFERSON DAVIS,
Secretary of War, Washington City, D. C.

CAMP VERDE, TEXAS, *September* 24, 1856.

SIR: The last mail brought me your instructions, through the quartermaster general's office, to deposit with the Treasury of the United States the sum of $9,920 77 of the appropriation for the purchase of camels, now to my credit on the books of Messrs. Riggs & Co., bankers, of Washington city. I have accordingly directed the transfer to be made at once to the assistant treasurer of the United States at New Orleans, the most convenient point for me to draw upon, and have advised that officer of the fact, requesting him, upon receipt of the money, to place it to my name under the head of "appropriation for the purchase of camels."

The camels are doing well, though beginning now to show a little the effects of the climate and of the unusual heat and drought of the past summer. One of the Bactrians and four of the Smyrna camels have particularly suffered from heat. The shelters for them are coming on rapidly, (thanks to the energy and interest of Captain Palmer, and of his Lieutenants Chamblis and Van Camp,) and I hope soon to have completed the accommodations for them, and for those expected in December.

Since my arrival in Texas I have endeavored to obtain from the stock-raisers and farmers of the State as much *practical* information as possible in regard to animals, and to their care and management in this climate. I have thus obtained much useful knowledge that my own observation and experience subsequently has approved. Among the opinions advanced to me, and it seems universal among old residents, for I have not yet heard a dissent from it, is one that will affect materially our experiment, and that bears also with force upon the mounted service in Texas. This opinion is, that no animals, full grown, brought into Texas from other countries, or from the old States, are here as vigorous and as serviceable as they were in the countries or States they left; the process of acclimation impairing, apparently, vital energy and endurance. This deterioration does not, however, extend to animals born in Texas or brought into it very young. On the contrary, they are said to equal and often to surpass the parent stock. If this be so, we must look to the produce of the present importations for a fair exposition of our views, accomplishing in the meantime as much as we can with deteriorated animals in demonstration of the experiment. Of course, from my short residence, I am not competent to decide upon the correctness of this apparently universal sentiment; but grant it to be true, I am fully satisfied that the camels we have, though deteriorated, will amply sustain the positions we have assumed in regard to their probable usefulness and advantage, if they can be successfully introduced upon the continent. Indeed, I think we may almost claim to have already done much towards it. On the 28th of August I sent down six camels under my clerk, Mr. Ray, to San Antonio, for oats, in company with three wagons from this post. The camels could, as it turned out, have gone down leisurely in two days, but governed in their movements by the wagons, (though they were empty,) they went down in three, the wagons being restrained in their march by the want of water along the route. On Monday, September 1, Captain McLean, assistant quartermaster at San Antonio, sent back the camels to me at 12 m., with 3,648 pounds of oats, an average of 608 pounds to each animal. At 6 p. m. on Wednesday, the 3d of September, the camels were again in this camp and had delivered their loads, having travelled leisurely and with much less weight than they could easily have transported. On Tuesday, September 2, the wagons were returned by Captain McLean at 12 m. On Saturday, September 6, they arrived in camp at $12\frac{1}{2}$ p. m., only one wagon carrying 1,900 pounds, and the others averaging about 1,800—the loads that experience has taught can be safely transported in them over this rough and thinly settled country. From this trial it will be seen that the six camels transported over the same ground and distance the weight of two six mule wagons, and gained on them $42\frac{1}{2}$ hours in time. Remember, moreover, that the keep of a camel is about the same as that of a mule, (if any difference it being rather in favor of the camel, as it eats no more, and ruminates like a cow,) and that there is no heavy outlay for wagons, harness, &c., (the only equipment being a very rude pack-saddle that can be made by the camel drivers themselves,) and you will have all the data necessary for a comparison of the two methods of transportation just related. Now, I do not mean to be understood from this statement as advancing any general abstract opinion that six camels are equal in transportation to twelve good mules and two strong, well-built wagons. But I mean to say that, viewed in relation to this vast unsettled country, where the roughness of the roads limits materially the loads placed in the wagons, and where the general want of water throughout regulates the day's journey of mules, six camels will accomplish as much as two six-mule teams, and in less time, and at much less expense. Another test of the advantage of the animal is before me, in a trial of them over a straight road hence to San Antonio, by which some miles in distance are saved, but which, lying over the mountains, is, from its roughness, impracticable for wagons.

On the 8th of September I had an opportunity of experimenting with one of the dromedaries. Lieutenant Chamblis went out with a small party, and with him I sent a dromedary to transport the provisions and forage (corn) for the men and horses, seven of each. The next day he returned, and from his report and that of the men the trial was very successful, the dromedary following the horses wherever they went, not only keeping up with them, but showing that, if not restrained, he would have gone ahead of them. The weight he transported was between 300 and 400 pounds.

For several months to come it will not be proper to put the camels and dromedaries to work regularly, on account of their long sea voyage, their want of acclimation, and the near approach of the rutting season; but from time to time I can find opportunities, as I have already done, to test their adaptation to the military service, and their usefulness and economy in transportation generally. Meanwhile there is ample occupation in studying their equipment with a view to their improvement, and in instructing some of Captain Palmer's men in their management, and in packing, that they may be used on scouts and in expressing.

Will you send me the treatise on the "Zembourek" or "dromedary artillery," either the original French or my translation; the original French I would prefer, as I had not time to make with my translation copies of all the drawings.

With much respect, I am, sir, your obedient servant,

HENRY C. WAYNE,
Major United States Army.

Hon. JEFFERSON DAVIS,
Secretary of War, Washington City.

CAMP VERDE, TEXAS, *November 5, 1856.*

SIR: In my letter of the 24th of September last I wrote you that another test of the advantage of the camel was before me, in a trial of them over a straight road hence to San Antonio, by which some miles in distance are saved, but which, lying over the mountains, is, from its ruggedness, impracticable for wagons.

On the 1st of October a caravan of twelve camels left this for San Antonio, under my clerk and overseer, Mr. Ray, with instructions to take, going and returning, the straight road before mentioned. It did so; but on going down, after following it for some miles, its indistinctness induced Mr. Ray to turn aside, and it was not until the caravan had proceeded ten miles that he discovered his error and retraced his steps back to the point of deviation. Notwithstanding this increased journey, the caravan arrived in San Antonio on the 3d of October, (Friday,) in good condition, having accomplished the distance easily in two days.

On Saturday night (October 4) and Sunday morning it rained in San Antonio heavily, wetting the roads deeply, and making them muddy and boggy. Wagoning through such mud is labor lost; for the viscidity of this soil is such that it packs firmly on the wheel, and as with each revolution a new layer is taken up, the tire and felloes soon become encased in a thick, firm coating of pressed earth, rendering traction slow and painful. Travelling in such roads with anything like a load in a wagon is out of the question. This condition of the roads offered an opportunity for another test, the travelling of the camel in muddy weather, not contemplated by me when the caravan left, but · which the information and sagacity of Mr. Ray at once embraced.

Packing light loads upon the camels, averaging about three hundred and twenty-five pounds to each, he took advantage of a temporary cessation of rain between 12 m. and 1 p. m. on Sunday (the 5th of October) and commenced his return to camp. The rain continued with slight intermissions, but generally coming down in torrents throughout Sunday night and the succeeding Monday and Tuesday. On Tuesday evening (October 7) the caravan reached camp at 7 p. m., and delivered 3,800 pounds of oats, and a few miscellaneous stores that it had transported, the state of the roads having impeded but little its progress. Experienced disinterested persons said at the time that loaded wagons could not have travelled in such weather. I think they said right; but I prefer their opinion to my own, as it is unbiased by any prejudices in favor of the experiment. The usefulness of the camel in this interior country is no longer a question here in Texas among those who have seen them at work, or examined them with attention. As far as possible, I have endeavored to satisfy the very natural curiosity of all who have come to see them; but especially of those whose experience renders them competent judges of the anticipated advantages to be derived from their employment; and I am gratified in being able to state that the experiment is regarded by the latter class with interest and decided favor.

The camels are in good health, and doing well, with the exception of three—one Bactrian that has been teething, and two dromedaries, severely bitten by other camels. One has been bitten some time, the other last night.

The shelters have been much retarded by frequent and heavy rains; but, taking everything into consideration, we are getting on with them fairly. Captain Palmer is indefatigable in his labors, and carries on the works for me as rapidly as the necessary scouting and military duties of the post will permit. I find also a valuable adjunct in Assistant Surgeon J. R. Smith, attached to this post, who has entered into our views with the zeal of science, and with the judgment of practicalness.

With much respect, I am, sir, your obedient servant,
HENRY C. WAYNE,
Major United States Army.

Hon. JEFFERSON DAVIS,
Secretary of War, Washington City.

[Extract.]

CAMP VERDE, TEXAS, *November* 20, 1856.

SIR: It is with regret that I report to you the loss of two more of our camels—the Bactrian mentioned in my previous communications as ailing, and the camels reported in my letter of the 5th instant as having been severely wounded by a bite some time before. The enclosed report of examinations, *post mortem*, by Mr. Ray, who has the veterinary care of the animals, explains the causes of death in each case.

The other camel reported bitten on the night of the 4th instant has been cured.

*   *   *   *   *   *   *   *   *

Very respectfully, your obedient servant,
HENRY C. WAYNE,
Major U. S. Army.

Hon. JEFFERSON DAVIS,
Secretary of War, Washington City, D. C.

CAMP VERDE, TEXAS, *November* 19, 1856.

SIR: In obedience to your order, I have made "post mortem" examinations of a male Bactrian camel, named "Gusuf," which died on the evening of the 10th instant, and of a male Egyptian dromedary, named "Goumal," which died on the 17th instant, and have to report:

That the bowels of the Bactrian were in the state natural to an animal which has been dead some hours—i. e., inflated with air or gas; the stomachs were in a tolerably healthy condition, and the paunch nearly full of undigested food. On examining the viscera, the liver was found to be totally diseased, and, although dead only a few hours, putrescent and offensive. The organ in question contained large *cysti*, full of pus, and numerous *hydatids* permeated the whole of it, even to the extremities of the lobes. The lungs and heart evidenced no disease *per se*. The jugular veins being greatly distended were opened, and the serous portion of the blood was found to be separated from the rest, coagulated, yellow in color, and highly offensive.

From the appearance of the liver, its disorder appears to have been of long standing, and being aggravated by confinement on shipboard, change of food and climate, at last resulted in the death of the camel.

There seems to be the more reason for this belief, as, whilst on the ship, (and even as soon as received on board,) the above mentioned animal was ailing, refusing to eat, persisting in lying down, &c., indicative at that period of something wrong.

The cause of the loss of the Egyptian dromedary was an external injury, viz: a severe laceration and bruising of the inside of the left thigh, in close proximity to the joint, being the effect of bites from the Tunisian camel, "Mahomet," whilst they were at pasture, October 5th ultimo.

One of the tendons was torn out by the tusks of the attacking camel, the ruptured ends protruding from the wound; the flesh was much torn and bruised; the wound deep and ragged.

It had been under careful treatment up to the time of its death; but continuous and deeply seated inflammation set at nought all means used for its relief.

Being unable to walk, kneel down, or graze, and pain producing loss of appetite, it died on the 17th instant, nearly as much from exhaustion and inanition as from the wound itself.

On making a longitudinal incision on the external side of the injured thigh, to the depth of three inches, a large quantity of pus exuded from the opening. Commencing the same operation on the inside of the limb, and at the exact spot of the original injury, the knife had to be thrust almost to the bone ere the pus showed itself. Laying the thigh open, the whole of the muscles, integuments, and flesh in the interior of the limb and around the bone were found to be totally destroyed and converted into putrescent matter. The quantity of pus contained in the cavity exceeded a half gallon, and mixed with it were numerous indurated lumps.

Inflammation commencing at the bone, and externally demonstrating little or nothing until so far gone as to render the usual remedies useless, has rendered the cure of a limb so crushed and torn as this was in the first instance difficult, if not impossible.

Had the thigh been opened prior to the animal's death, it could not have saved the camel for any useful purpose, the destruction of the substance of the limb being so great, and the animal in an extreme state of emaciation.

With much respect, I am, sir, yours, most obediently,

ALBERT RAY.

Major H. C. WAYNE.

CAMP VERDE, TEXAS,
December 4, 1856.

SIR: As the political changes of the coming year may terminate your official connexion with the War Department, and alter the policy heretofore observed in our experiment, I have thought it advisable to make a few suggestions at this early date, that if you agree with me a system may be organized, that the matter may be left to your successor in as complete a form as possible. My observation of and experience with civil employés in Texas satisfies me that the accomplishment of your views for the uses of the dromedaries and burden camels can only be attained through military responsibility and accountability. I would, therefore, respectfully propose that the camels be turned over to the charge of an intelligent regimental captain, who would take an interest in our views, and who, by military control of the men attending the animals, will efficiently carry them out. The prejudices of regimental officers against the exercise of command over them by an officer of the staff precludes me from the control of enlisted men. I have no desire to hold a questionable position. In making this proposition I sacrifice personal wishes to what I conceive to be a necessary duty. At all times, however, I shall be ready to contribute to the experiment whatever of knowledge and of systematic employment I possess and have digested.

The animals are now well sheltered, and everything prepared for breeding and using them in accordance with the views from time to time communicated to you. A better spot than this for all purposes that induced their importation and for propagating them could not be selected.

The experiment to be fairly determined will require time, five or six years at least; and as this is an important military point, and will be so for ten years to come, the presence of troops here for the length of time necessary to demonstrate the experiment may be regarded as a certainty.

Should this proposition meet with your approval, I would further recommend that my present overseer, Mr. Ray, be continued in service with the camels on account of his knowledge of their habits, and for his veterinary skill, his position to be that of veterinarian. The present commander of the post, Captain Palmer, second cavalry, and his officers have taken a good deal of interest in the matter, and are sufficiently informed upon it to carry it on, aided by Mr. Ray's experience.

The usefulness of the camel for all military purposes, and its economy, I hold to be fully shown already, though they have necessarily been handled with extreme care. Their condition is excellent. Their acclimation I regard certain. By the time, though, that your answer reaches me, this portion of the experiment will be definitely settled. The meteorological register of the medical officer here will show the climate they have gone through in the past month; and in six weeks more they will have passed the severity of winter.

Requesting your earnest attention to this letter, I am sir, with much respect, your obedient servant,

HENRY C. WAYNE,
Major United States Army.

Hon. JEFFERSON DAVIS,
Secretary of War, Washington City.

PURCHASE OF CAMELS FOR MILITARY PURPOSES. 165

No. 1.

ANIEH DROMEDARY—[Heap.]

BECHARIEH DROMEDARY.—[Heap.]

PURCHASE OF CAMELS FOR MILITARY PURPOSES.

No. 3.

"COURIER OF THE DESERT."—[Vernet.]

No. 4.

DROMEDARY FROM MUSCAT, (FEMALE.)—[Heap.]

No. 5.

DROMEDARY FROM LOWER EGYPT, (FEMALE)—[Heap.]

No. 6.

ARVANA CAMEL FROM ASIA MINOR.—[Heap.]

PURCHASE OF CAMELS FOR MILITARY PURPOSES. 171

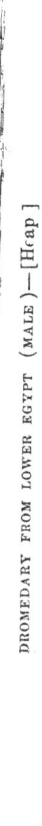

DROMEDARY FROM LOWER EGYPT (MALE).—[Heap.]

No. 7.

172   PURCHASE OF CAMELS FOR MILITARY PURPOSES.

No. 8.

DROMEDARY FROM MOUNT SINAI, (MALE.)—[Heap.]

PURCHASE OF CAMELS FOR MILITARY PURPOSES. 173

No. 9.

FEMALE CAMELS AND YOUNG.—[Heap.]

No. 10.

WRESTLING CAMEL, FROM ASIA MINOR, (MALE.)—[Heap.]

PURCHASE OF CAMELS FOR MILITARY PURPOSES. 175

No. 11.

BACTRIAN CAMEL, FROM CENTRAL ASIA, (MALE.)—[Heap.]

176 PURCHASE OF CAMELS FOR MILITARY PURPOSES.

No. 12.

BACTRIAN CAMEL FROM CRIMEA, (MALE.) —[Heap.]

PURCHASE OF CAMELS FOR MILITARY PURPOSES.   177

No. 13.

BACTRIAN CAMEL, BLANKETED, FROM CENTRAL ASIA, (MALE.)—[Heap.]

Ex. Doc. 62——12

178 PURCHASE OF CAMELS FOR MILITARY PURPOSES.

No. 14. TULU, (HYBRID, MALE.)—[Heap.]

PURCHASE OF CAMELS FOR MILITARY PURPOSES. 179

No. 15.

EMBARKATION OF CAMELS.—[Heap.]

180 PURCHASE OF CAMELS FOR MILITARY PURPOSES.

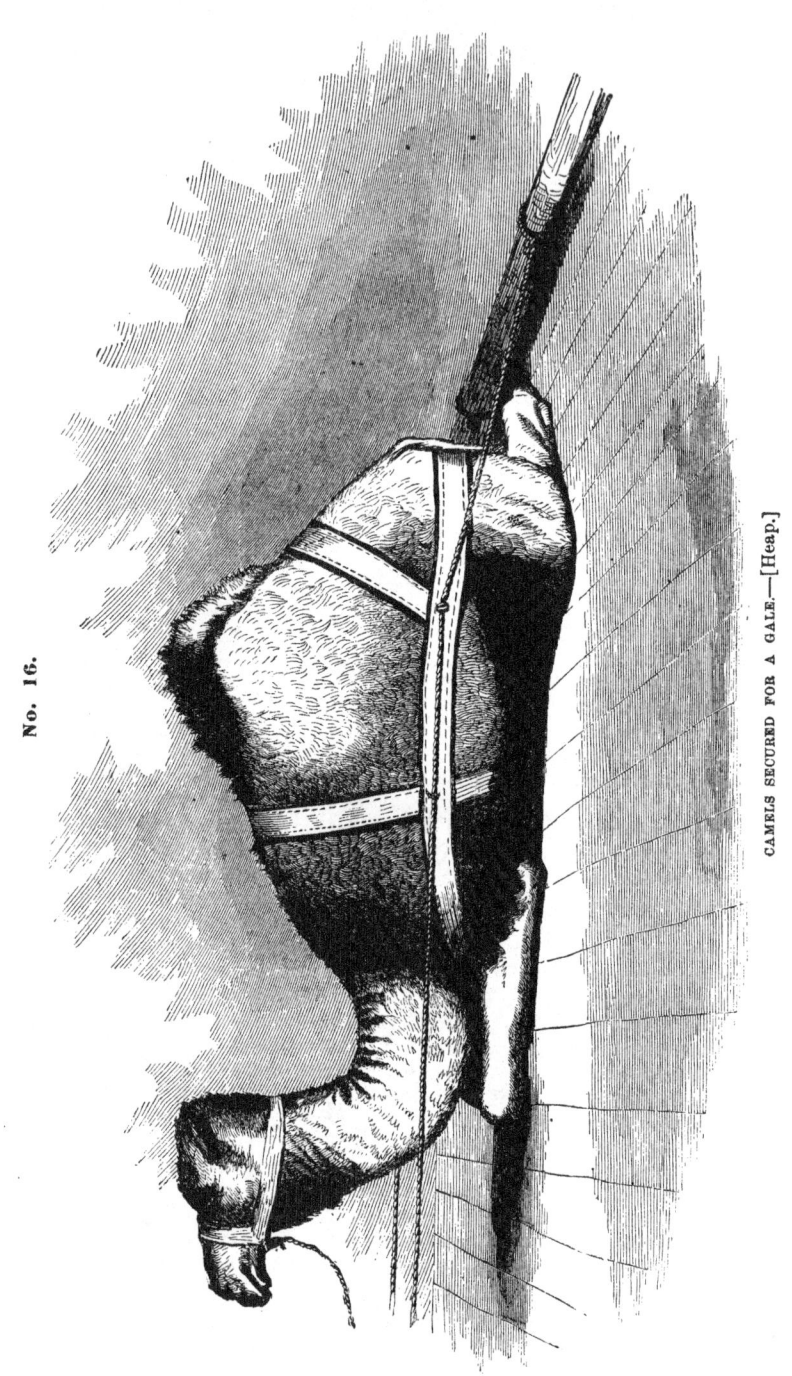

No. 16.

CAMELS SECURED FOR A GALE.—[Heap.

PURCHASE OF CAMELS FOR MILITARY PURPOSES. 181

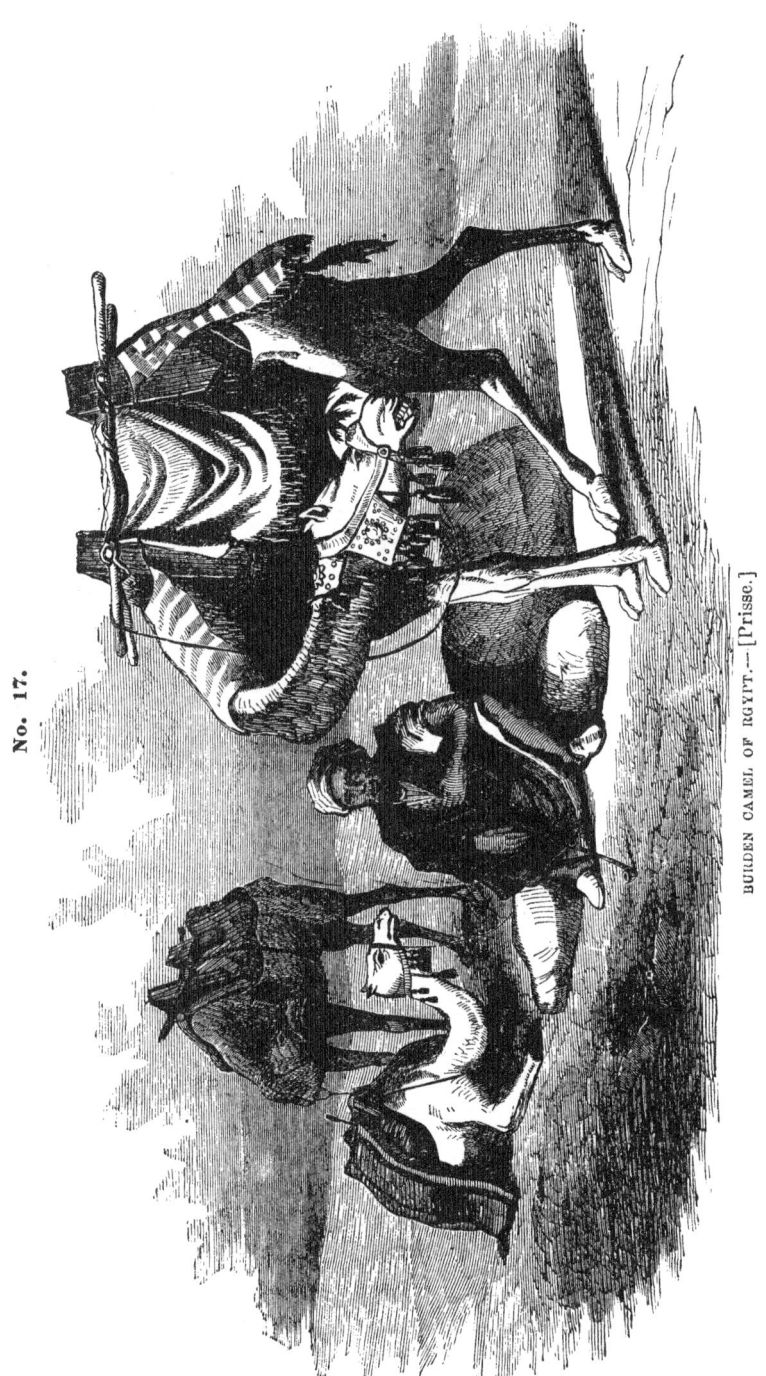

No. 17.

BURDEN CAMEL OF EGYPT.—[Prisse.]

182 PURCHASE OF CAMELS FOR MILITARY PURPOSES.

No. 18.

BURDEN CAMEL OF EGYPT.—[Prisse.]

PURCHASE OF CAMELS FOR MILITARY PURPOSES. 183

No. 19.

DROMEDARIES OF EGYPT.—[Prisse.]

184 PURCHASE OF CAMELS FOR MILITARY PURPOSES.

No. 20.

DROMEDARIES OF EGYPT.—[Prisse.]

PART II.

PAPERS RELATING TO THE SECOND EXPEDITION FOR CAMELS AND DROMEDARIES.

PAPERS RELATING TO SECOND EXPEDITION.

WAR DEPARTMENT,
Washington, June 18, 1856.

SIR: Lieutenant Porter goes out in the "Supply" again, with the intention of importing another load of camels and dromedaries, and as there will likely be some difficulty in obtaining any of the latter class of animals without your co-operation, I beg leave to trouble you in the matter, and request that you will afford the required assistance.

Lieutenant Porter informs me that there is still a permit for ten dromedaries, which he was unable to purchase owing to the shortness of time, and not getting the viceroy's permission until after the vessel had been in Alexandria sometime, which permission was obtained, I am informed, through your representations, and, consequently, you are well informed about the whole matter.

It is my desire that you should get the permit for the ten dromedaries renewed, so that there will be no mistaking the views of the viceroy in case the "Supply" should go to Alexandria, and that she may be enabled to sail from there as soon as possible; it is also desirable that you should communicate the result of your application to Lieutenant Porter, at some point where the ship may stop, so that he may shape his course accordingly, and you will much oblige me if you will direct your communication to Spezzia, care of Wm. Long, naval storekeeper, and to Mr. Offley, the American consul at Smyrna, to be left until called for by Lieutenant Porter.

In case the viceroy will not renew the permit to export the ten dromedaries, you will please endeavor to obtain permission to pass ten camels, which will be bought at "Hedjas," or some other point outside his dominions; ten are as many as will be required, and the permit having already been granted, it is only desirable, at present, to get that number, and I should think the viceroy would make no objection whatever to this request

Will you please communicate freely on this subject with Lieutenant Porter?

Very respectfully, your obedient servant,

JEFF'N DAVIS,
Secretary of War.

EDWIN DE LEON, Esq.,
Consul General, Alexandria, Egypt.

WAR DEPARTMENT,
Washington, June 26, 1856.

SIR: After fulfilling the orders of the Navy Department, you will proceed, as authorized, with the ship Supply to procure an additional number of camels for the military service of the United States.

It is desirable to procure ten dromedaries, of the swift kind, from Egypt. Mr. Edwin De Leon, consul general at Alexandria, has already been written to on the subject, and has been requested to give such aid as he may render, and you may require, in obtaining them. After procuring the dromedaries, you will complete your cargo at Smyrna with such specimens of the burden camel as seem best adapted to the soil and climate of the United States, and, especially, you will avail yourself of any opportunity which may offer to obtain fine animals of the Bactrian variety, and complete your list by selecting young camels of the approved crosses.

It is desirable that you should expedite the matter as much as possible, so as to reach the United States in the early part of December. Inform me through the mail of your proceedings, particularly when you leave for the United States, so that due preparations may be made for the arrival of the camels.

You will receive, for the purpose of carrying out this experiment, ten thousand dollars, which will be charged to you on the books of the treasury, and, as the War Department is not prepared at this moment to furnish you with letters of credit abroad, you will have to draw the amount here, and make arrangements with some banking house in the United States to furnish you with letters of credit on England, taking certificates at the time of the difference of exchange, so that it may be allowed in the settlement of your accounts. If you cannot make any such arrangement and find it necessary to turn your funds into such money as will pass current at the places to which you are going, you will exchange for French money at New York, taking certificates of the premium you pay, and the amount will be allowed in the settlement of your accounts. The latter is the least expensive though not, perhaps, the most convenient mode of arranging the matter.

Very respectfully, you obedient servant.

JEFF'N DAVIS,
Secretary of War.

Lieutenant DAVID D. PORTER,
  United States Navy.

QUARTERMASTER GENERAL'S OFFICE,
Washington City, July 14, 1856.

SIR: On the 12th instant you were addressed by telegraph, and authorized to employ Mr. Heap at a compensation of two thousand dollars a year and his necessary expenses.

A remittance will be made to you of ten thousand dollars, for the purchase of camels and the expenses connected therewith.

I am, sir, &c.,

THOMAS S. JESUP,
Quartermaster General.

Lieut. D. D. PORTER,
United States Ship Supply, New York.

CONSULATE GENERAL OF THE U. S. OF AMERICA IN EGYPT,
Alexandria, August 14, 1856.

DEAR SIR: I have the honor to acknowledge the receipt of your communication of June 18, 1856, and it will afford me great pleasure to give Lieutenant Porter all the aid in my power for the furtherance of his mission.

When I obtained from the viceroy of Egypt the temporary suspension of the rigid prohibition of the exportation of animals from his dominions, it was distinctly stated and understood that it was to be regarded as an act of international courtesy for this special occasion only, and not again to be demanded, for reasons which will be obvious to you, and which I have already explained. The order which Lieutenant Porter retains is therefore valueless now, nor could I in good faith ask for its renewal.

The viceroy has promised to give the necessary firmans to the local authorities authorizing the passage through Egypt, and the embarkation at Alexandria, of as many animals as we may purchase from the Hedjaz, or elsewhere beyond his limits.

I have also obtained such assistance as will render Lieutenant Porters' task less difficult, by entering into preliminary negotiations with one of the Arab Sheiks from the Hedjaz, who offers to provide choice dromedaries from his own stock at reasonable prices.

In conformity with your request, I shall immediately write to Lieutenant Porter duplicate letters directed to Smyrna and Spezzia, enclosing also copies of this communication, and feel fully satisfied that (unless unforseen circumstances prevent) no impediments will retard his speedy and satisfactory performance of the duty assigned him.

The successful issue of the first essay must be very encouraging to you, sir, who have so long and energetically pressed this useful work to a conclusive trial.

The viceroy of Egypt has recently organized a dromedary corps, and as I suppose the details may interest you, subjoin such particulars as I have been enabled to obtain respecting it. But a few days since the corps passed through the town of Alexandria, and the noiseless progress of so large a body of men and animals was not the least curious part of the spectacle. A blind man would not have known anything was passing.

For a night march or a surprise this peculiarity would render such a corps most effective. The present force of this corps amounts to

480 dromedaries, which it is intended to increase to 1,000 or 1,200. Each animal carries two soldiers, armed with muskets, &c., and the saddles are so arranged as to admit of their firing in any direction. The baggage camels can carry from 300 to 350 pounds weight of guns, powder, &c., each, when not on a forced march, when the troop can easily travel from 35 up to 60 miles per diem.

This speed, of course, can be greatly increased on special occasions, for short distances, with decreased weight of baggage, when most extraordinary celerity can be obtained. Only a few attendants to feed the animals are required on long marches.

The viceroy is greatly pleased thus far with his new regiment, which is but a revival of the corps formerly well known in Eastern warfare.

As the burden camel of Smyrna seems to have obtained the preference of Captain Porter, I have confined my observations to the dromedary, though, if required, animals of that description used in Egypt can promptly and easily be obtained from Syria, just over the Egyptian frontier. With an expression of the hope that the results of this enterprise may requite your efforts in its behalf, and with personal acknowledgments for the kind manner in which you have been pleased to recognize such services as I have been enabled to render, I remain, very respectfully, your obedient servant,

EDWIN DE LEON.

Hon. JEFFERSON DAVIS,
   Secretary of War, Washington City.

UNITED STATES SHIP "SUPPLY,"
September 11, 1856.

SIR: I have just received a letter from Mr. De Leon, enclosing a copy of one he sent you, giving his views with regard to an expedition to the "Hegas" in Arabia, for the purpose of procuring dromedaries. I regret that time will not permit my obtaining your views on the matter, and I hope you will approve of the course I am about to take. I think you will do so, when you read my reasons for not going into Egypt. In the first place, Mr. De Leon states, positively, that the permission for the exportation of the ten dromedaries cannot be renewed, and that they must be procured outside of Egypt, in Arabia. This involves a travel of two thousand miles, and an absence of three months at least. The following estimate of expenses have been made with a view to finding out how much ten dromedaries will cost, and you will perceive that it will take nearly the whole amount of what I have on hand, with the prospect of a failure in getting what we want:

Hire of twenty dromedaries for three months, at fifteen dollars per month	$900
Hire of twenty men three months, at fifteen dollars per month	900
Provisions and forage	500
Presents to Arabs through whose districts we pass	500

Two dragomen three months, at forty dollars...............	$240
Cost and expenses of ten dromedaries of the best kind, three hundred dollars each..	3,000
Accoutrements for the same..	500
Occasional escorts from Arab tribes, presents to sheiks, &c.	600
Provender for animals..	400
	7,540

This would be a large amount to pay for ten animals, coming from a climate not at all like the one they are going to, and I think it more than probable that the whole thing would be a failure. Under these circumstances, I have concluded to go direct to Smyrna, and procure a good number of camels of superior breeds, and by obtaining young ones of one or two years, they can soon be broken in to act as a dromedary corps. Those animals used by the pacha of Egypt are not the blooded dromedary, but the common Arabian camel trained to the service. I could procure, without going out of Egypt, a sufficient number of blooded dromedaries with the amount I estimated for, three thousand dollars, but Mr. De Leon says in his letter, "when I obtained from the viceroy of Egypt the temporary suspension of the rigid prohibition of the exportation of animals from his dominions it was distinctly stated and understood that it was to be regarded as an act of international courtesy for the special occasion only, and not again to be demanded."

Under these circumstances, I think, sir, you will agree with me that it would be useless to go to Egypt, unless the consul could promise a certainty of getting what we want. As to making a journey of two thousand miles through a country where the tribes are in open hostility to each other, and where, when I was in Egypt, it was impossible to go, did not, I think, enter into your calculation. I would promise to go and get the animals if ordered to do so, but am afraid I should have to account for them as expended on the road, as they would all certainly be stolen after the money was paid down.

I think I can promise to bring from Smyrna such animals as will please you. Mr. Heap has already set out for the interior of Asia Minor, and will procure the best animals that money can purchase; and instead of ten dromedaries only, (which would make rather a poor show for so much money,) we will procure, I hope, forty-five camels that will fully answer all your expectations. As soon as I get through the delivery of my stores, and stop at some place to make some money arrangements, I proceed direct to Smyrna, where a letter from you will reach me in time to change my plans in case you think it desirable.

Very respectfully, your obedient servant,
DAVID D. PORTER,
Lieut. Com'g.

Hon. JEFFERSON DAVIS,
Secretary of War.

WAR DEPARTMENT,
Washington, October 8, 1856.

SIR: I have received your letter of the 11th ultimo, stating your views as to the best mode of expending the balance of the appropriation for camels; and, in reply thereto, I have to inform you that your views are approved, and that no change is desired in the proposed mode of execution.

Very respectfully, your obedient servant,
JEFF'N DAVIS,
Secretary of War.

Lieut. DAVID D. PORTER, *U. S. N.*,
Commanding storeship Supply.

UNITED STATES SHIP SUPPLY,
Smyrna, November 14, 1856.

SIR: I have the honor to inform you of our arrival at this place, and that we shall sail to-morrow for the United States. Our voyage here was a very long one, having met with unprecedented bad weather. Directly ahead for twenty-one days, we were struggling against gales of wind; and in all that time only made thirty-five miles. Fortunately, I had sent Mr. Heap on ahead, and when I anchored in Smyrna he had all the camels purchased and fully equipped with new saddles, covers, &c., and there was nothing left to do but ship them. Mr. Heap has purchased a beautiful lot of animals, all young, (between three and four years old,) and few of them have ever been under the saddle. He selected the best of about three hundred good ones that were sent in. There are two Bactrians, males, three male Arabian, one Tulu or cross between the Bactrian and Arabian, one female of the same kind. All the rest are young females of the Arabian breed; some of them will produce young in four or five months.

Six of the camels have been presented by the sultan, through our minister at Constantinople, or Mr. Brown; one of them is a Bactrian, the others of the Arabian breed. We shall sail with forty-four camels in all, which is eleven more than we started with last year. I have had to make some little alterations in the vessel to accommodate them, and have arranged the decks better than I had them on the last voyage, so the animals will be much more comfortable.

Camels are much dearer than they were last year, owing to a cessation of the war, and the great demand for transportation of merchandise into the interior of Asia Minor; but notwithstanding the additional number of camels, the expenses will not amount to more than they did last voyage, and we have a much finer lot of animals.

I think our present home voyage will be about the same as the last, and if the steamer will be ready on the 20th of January, I hope by that time to get to the mouth of the Mississippi, and turn the camels over to whom you may direct. I have employed eight good men, who will go with them into Texas, and be discharged there when the government no longer need their services.

I have disposed of four of the guns, two to the ex-governor of Smyrna, and two to the present governor, through both of whom came the present of the six camels from the sultan, and who have been very civil. I shall send the rest to Mr. De Leon for the pacha of Egypt, which I hope will meet your approval.

I have the honor to remain, sir, very respectfully,
DAVID D. PORTER.
Hon. JEFFERSON DAVIS, &c., &c.

WAR DEPARTMENT,
Washington, December 13, 1856.

SIR: I enclose herewith the copy of a letter from Lieutenant D. D. Porter, received to-day, by which you will perceive that he expects to be at New Orleans with the storeship Supply and a cargo of forty-four camels by the 20th of January. I am desirous of seeing you here; and if you can make arrangements conveniently to leave Texas, repair to this city, and return to New Orleans by the time the vessel will arrive there, you will consider this an order to cover your transportation.

Very respectfully, your obedient servant,
JEFF'N DAVIS,
Secretary of War.
Major H. C. WAYNE,
U. S. Quartermaster, Camp Verde, Texas.

UNITED STATES SHIP "SUPPLY,"
Malta, December 3, 1856.

SIR: I have the honor to inform you of my arrival at this port, after a voyage of fifteen days from Smyrna. The subject which will interest you most is the welfare of the camels, and I am happy to say that they are all well and in fine condition, though they have gone through more hardships than camels ever went through before. We were driven back to this port by the severest weather it has ever been my lot to meet with before at sea. Gales and hurricanes have been tossing us about ever since I left Smyrna, and thirteen days out of the fifteen have been passed under close-reefed topsails, under water half the time, and officers and crew knocked up and worn out. For myself, I have not had my clothes off or been in a bed during the whole period. The camels were strapped down all the time, and so secured that not an accident happened to them beyond a temporary loss of the use of their legs. I put my helm up for Malta (having passed it) on the 1st December, in a hurricane, and in six hours succeeded in getting safely into port, one of the only vessels of the many that were driven in that met with no loss of sails or spars; and now the camels are as well and comfortable as if they were in their native land.

I almost regret having undertaken a winter trip home, though in some respects it is the best time; but no one ever heard of such weather in the Mediterranean. From the time we left Naples until we arrived here on our return voyage we were forty-eight days at sea, thirty-seven of which we were struggling against heavy gales; but I presumed it would gratify you to be able to say that you had introduced eighty camels into the country before the close of the administration, and I hope still that such may be the case. The adverse gales will make some difference in the time I appointed for getting to New Orleans, and I think it likely that we may not reach there before the 10th of February, by which time I hope the steamer may be ready to receive the camels.

This is a beautiful lot of animals that we now have, much larger and finer than the first, and I feel some anxiety in getting every one of them over; consequently I shall not hurry until there is every prospect of good weather to try and slip out of the Mediterranean; once in the Atlantic I shall feel quite secure. There will be some additional expense, (for repairs to camel gear, and for the animals' comfort, &c.,) but it will still leave a surplus of the amount I brought with me, including Mr. Heap's pay, and all else.

I am instructed to stop at Tangiers on my way home to take on board the remains of a late consul there, and will leave no effort untried to do so, though it will be rather a difficult thing at this season. No ships ever go there in this month. If I am driven through the straits by December gales and easterly weather, I hope you will make my peace with Mr. Dobbin, for I could not possibly return there (after having been driven into the Atlantic) without detriment to the enterprise on hand. I shall inform you again, at the first stopping place, how we are getting along, and when you may likely expect us in New Orleans.

Very respectfully, your obedient servant,
DAVID D. PORTER.

Hon. JEFFERSON DAVIS,
    Secretary of War.

INDIANOLA, TEXAS, *January* 4, 1857.

SIR: Your letter of the 13th of December last, enclosing a copy of Lieutenant Porter's letter to you, met me at San Antonio, as I was leaving for this place. The copies addressed to me here were received on my arrival last evening, and this morning the steamer brought me from Colonel Tompkins your telegraphic despatch of the 29th ultimo.

Should the business of the court of inquiry not detain me long, I will, with your permission, return to the Verde to pay my men for December, and to close my papers for the past quarter, which will occupy me about two days, and then repair to Washington.

* * * * * * * *

If detained by the court beyond my expectations, I will, in such case, yield to the necessity, and proceed hence direct to Washington, leaving my business at the Verde to await my return. In either case I hope to see you by the 28th instant.

In the event of the camels arriving at Indianola during my absence, I will leave here a competent person to take charge of them, under Captain Van Bokkelen's superintendence.

With much respect, I am, sir, your obedient servant,
HENRY C. WAYNE,
Major United States Army.

Hon. JEFFERSON DAVIS,
Secretary of War, Washington City.

[Extract.]

UNITED STATES SHIP SUPPLY,
Mouth of the Mississippi, January 30, 1857.

SIR: I have the honor to inform you of the arrival of the "Supply" at this place, with camels all in good condition, except one that has a sore on the back, but is rapidly improving.

I regret to say that I have not been as fortunate this time as I could have wished, having lost three camels on the voyage, among them the two Bactrians. After going through safely all the bad weather we had encountered, one of them died suddenly in Malta, and the other two fell over dead, without a moment's warning, when eating their food and apparently in perfect health. There was no way of accounting for it, unless they swallowed something in their food; the first one, I think, died from fright, owing to the excessive motion of the ship, and would never eat afterwards.

The remainder have stood the voyage well, better even than the last had, and none of them have been sick a moment.

Very respectfully, your obedient servant,
DAVID D. PORTER.

Hon. JEFFERSON DAVIS,
Secretary of War.

WASHINGTON, *February* 12, 1857.

GENERAL: In compliance with the direction of the Secretary of War I have the honor to submit herewith a *projet* for the future management of the experiment of introducing the camel upon this continent.

That it may be fully appreciated, I will premise that from my first connexion with the experiment, in 1848, to the present time, I have never entertained the idea that the benefits to be derived from the introduction of the animal among us could be extensively realized in our day. I regard it more in the light of a legacy to posterity, of precisely the same character as the introduction of the horse and other domestic animals by the early settlers of America has been to us. With this view, it seems to me that while at the same time we carry out the immediate purposes of utility and economy specified in the resolution of Congress authorizing the experiment, the uses of the camels imported should be in subordination to the breeding of and establishing the stock among us. Indeed, the breeding and the character of the stock that may be produced are essential features of the experiment itself. The transportation of the animal from the old to the new world has been fully and successfully demonstrated. The acclimation has been partially, and so far fortunately, accomplished—so fortunately that I have no doubt of its complete success. The breeding and the character of the stock yet remain to be shown; and for this time and careful management are required. The military benefits to be derived from the introduction of the camel, are in my view, of little moment in comparison with its bearing upon trade and communication throughout the vast interior of our continent; and to the army has been committed, it seems to me, the charge of an experiment which, in its action upon the development of our country, if successful, may be regarded as initiatory of railroad connexion, not only across, but in the northern and southern directions of the continent.

I would respectfully suggest, therefore, that the camels imported have a fixed home for three or four years, at least, at some point on the frontier, where they may be carefully tended, and from which they may be used from time to time in transportation and scouting. The point at which they are now established presents excellent opportunities for all the requirements of the experiment, and particularly for comparison with the ordinary means of transportation through an arid and broken country, with range of service embracing journeys of from sixty to six hundred miles. I recommend, then, that they be kept where they are.

For the care and management of the camels enlisted men are necessary—say twenty-five, including three or four good non-commissioned officers. For this purpose, unattached recruits may be assigned, perhaps, as to the cavalry and artillery services at the Military Academy. My observation and experience with civil employés in Texas satisfy me conclusively that the successful accomplishment of the experiment can only be justly attained by the rigidness of military responsibility.

The officer in charge of the experiment should be left very much to the guidance of his own judgment and discretion, with as few military superiors over him as may be consistent with the laws and rules of service, both as a matter of justice to his individual reputation, and for the stronger reason that with a division of control and accountability responsibility ceases.

These main features established, the details of the arrangement will

rest with the officer selected for the duty, subordinate to the authority controlling the experiment.
Very respectfully, your obedient servant,
HENRY C. WAYNE,
Major United States Army.
Major General THOMAS S. JESUP,
  Quartermaster General U. S. Army, Washington, D. C.

WASHINGTON, *February* 21, 1857.

SIR: The court of inquiry referred to in my letter of the 4th ultimo adjourned on the afternoon of the 10th January, and the next day I commenced my return to the Verde, where I arrived on the morning of the 17th of the same month. Adjusting my business on the 17th and 18th, I began my journey for this place, under your orders of the 13th and 29th December, 1856, on the 19th January, 1857.

During my absence at Indianola, the remaining Bactrian died. Making in all five animals that we have lost, up to the time of my departure—two by violent injuries, one by epilepsy, a disease to which the camel is said to be peculiarly liable. and two, the Bactrians, by what I believe to have been the acclimatory disease of Texas, known as the "Spanish fever." These two Bactrians are the only animals that have shown any serious effects of climate in Texas. This is attributable, I think, to the unusual and excessive heat of the past summer, to confinement on ship-board, and to an error, I believe, we committed in blanketing them two warmly on the voyage. Accustomed to rather a cool climate, their systems yielded to the combined injurious effects of confinement on ship-board, sea voyage, over care, and acclimatory process in a new, and unfortunately, unusual hot summer temperature. The remainder of the camels I left in as good condition, apparently, as animals could be. I could notice no difference in condition between the dromedaries from Egypt and the burden camels from Asia Minor, though on the night of the 17th (the day after my return from the coast) the thermometer went down to 8° (Fahrenheit.) The climate seems to agree with them equally well, and I have been much gratified by the assurances of many gentlemen in Texas, (among them the present able commander of that department, an old and experienced Texan,) that we have been more fortunate with our camels than is usual with the same number of horses or mules, brought from other States.

At Indianola I arranged with Captain Van Bokkelen for the care of the new lot expected; and at New Orleans I left my clerk and overseer, Mr. Ray, to receive them from Lieutenant Porter, upon the arrival of the "Supply" in the river, and to conduct them to Texas on the steamer awaiting there for that purpose.

On the 13th May, 1856, the first camels were landed on the shores of Texas; and after our now eight months' experience with them, (from my own continuous observation, and from recent statements to me from Captain Palmer and Assistant Surgeon Jos. R. Smith, copies of which are enclosed,) I think we may regard the acclimation of the camel as decided, and that it will flourish with us as well as it does in Asia or Africa. In my own mind I have no doubt of the complete success of the experiment, under good management for the future; but as we cannot expect the public to adopt our conclusions as facts, the remaining points of breeding, and the character of the stock bred, must be demonstrated practically, with as much care as if we had not such good reasons to anticipate their favorable issue.

So far the results of the experiment, within the limits time has permitted it to be carried, have fully sustained the views that we entertained in regard to the usefulness of the camel, and which induced us, in our respective spheres of action, to press it upon the attention of Congress. In conducting the experiment, I have endeavored to act with great caution, and rather to err on the side of excessive care than to jeopard success by any effort at display. I know what the animal is capable of doing, *and does* in Asia and Africa, and I am firmly convinced that it can do as much in America. But there is a large portion of the community always opposed to what they call "novelties," and ever ready to seize upon any want of success in any of them essayed, to maintain their own reputation for sagacity; and another class who, though they may wish well, are timidly doubtful; and still another class, whose misgivings are founded in reason. The prejudices, fears and objections of all these classes, are to be met only by successful demonstration; and to attain this in our experiment, I have treated the camels with perhaps more care than their naturally hardy constitutions really required. We have camels that, for short distances, will easily transport twelve and fifteen hundred pounds; yet never, but in one instance, has there been put upon them more than about six hundred pounds. The exception referred to was during my stay in Indianola, and within the first month or six weeks after landing. Needing hay at the camel yard, I directed one of the men to take a camel to the quartermaster's forage-house, and bring up four bales. Desirous of seeing what effect it would produce upon the public mind, I mingled in the crowd that gathered around the camel as it came in town. When made to kneel down to receive its load, and two bales, weighing in all 613 pounds, were packed on, I heard doubts expressed around me as to the animal's ability to rise under them; when two more bales were put on, making the gross weight of the load 1,256 pounds, incredulity as to his ability to rise, much less to carry it, found vent in positive assertion, and as I had then become recognized, I observed that I was regarded by some compassionate individuals as about to make a splendid failure; to convey to you the surprise and sudden change of sentiment when the camel, at the signal, rose and walked off with his four bales of hay, would be impossible. It is sufficient to say that I was completely satisfied. The circumstance was chronicled in verse by one of the poets of Texas, and published in the Indianola Bulletin or Victoria Advocate, I forget which, and in it was amusingly described the incredulity and surprise, almost dismay, I have endeavored to portray. I am sorry I have not the verses by me to enclose them to you. I would have put on two more bales, about eighteen hundred pounds, but four bales were sufficient for my purposes, and the animal had no particular effort (objectionable after so long a sea voyage) to make under them.

I have not reported to you every instance of use to which the camels have been put, thinking it to be unnecessary; but their service has been in character with my reports of the 24th September and November 5, 1856. At the commencement of December their use in caravan was suspended, the rutting season then beginning, and will not be resumed on account of it until March. Captain Palmer and Assistant Surgeon Smith are now superintending, as requested, the breeding. Two births, still-born, the get of last year, have been reported to me. On this bad fortune, and the probability of its being the case with all the females impregnated last year, Dr. Smith expresses an opinion that seems reasonable. [See his letter herewith.] I have never, myself, hoped for anything from the crossing of last year, but regard that portion of the experiment as commencing with the present season, after the acclimation, and in the usual condition of the animal.

As soon as the lot recently brought over have been landed in Texas, and have recovered the use of their legs—say in three or four weeks—they should be taken up to the Verde, where the others are, and where they could be properly sheltered and cared for.

With much respect, I am, sir, your obedient servant,
HENRY C. WAYNE,
Major United States Army.

Hon. JEFFERSON DAVIS,
Secretary of War, Washington.

CAMP VERDE, TEXAS, *January* 29, 1857.

MY DEAR MAJOR: The day after your departure from San Antonio, I started for the Verde by the Cibolo, and arrived in safety, finding everybody and everything doing well. Mild weather still continues, the thermometer not having been below 40° since I saw you. In fact, I think the severity of the winter entirely passed, and the camels, I think, have suffered none from the cold. The night after my return another camel was born dead, and, as far as I can judge, I think that the most, if not every one, of the camels begotten on ship-board will be still-born. The reason is obvious, the unusual and unnatural sea voyage.

*   *   *   *   *   *   *   *   *

With great respect, truly yours,

JOS. R. SMITH,
Assistant Surgeon.

Major HENRY C. WAYNE,
United States Army, Washington City.

CAMP VERDE, TEXAS, *January* 30, 1857.

DEAR MAJOR : * * * * * * *
The camels are doing very well. Another of the females has had a "still-born" young one. Alexander (the Armenian interpreter, H. C. W.) thinks the mother must have been hurt or frightened to produce this. Alexander says that nearly all the female camels are *enceinte*. I think they are doing very well.

* * * * * * * * *

Very truly, yours,
J. N. PALMER,
U. S. Army, Captain 2d Cavalry.

Major HENRY C. WAYNE,
United States Army, Washington City.

ASSISTANT QUARTERMASTER'S OFFICE,
Indianola, Texas, February 10, 1857.

SIR: I have to report that 41 (forty-one) camels, in good order, were landed this day from the steamer "Suwanee."

* * * * * * * *

I am, with respect, your obedient servant,
W. K. VAN BOKKELEN,
Captain, Acting Quartermaster.

Hon. JEFFERSON DAVIS,
Secretary of War, Washington.

PART III.

THE ZEMBOUREKS,

OR THE

DROMEDARY FIELD ARTILLERY

OF

THE PERSIAN ARMY.

BY COLONEL F. COLOMBARI,

GRAND OFFICER OF THE ORDER OF THE LION AND SUN OF PERSIA, DECORATED WITH SEVERAL OTHER ORDERS, AND MEMBER OF THE GEOGRAPHICAL SOCIETY.

EXTRACTED FROM THE "SPECTATEUR MILITAIRE," 1853.

TRANSLATED BY BREVET MAJOR HENRY C. WAYNE, U. S. ARMY, 1854.

INTRODUCTION.

The subject of this essay is the dromedary artillery, styled in Persian *Zembourek*, from the word *Zembour* (a wasp.)* It has been used with advantage for a long time in the Persian army, and has often contributed to the achievement of signal victories over neighboring powers, and in the civil wars which followed the fall of the Shahs Sophis, and which continued until the accession of the reigning family of Kadjars.

Repairing, in 1838, for the second time, to Teheran, at the head of a regiment of *behaderan khassa*, (grenadiers of the guard,) to be presented to H. M. Mehemed Shah, I saw a detachment of the dromedary artillery parading in a review. Struck with its singular appearance, I made, on the spot, a few rough sketches of it. Up to that time I had served only in the war in Kurdistan, a mountainous country, not admitting the employment of dromedaries; nor was it until subsequently, in 1841, when I became attached to the person of the king, that I could measure exactly their usefulness. The prime vizier, wishing to introduce reforms into the corps, charged me with the reports in relation to it, which gave me an opportunity of making numerous investigations, and of thoroughly ascertaining everything relating to the history of the zemboureks, and of their service since organized, a period of one hundred and twenty years. The greater number of Europeans who have described this artillery, and given sketches of it, have done it in so incomplete and inexact a manner, that it is fair to presume that they never saw it. We will not, however, pursue further this criticism, as it would draw us beyond the limits we have prescribed to ourselves.

I have thought it best to give, first, a few particulars of the natural history of the dromedary, which are little known, avoiding repetition of those found in special treatises.† From the earliest ages, dromedaries have been used in Asia for military transportation. Titus, Livy, and Diodorus Siculus even, give accounts in detail of expeditions in which the dromedary was used as an immediate auxilliary to

---

* The name of this insect is given to the dromedary artillery, to indicate, by a metaphor common in the East, the constant and incessant annoyance of this light artillery to the troops it is ordered to pursue and attack.

† We cannot too highly recommend the excellent work on this subject by General Carbuccia; a work as interesting as it is instructive.

soldiers armed with lances and javelins. Therefore, I shall not treat of its actual use in facilitating the march of troops. A still more important duty has been assigned to it within a century—that of transporting the thunderbolts of war. It was Persia which first so used it; and this light artillery has never since ceased to render to it important services in its expeditions. Though I have aimed at brevity in my narrative, I have found it impossible to omit some particulars relative to a nation whose genius and customs differ so much from our own.

Within a few years the dromedary artillery has had to sustain a rivalry with field artillery, in consequence of the introduction of the European system into Persia. As in all similar cases, it was temporarily supplanted by the novelty; but the excitement over, it was perceived that the continual difficulties which were encountered in an arid country, unprovided with roads, rendered the use of the dromedary highly important, and the artillery of the zemboureks was reorganized. It is of this reorganization that I shall treat, describing the attempts made by the reigning family to introduce the European military system into Persia*, and concluding with a few general reflections upon the result of such efforts in Musselman countries.

PARTICULARITIES OF THE NATURAL HISTORY OF THE DROMEDARY.

There is but one species of camel indigenous to Persia; it is the dromedary with one hump. It is commonly known under the two denominations of *Dévèh* and of *Choutour*. The first is a *farsi* (Persian) word used among the tribes speaking the Tartar language, and is derived from the Persian word *der* or *deviden*, (to run, to make haste.) The second, *Choutour*, is used by the Persians who speak the *farsi*, and is derived from the Zend word, *Aster, Oustour,* or *Choutour*.†

The *Choutour-bad don Kouhé*, or camel with two humps, is not indigenous, and has always been brought into Persia, either from Tartary, Georgia, or other countries.‡

Following a due north and south line, we find these animals distributed as follows: From Orenburg to the southern shore of Lake

---

* Omitted, as it does not bear upon our immediate purpose.   H. C. W.

† The wealth of the caravans of dromedaries loaded with merchandise which arrive from Khiva at Asterabad, has given to the latter town the name it bears: *Aster*, dromedary; *abad*, town.

‡ A number of camels with two humps are brought from Trans-Oxana (Touran) into Persia, and yet they are never seen employed in the transportation of merchandise. The reason for this I understand is, that they are kept only for breeding, and that their issue takes always after the mother, which is selected from the females of the Persian dromedaries. Indeed, either by the influence of a warmer climate, or from a change in diet, the camels brought from Trans-Oxana, after being some time in Persia, lose gradually one of their humps. This agrees with the anatomical observation of Buffon, who distinguishes two kinds, and not two species; the one with one hump, which he calls the *dromedary;* the other with two humps, which he designates the *camel*.

There is sculptured on the first flight of the great staircase at Persepolis, a man in foreign costume, leading a camel with two humps by a cord through the nose, with no other trappings than a collar, to which is attached a small bell. This camel driver is one of those coming to present to the great king as offering the products of their native countries. A certain indication that the camel with two humps was of foreign origin.

Aral, the camel with two humps; from Lake Aral to the sea of Oran, the dromedary with one hump.

The dromedary is of two kinds, one strong and massive in form, which inhabits the north in the provinces of Azer-bijan, Irak-Adjemi, Asterabad, and Khorasan; the other weaker, but more active, found in the southern provinces of Khoosistan, Farsistan, Kerman, Yezd, Laristan, &c. The only provinces in which the camel is not raised is Koordistan, which is the extreme frontier, adjacent to Turkey, Ghilan, and Mazanderan, where the transportation is done by oxen, mules, &c.

The dromedary is not found wild. It lives for thirty years, but rarely attains that age, being either sacrificed in honor of some great personage,* or sold to the shambles. Their docility is proverbial; to such a degree that the Oriental fabulists say that the dromedary would be led by a mouse. Bad treatment makes them stupid; they become confused by it, but they are sensible to kindness. They retain their spite for a long time, and often revenge themselves upon those who maltreat them.† Before they are five years old they are trained to carry the pack-saddle. When too heavily loaded they utter plaintive cries, and even shed tears, and it is only by blows and by pushing them up from behind that they can be induced to rise. Arrived at the end of the stage, they are unloaded, with the exception of the pack-saddle, which is left on to prevent the animal from becoming chilled, the nights in Persia being cool even in summer. Throughout the year they sleep in the open air, care only being taken to shelter them from the wind, by placing them behind a wall, in the courtyard of a caravanserai, or in some low spot. Covered with large pieces of carpet and matting, and thus protected, they sleep even upon the snow.

When rutting they are vicious, and sometimes ferocious. They are then removed from their companions and the lower jaw and knee are tied together. If fond of the driver they will permit him to approach, and will receive food from him, but if they entertain any spite against him they will endeavor to avenge themselves by refusing food, by attacking, biting, or knocking him down, and will kill him if not prevented. Luckily, the rutting season is not the same for all in a herd of dromedaries; not more than two or three in twenty are in this condition at the same time, which allows of all necessary precautions being taken to avoid accidents; but if they become unmanageable they are castrated, and are only used in caravans for transporting mer-

---

* To do honor to distinguished guests in Persia it is customary to sacrifice a domestic animal in their presence, such as a sheep, goat, ox, or dromedary. The head of the slaughtered animal is thrown under the horses feet of the chief as he passes, and the flesh is distributed among his people.

† Reliable witnesses have assured me that a dromedary once, in revenge for bad treatment, deliberately rose from his place for the night, and going to his driver, lay down upon him with all his weight. The driver was found the next morning crushed under him. This same dromedary was sold to another master, who was probably more gentle, as he never afterwards exhibited any viciousness.

The *dēvēdjis* or *chuturbân*, (camel drivers,) have often told me that they were obliged to exhibit no preferences for any of their dromedaries, for fear of exciting jealousies among them; not only with the intention of preserving harmony, but to prevent their pining away.

chandise; this operation is performed at any age. The dromedary is so awkward in copulating that his driver has to direct him in the act.*

The flesh of the dromedary is served at the table of royalty, not as a rarity, but as a meat privileged by the Prophet.† The dromedary travels over ground of every description; they are very sure-footed, even when ascending slopes; they choose their steps with admirable instinct, and often when the ascent is very steep, they kneel and walk upon the callosities of the fore legs, trying thus to reach the summit by maintaining a horizontal position. Going down hill fatigues them, particularly in stony soils, and the rider has often, in such cases, to dismount; but in sandy soils they have a great superiority over all other animals.‡

They kneel down and get up easily, but this movement should not be repeated too often, especially after a long journey, and if they are loaded, for they will finally refuse to move and will not stir until they have rested. In the spring they shed their hair, which is pulled off in great handfuls, and is used for weaving carpets and other finer fabrics. In the north of Persia the young dromedaries are weaned when a year old, which is the cause of their being stronger than those of the south, where the milk is used by man. As soon as weaned they are turned out into the fields to feed. They seem to prefer the thistle and wormwood, (*aszantin*,) and find subsistence where the eye of man can only detect an arid soil. They resist hunger, and especially thirst, for several days. In winter they rarely drink, the snow which they eat sufficing them. When they have to work they must be fed either with bran or barley, and straw. They are fed in the evening, and a single feed lasts them for twenty-four hours. An hour after feeding they begin to ruminate, to finish only the next day at nearly the same hour. They eat ordinarily a *meni-tabrisi* (about six pounds) of barley, and about nine pounds of straw a day. Along the Gulf of Persia they are fed with dry fish§ or date nuts. They are driven by a cord fastened over the head, and are controlled in their movements by different whistles or gutteral sounds, sometimes by the whip.‖ Most dromedaries can make forced marches of fifteen *farsengs*

---

* This statement, in spite of its absurdity, is strictly true, and the Persians have assured me that it is always necessary.

† My Musselman cook has often passed it off upon me for beef, in order to get the advanced price for it.

‡ Rains are rare and last only a few hours, the earth absorbs them and immediately becomes dry. When the snow melts, however, and mud is formed, the dromedary then travels with great difficulty, particularly in going down hills.

The grand vizier, Hadji-Wirza-Agassi, gained great reputation by inventing a shoe for the dromedary. It was made of very thick leather, to which was attached a large horse-shoe, and was fastened on just above the hoof. This enabled the animal to travel over rocks. It appears, however, that shoeing the dromedary was practiced long since by the Kalmucks and Tartars inhabiting the Russian-Chinese frontier. We find in Corneille Le Brun (Vol. 1, p. 121) that the camels that traverse Lake Baïkal, on the route to China, are shod with boots ironed in such a manner as to enable them to walk on the ice.

§ Horses are in like manner fed with fish.

‖ They are so sensitive in the legs that the slightest blow makes them kneel; in consequence the drivers who have charge of large droves of dromedaries, employ the following means for stopping those that will not halt when ordered: whirling their *tchomach*, (a kind of stick with which they are armed,) they throw it with great skill at the legs of the refractory, which immediately stops them.

(fifty-four to sixty miles) a day. I have been told that some can accomplish twenty-five *farsengs*, which would be more than ninety miles, carrying, however, only a rider.*

The dromedary is not timid, and is easily accustomed to the sound of the drum and of cannon. They sometimes, however, take to starting, and are then seized by a kind of panic, from which it is difficult to recover them. On such occasions, if there are many in company, they huddle together, but do not run away.

The dromedary generally ambles. Their rapid gait is the trot. As for the gallop, they take it with difficulty, and only for a short time. All of their motions are rough and disagreeable; in pacing they have a rolling, pitching motion, which sometimes produces nausea; when trotting, their jerking step is apt to chafe, until familiarized to it by custom.

The dromedary is subject to several diseases of the skin and muscles, which are all cured by rubbing with grease, tar, or petroleum; by the use of *guili-ermeni*, (a very astringent red earth,) (sandix? H. C. W.) or by searing with a red-hot iron, which is the sovereign remedy. The Persians say, that to be proof against disease the dromedary should be covered with burns, and that it does not impair their value.

Government buys the dromedaries for its service at from 10 to 15 *tomans*, ($23 to $35.) There are some which cost more, but never to exceed 25 *tomans*, (about $56.) They are hired for 20 or 30 *châhis* a day, (from 22 to 33 cents.) Their ordinary load is about 120 *meni-tebrizi*, (somewhat more than 720 pounds.) I have seen some carrying the top of a large tent which weighed more than 1,000 pounds. An Asiatic proverb says: "When you want to travel, take a dromedary, for he will cross forty mountains without showing fatigue."— (*Tartar songs by M. Chodzko.*)

True child of the desert, the dromedary, in spite of its docility, can never be trained to the same regularity of movement and alignment as the horse. Its ungraceful figure, long neck, the slowness and awkwardness of its movement in turning about, the apathy which prevents it from sharing the excitement of the rider in presence of danger, and, in fine, its rough, jolting gait, cause it to be despised by the European military men who have not the same difficulties to contend with as the Asiatics and the Africans.

THE DROMEDARY AS A MEANS OF MILITARY TRANSPORTATION.

Each tribe in every part of Persia, from the extreme northern to the southern frontier of that vast kingdom, possesses a number of dromedaries, which constitutes the larger part of its possessions. From the earliest ages they have been used as a means of transport-

---

* Hussein-Khan, who came to France in 1836 as ambassador, and who had been nominated governor of Yezd, presented to the grand vizier a hundred dromedaries from his province, which were so swift that horses that followed them at a gallop remained so far behind, after an hour's running, as to be unable to overtake them. This trial was made before the whole court and in presence of the king.

ation in caravans, and also in the service of military expeditions. There is not a common *mirza* attached to the *defter** who has not dromedaries of his own. Far from being an expense to their owner, they are employed to his profit in transporting military supplies in war and merchandise in peace; whence it is that the government is never apprehensive of the want of the means of transportation in its expeditions.†

The dromedaries attached to regiments belong to the colonel, who, as required, employs them in transporting hard bread or flour. It is to the interest of this officer to treat his men well, as he is always chosen from the chiefs of their tribe; they are really his clansmen. He must seek to be beloved by them to keep his office.‡ He must know, moreover, how to enhance his services with the king, the means by which grants of villages, honors, and titles are obtained. The colonel furnishes, also, the dromedaries required for the transportation of the sick and wounded; the government, therefore, is never troubled with these details. The Persian soldiers carry neither knapsack nor haversack. At the beginning of the campaign each foot soldier receives from the government a *toman* (about $2 25) to procure a baggage animal. Five men unite to buy an ass, if the expedition is into a mountainous country; and 10 *tomans* to buy a dromedary, if the campaign is in a level one. The animal is loaded with their tents, clothes, and guns, and sometimes with provisions to sell. This traffic is very profitable, for often they return home with large sums of money acquired by it, and also by other lawful means. The colonels are also charged, at government expense, with the transportation of munitions of war, and are held responsible for them.§

To give all the details of the system would force me beyond the limits I have prescribed to myself.‖ A few notes which I add will enable the reader to understand how this system, in spite of the long train it involves, gives to the army greater mobility when once in motion, and is exactly suited to the Persian method of warfare.

The dromedary, then, has always been employed in Persia as a means of military transportation.¶ This animal, steady as well as patient, and capable of performing long and toilsome journeys, is especially of indisputable service in this vast country, where the villages are at long distances from each other, and where in the country between them there are neither roads practicable for carriages nor bridges to cross the deep ravines worn by torrents. The mountain

---

* A civil officer who attends the king in his campaigns. The shah of Persia is always accompanied by his ministers, even in his longest expeditions.

† It may be said that every man in the country understands the nature, hygean, defects, and good qualities of the dromedary. There is no necessity, therefore, for any instruction of the Persian soldiers in these particulars.

‡ It has more than once happened that an avaricious colonel, who has neglected his men, has been contumeliously dragged by them to the feet of the king, where he has cruelly expiated the privations he had imposed upon them.

§ When the king heads the expedition, the munitions of war are transported by the dromedaries attached to the *karkhané*, (arsenal.)

‖ Omitted, as they do not bear upon our immediate purpose.—H. C. W.

¶ Parmenion took possession of the camp of the barbarians, with all its baggage, elephants, and dromedaries, (Arrian, book III, chap. 5.)

ranges are only broken by *dèrè*, (passes,) narrow valleys, which open upon a desert covered with crystallized salt, under which are here and there enormous quicksands, in which sometimes man and beast are swallowed up without the possibility of receiving assistance. Elsewhere this desert is covered with moving sands,* in which an oasis occasionally appears as an island in the sea. Indeed, a large portion of the soil is without vegetation, without water, and perfectly uninhabitable.

THE EQUIPMENT OF THE BELOUTCHIS, AND THEIR INCURSIONS INTO PERSIA.

The successive use of different arms has modified, accordingly, the equipment of the dromedary. We will endeavor to describe the changes it has successively undergone.

Before the invention of fire-arms, the dromedary was, according to the accounts of Grecian historians, and apparently, mounted and equipped as they still are now by the Beloutchis, who have not all profited by the improvements in arms. When these Nomads, who are constantly at war with Persia, wish to make an incursion into Kermân, they are organized in the following manner: Each dromedary is mounted by two men, who ride back to back upon a wooden saddle. The front one guides the animal by a rope bridle fastened to the headstall. He is armed with a bow and arrows;† a sword hangs by his side; and a shield, covered with leather, is thrown over his shoulder. The other, facing the tail of the animal, has no projectiles; he is there to cover the retreat, and, in consequence, is armed only with a long *kama*, (poignard,) or sabre, and with a long lance. Their provisions consist of barley bread for fifteen days, curdled milk in a skin bag, and a leather bottle of water suspended under their animal's belly. To which is added, whenever they can get it, lumps of *asafœtida*, of which they are very fond. A number of dromedaries thus equipped leave the province of Bampour, cross the desert, and fall suddenly upon the provinces of Kermân, or Yezd, carrying death and destruction into all the villages through which they pass, and plundering and massacreing the caravans.‡ The governors of these two provinces send in pursuit of them horsemen and dromedaries, better

---

* When Pottinger entered the great desert of Kermân, he saw that its surface differed from those of the deserts of Africa and Arabia; there was something in it more formidable. The particles of sand are so light and fine, that, held in the hand, they are scarcely perceptible to the touch. Impelled by the wind, they form hills, of which one side, almost perpendicular, resembles a brick wall, as much in form as in color, from the reddish hue of the sand. The side exposed to the wind presents, on the contrary, a gentle slope. The traveller has to find his way through these ranges of sand-hills in the narrow passes or ravines between them. It is very difficult to cross these ranges, particularly to climb their steep sides; and one is often baffled in the attempt, and obliged to turn them. They are from 10 to 20 feet in height. The dromedaries actively scale the sloping side, their large feet preventing them from sinking into the sand. Arrived at the top, they kneel and slide down, carrying the sand with them; the first thus opening a breach through which the others follow. The sand flying through the air gives to the atmosphere the appearance of a thick fog, and, penetrating the mouth, the eyes, and the nostrils, produces a painful irritation and excessive thirst.

† Within a few years some of them have been seen armed with long match-locks.

‡ The Beloutchis do not regard themselves as lawful possessors of booty until they have slain its owner.

Ex. Doc. 62——14

armed, undoubtedly, but who, however, do not always succeed in capturing them; for at the approach of danger, the Beloutchis rapidly retreat, taking off everything they can carry. If they cannot escape, they fight to the death. The Persians have several times endeavored to subjugate these troublesome neighbors, but always unsuccessfully.

In 1838, Mehemed Shah sent against the Beloutchis the Emir Top-Khané, (commander of the artillery,) with a corps of 500 cavalry, 2,500 infantry, and four field-pieces. Arrived at Bampour, after encountering a thousand difficulties, the soldiers found no enemy. They had dispersed. The army, in the midst of those vast deserts, before a deserted town,* had to retrace its steps to save itself from destruction, although it was partly supplied by the province of Kermân.†

These facts have been stated to show of what utility the dromedary, mounted with armed men, has been in all ages, and the conclusions we should draw from them in considering their applicability to artillery purposes for the defence of an exclusively desert frontier of 480 *farsengs* (1,800 miles) in extent.

---

* This extreme measure has been resorted to by the Persians from the earliest ages. If they did not follow the advice given to them by Memnon, the Rhodian, at the time of Alexander's expedition, it was either because they had great confidence in the number of their troops, or, which is most probable, because they wished to destroy that skilful general in the opinion of Darius.—(*Arrian, Voy.*, chap. 4.)

Pietro del Valle tells us that Shah Abbas, on the 30th of August, 1619, ordered the inhabitants of Tabriz to desert it, and to betake themselves to a place of safety, with all their furniture and property, abandoning their houses empty to the Turks, with whom he was at war.

The present King, upon the news of the death of his father, Mehemed Shah, set out from Tabriz, at the head of 20,000 men and s x field-pieces, for Teheran, to take possession of his throne. Having been in attendance upon him in his father's lifetime, and having known him since he was five years old, I thought it my duty to go out to meet him, and, accordingly, set out on the 9th October, 1848, for Casbin. Upon my route I found only deserted villages. The houses empty, and the doors unhinged. (Such is the fear which the march of a *corps d'armee* inspires, that the unfortunate villagers, knowing by sad experience that they are pillaged and robbed by the troops of the country as they would be by those of an enemy, run away, carrying off their movables, or concealing them in places prepared expressly for such contingencies. The houses which they abandon, being built of sun-dried bricks, are easily repaired; and, besides, they prefer to run the risk of losing their houses, which they can again rebuild in a few days, than the loss of what they have laboriously acquired by years of toil.) A few fields of standing crops, which there had not been time to harvest, alone remained. Meeting with no villagers, and perceiving the impossibility of procuring provisions for myself and escort, I went some leagues out of my way to the house of Mehemed-Kherim-Khan, brother of the *begler-begui* (prefect) of Teheran, who offered me hospitality, and gave me provisions to continue on my road, assuring me that for four leagues around I would find only deserted villages. Indeed, until arriving at Kichlah I met no one. This town being surrounded by a crenelated wall, its inhabitants had entrenched themselves within it, and barricaded the gates against marauders. I had to parley a long time before I could gain an entrance. Explaining to them my rank in the army, and that I was a European, which always inspires them with confidence, they greeted me as a liberator, and asked me to defend them until the arrival of the Shah. I was so fortunate as to succeed, by threats, in dispersing the troops which had collected around desiring to pillage the town. The arrival of Nasraden Shah put an end to this petty siege. The town of Casbin, to avoid the heavy losses always sustained by the march of troops through the country, offered to the young monarch a considerable sum if he would be so good as not to stop there. The King accepted the offer, and only passed through it. A month after these events, I repassed the same place. They had resumed their usual appearance, and were as populous as ever.

† This is the same country of the Gedrosians, in which a portion of Alexander's army was destroyed by hunger, thirst, and disease. Dromedaries were employed by the governors of Caramania to carry provisions to the troops, and so saved the remains of the army.—(*Plutarch, Book IX, chap. 10.*)

INTRODUCTION OF FIRE-ARMS INTO PERSIA.

Under the reign of Shah Abbas 1st, of the race of Sophis, the Persians adopted the match-lock, of which they had learned the use from the Turks.* It was probably at this period that the idea was conceived of mounting upon dromedaries the small cannon which they now carry. We cannot, however, unfortunately, do all the justice which is due to it, nor give minutely the services it rendered to Persia before the invasion of the Affghans; for the historians and chroniclers, according to the customs of their country, attribute to the monarch alone all the successes obtained in battle, avoiding the mention of anything which does not refer exclusively to the person of the King. Thus, the historian of the *Zoubd-oul-tevarin* relates, as an apology for defeat, and to conceal the inferiority of the Persian arms, that when battle was offered by Selim to Shah Ismail, in 1514, (920,) upon the frontiers of Azerbidgan, "the cannon of Selim were strongly bound together to stop the charge of the Persian cavalry, and the sabre of the prince who commanded cut the heavy chain by which they were united. But all was useless; from that moment the day was irretrievably lost." This rhodomantade apparently would indicate that the Persians finally perceived that the valor of their brave cavalry was not sufficient of itself to conquer an enemy supported by such terrible auxiliaries.

It is a fact, that, from the reign of the Shahs Sophy, until that of the Shahs Kadyar, the Persians possessed only some old pieces, captured from the Portuguese, at the taking of Hermouz, † and those which are now seen exhibited as trophies upon the royal squares of towns. These last are ungainly masses of bronze, cast, in the time of the Shah Abbas, by the English who were in his service. ‡ These pieces, on account of the difficulty of transporting them, and their bad quality, § dissatisfied the Persians, and made them value more their

---

* Pietro del Valle, who followed the camp of King Abbas 1st, in 1619, in an expedition against the Turks, thus speaks in his naive manner: "The king from day to day discontinues as much as possible the use of the bow and arrow as good for nothing and a great incumbrance, in order to introduce fire-arms gradually throughout the army, because he perceived, and justly, that in comparison with them, other projectiles were trifling and harmless."

† According to Pietro del Valle, eighty pieces of all calibres were taken from the Portuguese by the Anglo-Persian army, which divided them.

‡ This statement seems to be sustained by the following passage by a contemporary writer, in a memoir upon the travels of Sir Robert Shirley: "The powerful Ottoman trembles at the operations of the Shirley's, (the English in the service of Shah Abbas 1st,) and already we may hope that his destruction is nigh at hand. The victorious Persians have learnt from Shirley the art of war; lately they were as yet ignorant of discipline; now they have five hundred pieces of cannon, (this number seems to be exorbitant for that period, unless there is comprised in it also all the falconets which are at present seen in the royal square at Ispahan,) and 60,000 men armed with muskets. When they possessed only the sword, they made the Turks tremble; now they have become more formidable, as their attacks are made from greater distances, and they can use their new arms with skill."—(*Purchaser's Pilgrims, vol.* 11, *p.* 1806.)

§ I introduce here a conversation held in the presence of Pietro del Valle, between Shah Abbas 1st and the English resident at Ispahan. Shah Abbas, after pointing out to the resident a heavy Portuguese cannon, said that he could not make use of such heavy artillery; that it delayed his march; that the advantage which his troops had over the Turks was in

dromedary artillery, which without any hindrance, followed them with the utmost rapidity from one end of the kingdom to the other.

THE ARMY IS NEGLECTED.—REVOLT OF THE AFFGHANS.—BATTLE OF GOUL NABAT.—FIRST USE OF ZEMBOUREKS.

I cannot omit a brief sketch of the lamentable history of the Shah Sultan Hussein, one of the last princes of the family of Sophy, that reigned in Persia, for it was under his reign that the Affghans used the dromedary with the greatest success in the execution of some of their boldest attacks. This weak monarch, guided by the advice of the Mollahs and eunuchs, plunged his country into the most deplorable condition. In the first years of his reign he so abandoned himself to the pleasures of the harem, that the epoch received the name of the "hunt for virgins"; * afterwards, age having subdued his passions, he became as fanatic as he had been profligate. The enormous expenses of his harem, † the gifts to mosques, and the fees to priests, by dissipating the revenues of the state, rendered it impossible to maintain an army capable of defending the independence of the nation, or even of suppressing revolts. The astrologers predicted from the phenomena happening at that time ‡ inevitable misfortunes, which the Mollahs, however, promised to avert by public prayers. The eunuchs, the courtiers, the swarm of princes and princesses, § and even the physicians, who promised to re-establish the exhausted powers of the king by prescriptions into which diamonds and rubies

---

rapidity of movement; that to besiege a town, he would prefer to transport metal on the backs of camels, and cast before it a heavy piece of artillery.

In 1838, at the siege of Herat, the king, Mahemed Shah, observing that his field artillery did not produce the desired effect upon the fortifications of the town, had a bronze piece of 48 cast. It was bored, turned, and mounted in the same manner as the finest piece from the arsenal, and all of it done before the besieged town. When the siege was raised, (which lasted ten months,) the king had it sawed into pieces and transported to Teheran. As a memorial of this deed, the mouth of the piece was placed in the royal square at Teheran, where it may still be seen.

* The historians of the time relate that the governors of the different provinces had orders to send to the Shah all the beautiful girls they could find, and that they had obeyed with so much zeal, that in a single month there were presented to the king thirty cradles containing as many little princes and princesses.

† This prince, contrary to the custom of his predecessors, preserved all of his women and children. Until then, it had been the barbarous practice to put to death all the women who became needless to the pleasures of the Shah; and to put out the eyes of the male children for the purpose of destroying their pretensions to the throne, and so assuring it to the heir designated by the king.

‡ The author of a Persian manuscript says, that the sun was obscured during ten days, and that the horizon in all that time was of a red and bloody hue. Father Kruzinski, an eye-witness, observes that in the summer of the year 1721 the clouds were thicker than common, that the sun had a color red as blood, which lasted for nearly two months. He adds: "that the astronomers declared that it announced a great effusion of blood; and that this prediction increased the general consternation."

Tabriz was completely destroyed by an earthquake, by which a large number of the inhabitants lost their lives. According to the memoirs of Kruzinski, (p. 186,) there perished by it near 80,000 persons.

§ He had one hundred and eighty children.

entered,* rivalled each other in their rapacity in impoverishing the public treasury. By the intrigues of the courtiers, the king was induced to put away the only two honest and able persons who were devoted to him—two brothers—Feth-Ali-Khan, the grand vizir, and Loutf-Ali-Khan, general-in-chief of his armies.

The Kurds, the Lesguis, the Affghans, as well as the Sheik of Muscat, took up arms, not only to shake off the Persian yoke, but each to be the first to seize upon the tottering throne. Mir Vais, the Affghan, had, by his intrigues at court, and by his arms, succeeded in freeing all Affghanistan. His son, Mahmoud, twenty-three years old, having by a murder revenged the usurpation of his uncle, Mir-Abdallah, and caused himself to be recognized as the king of that country, put in execution the plan of his father, and marched, with the boldness that characterizes the nation, against the King of Persia, whom he attacked in the very heart of his dominions. After incredible fatigues and privations of all kinds, he crossed the desert of Sistan and of Kermân with his army of 15,000 men, the largest part transported on dromedaries. Obliged to carry forage, and even water,† he came, not without, however, a great loss of men and horses, to besiege the town Kermân. Repulsed the first time by Loutf-Ali-Khan, he profited by the disgrace in which the latter had fallen; and, undismayed by the difficulties he had experienced in his first expedition, he retook the same road, set a ransom on the governor of Kermân, did not stop to besiege Yezd, seized upon all the horses to remount his troops, and to mount those who had been provisionally mounted upon dromedaries, and taking the shortest route, although the most arid, pitched his camp upon the summit of Goul-Nabat, at three leagues from Ispahan, which then contained 600,000 souls.

The court and the inhabitants of Ispahan were stupified by this bold attack. The town was completely without provisions and the supplies necessary to sustain a siege. The troops which should have defended it were disbanded or scattered along the frontiers; the panic increased, and money was offered in order to gain time. Mahmoud refused it, answering that "everything belonged to him, even the crown." This arrogant reply left no other alternative than a resort to arms. Recovered from their first stupification, and considering the small number of their assailants, the Persians collected all who were capable of bearing arms and marched against the enemy.

We shall perhaps trespass upon the patience of the reader by

---

* When the Affghans, masters of Ispahan, taxed all the grandees oft he kingdom at a high rate, the Hakim-Bachi (first physician to the king) was taxed at 20,000 tomans, (about $463,000.) This man had been for a long time the sole favorite of his master, and was reproached for using his influence with him only to amass immense wealth. The overseers of the tax weighed jewels without taking into account the value of the precious stones in them, estimating them at two crowns the miskal, (about 80 grains troy.) I am told that what was taken from this man was not less than 100,000 tomans, ($2,315,000.)

† It is stated in the reports of the embassy of Douri-Effendi, minister from the Porte to the court of Persia, "that the Affghans were mounted by twos and threes upon camels, animals accustomed to bear thirst, and to subsist upon little Arrived at the edge of the desert, they were loaded with water, and each soldier filling the entrails of sheep, which they carried for this purpose, wound around their bodies in the manner of a sash, the army entered upon the desert."

giving a minute detail of the relative positions of the two armies; but the zemboureks having played the principal part in this action, it seems to us indispensable to do so.

The royal army which marched out of Ispahan on Sunday the 8th of March, 1722, (1135,) amounted to more than 60,000 men and 24 pieces of cannon.

The two armies were disposed as follows: the Persian right wing was composed of 2,000 *goulams*, (mounted body guards,) armed in part with bows and arrows, and in part with guns or pistols, under the command of Rustem-Khan, their general; of 3,000 Arab cavalry, under the orders of their Vali; of a great number of *Khans*, with their retinues, mounted. The left wing consisted of officers of the king, of noblemen of the court, on horseback, of the Vali of Loristan, Ali-Merdan-Khan, with 5,000 horsemen in his train,* and of more than 8,000 militia on foot, armed with muskets. The centre contained the reserve, and was commanded by Sheik Ali-Khan, general of cavalry. He had under his orders some *Khans*, with their retinues, about 4,000 horse guards, and a like number of foot guards; these last armed with guns and sabres. The front was covered by a battery of 24 cannon. The command in chief was divided between the Vali of Arabia, who commanded the right wing, and the grand vizir, Attemat-Doulet, who commanded the left wing.

The Affghan army was divided into four divisions. The largest formed the right wing under the orders of Emanoullah Khan. The left wing was composed of a body of new levies recruited among the Guebres, fire-worshippers, the Bloutchis, and the Indians,† commanded by Nasr Oullah. Mahmoud reserved to himself the centre with a "corps d'elite" called *pehlevans* (heroes.)‡ Behind the right wing of the Affghans kneeled 100 dromedaries, each carrying a gun.

Eye-witnesses tell us that "the length of the journey and the celerity of the march had not permitted Mahmoud to bring with him any cannon, but a singular kind of artillery supplied in some measure this deficiency. They were arquebuses pivoted, as large as those called by our seamen 'swivel,' which can carry at a load a handful of musket balls. Each of these guns mounted on a saddle formed, with its gunner, the load of a dromedary, and it was upon the backs of

---

* He was accompanied by his two daughters who followed him everywhere, and fought in men's attire and clothed in armor. I saw at Teheran one of the daughters of Feth Ali Shah, wife of the Vali of Senna, who had several times accompanied her sons in their military expeditions; she was a good shot with a pistol, and wielded the lance skilfully. These eccentricities, so exceptionable to musselmen, are seen only among the nomadic tribes, in which the women go with the face uncovered.

† It is very probable that the greater part of these recruits were raised among the Loutis (sans culottes) vagabonds, who are always ready to serve, for plunder, the first daring fellow that offers. There are large numbers of them in all the towns of Persia, and it is often necessary to turn out the military against them. During my residence in Persia, one of them was seized, who had been proclaimed king by his companions, and, by order of the Shah, his teeth were extracted, and set around his head in the manner of a crown.

‡ The duty of these was to begin the attack, and then to fall back in the rear of the line to encourage and sustain the different corps, to kill the runaways, and to succor the wounded.

these animals, trained to the exercise, that the guns were loaded and fired." This would seem to indicate that the Persians had it not then in their army, for M. Guiseppe, who was the interpreter of M. Gardone, French consul at Ispahan, speaks of it as a thing entirely new.*

The army of the Affghans amounted only to 20,000 men—that is to say, to about a third of that of the Persians. It consisted almost entirely of cavalry. Each man carried a sabre, a long lance which he wielded equally as well,† and was protected by a cuirass of very thick leather doubled, a buckler hung over the shoulder; several had long pistols in their girdles.‡

The action was commenced by the right wing of the Persians, who at first threw the Affghans into a little confusion. The vali, of Arabia, turning their flank rapidly, fell upon their camp, which the Arabs were so long occupied in pillaging that they did nothing else during the battle. Perhaps their chief saw with pleasure that the left wing, commanded by his rival, had been thrown into disorder. This body had charged the Affghan right wing, commanded by Eman-Oullah. As soon as this skilful warrior saw the enemy approach him, he fell back as if retreating. The Persians heedlessly pursued with ardor, but soon the enemy's ranks opened and discovered a line of one hundred dromedaries kneeling, each with a gun on his back, from which a fire was so well delivered that the front ranks of the charging column were cut down; and before the Persians could recover from the confusion into which this cannonade had thrown them, they were attacked by the Affghan cavalry and completely routed. Eman-Oullah pursued them for some time. Attacking then the Persian artillery in rear, he found it without defence, sabred the cannoneers, and turned the pieces against the Persian infantry, which formed the centre. The Persians were so astonished and panic-struck at seeing

---

* According to all the testimony I have been able to collect, it seems that the Affghans were the first who used the dromedary in the manœuvres of the *zembourek*, and who arranged the falconet on a saddle upon a movable pivot. The Persians, like the Indians, had used this kind of gun for a long time; but dromedaries or elephants were employed only to transport them, they being served, mounted on wooden carriages clumsily made, and standing on the ground.

† Fencing with the sword and the buckler is the favorite exercise of the Affghans Although skilful at it, their appearance when engaged is not graceful, for, gathering themselves in a peculiar manner under the buckler to protect the upper part of the body, they direct their attacks against the legs or bellies of their adversaries. I have often fenced with their best swordsmen, and satisfied myself that it is very difficult to touch them in that position.

‡ The Europeans who were at that time at Djoulfa, (one of the suburbs of Ispahan,) and who observed the two armies through their spy-glasses, thus speak of the difference between the two armies: "That of the Persians going scarcely beyond the ramparts, and composed almost entirely of the brilliancy of the court, and also of the rest of the empire, appeared less made to fight than to dazzle the eye. The richness and variety of their arms and uniforms, the beauty of the horses, the gold and precious stones with which the trappings were ornamented, the magnificence of the flags as seen in the distance, all united in forming a gorgeous and pompous spectacle. On the other side, there was an inconsiderable body of soldiers worn by fatigue and the heat of the sun. Their clothing, tarnished and torn by so long a march, scarcely sufficed to shield them from the weather; their worn down horses were only covered with leather and brass; the steel heads of their lances and their sabres were the only glittering things among them."

their own artillery turned upon themselves, that they fled from the field of battle in disorder, and the rout became general.*

From this account we see that the manœuvres of the Affghans were combined according to the effects that the zemboureks were to produce, and that the faults of the Persians contributed to the success of the plan. The Affghans, it is said, dared not pursue the Persians for fear of an ambush; but it is more probable that they busied themselves in plundering the wealth of the camp which the latter had just abandoned.† From an inexplicable weakness, Mahmoud, after he had won the victory, seemed frightened by his success. He withdrew into his entrenchments, and the next day permitted the Persians to return to the field and to carry off some of the cannon which had been left there. The events of the siege offer nothing of importance, and it would be repugnant to speak of the barbarities which were then committed.

The greater part of the Persian chiefs, as is the custom in such armies, returned home with their followers as soon as the battle was lost.

CONDITION OF PERSIA.—FORMATION OF A CORPS OF ZEMBOUREKS IN THE PERSIAN ARMY.—BATTLE BETWEEN THE AFFGHANS AND OTTOMANS.—BATTLE BETWEEN THE AFFGHANS AND PERSIANS.—THE PERSIAN ARMY FORCES THE SIRDAR PASS, (THE CASPIAN GATES.)—EXPULSION OF THE AFFGHANS.—CONQUEST OF THEIR COUNTRY.—BATTLES AND SIEGES IN WHICH THE ZEMBOUREKS WERE EMPLOYED.

Jahmasb Mirza, son of the Shah Sultan Hussien, succeeded, after running great risks in escaping from Ispahan, during the siege, with 300 horsemen. His object was to recruit, in the towns remaining faithful to the shah, an army for the relief of the capital, and the delivery of his unfortunate father. But his inexperience, and the luxurious habits acquired in the jealous seclusion of the harem, rendered him unfit for the accomplishment of so difficult a mission. And he would not have succeeded in relieving his country from its abasement but for a combination of favorable circumstances. First, the error of the rebels in alienating the people by repeated mortifications; and secondly, the meeting with a chief of his partizans, named Jahmasb-Konli-Khan,‡ who became afterwards the greatest general of his time. Since the death of Abbas the Great, the Persians had sunk into apathy and complete demoralization, of which the court set the example. In this state of things the frontier provinces of Turcomania, constantly disquieted by barbarians and reduced by the neglect of their nobles to defend their independence themselves, had alone preserved sufficient energy to aid the efforts of their general. Geor-

---

* See the memoirs of Kurzinski, page 205, and the History of Persia by Sir John Malcolm.

† According to the accounts of that time the Persian army lost on that day 6,000 men, the greater part being from the body guards. The cannoneers having been surrounded; were sabred with their commander. A Parisian, named Philip Coulon, who had passed from the service of Russia to that of Persia, and held an important office in its artillery, perished also. The loss of the Affghan army did not exceed 2,000 men.

‡ Who afterwards proclaimed himself king, took the name of Nadir-Shah, and was the modern hero of Persia.

gia, Azerbidjan, as also a part of Irak-Adjemi, were occupied by Ottoman troops; all the shores of the Caspian sea, from Bacou to Mazanderan, were held by the troops of the Czar; Arabia and the coasts of the Persian Gulf had declared themselves independent; and the Affghans had subdued, by the force and terror of their arms, all the rest, except the country lying on the two slopes of the mountain chain of Elbourg, from Isheran to Meched.* The position of Jahmasb-Mirza, it is thus seen, was identically the same as that of Darius Codoman; and if he had been pursued by the Affghans as Darius was by Alexander, his end would have been as tragical. A new Bessus, Jamasb-Konli-Khan betrayed also his master; however, before he did it he freed his country. Without wishing to extenuate, in the least, the odium of this treason, we will suggest, however, that he may have been led to it by the incapacity of the young prince. Be this as it may, Jamasb-Konli-Khan set about subduing all the towns of Khorassan which had not openly pronounced for Jamasb-Shah; (the young prince took this title as soon as his father had abdicated in favor of Mahmoud the Affghan.) He trained his troops for war, and rallied many tribes in his cause. The detail of these wars is very interesting, when compared with those of the time of the Macedonian invasion. Their examination proves clearly that the flight of Darius from Margiana was not an inconsiderate act, nor the pursuit of Alexander an imprudence, having for its object only the gratification of vanity. The Persian monarch knew that as long as he could hold the shore of the Caspian sea and Khorassan,† he could preserve the hope of reconquering his empire. There only is found the sap of the warlike races of Asia. With the exception of the religion, the people have remained the same. There also will probably be decided in our time the fate of Asia.

But these speculations, into which we have been insensibly drawn, have carried us away too far from our artillery, to which we will return.

As soon as Tahmasb-Kouli-Khan thought himself sufficiently strong to make head against the Affghans, he descended from the mountains, and crossing the plains which separate Meched from the province of Herat, he carried the war into the enemy's country. This stratagem produced all the results he anticipated; first, he attacked his enemies where they were wholly unprepared for defence, and by this means depriving the Affghans, who occupied Ispahan, of the assistance which they expected; he forced them to return with their cavalry to attack him in their turn upon ground favorable to his troops. A thing not less important was also a near acquaintance with his adversaries, whose deeds rumor had greatly exaggerated, and of putting to profit, as we shall see, everything which could be advantageous to his troops. Let us hear what the historian Mirza Mehdi says: "The Persian general, quitting the town of Asfendin, entered the enemy's country with his army. Having formed his troops in column, he marched them against Mandjanabat. A sandy desert

---

* Ancient Hyrcania, Margiana and Parthia.
† Nadir-Shah surnamed this province "the Sword of Persia."

lying before this place, he was obliged to dismount his cannon from their carriages, and to load them upon dromedaries. Tahmasb-Kouli-Khan himself mounted upon one of these animals, and giving the example of an indefatigable courage, *seemed like the sun upon the throne of the firmament.*" During the same expedition, at the siege of the fort of Senan, the general was in a battery, when a heavy gun burst and endangered his life. This incident, with the difficulties he had experienced in transporting heavy artillery, caused him to appreciate the advantages he would find in the organization of a dromedary artillery, which could accompany him everywhere without hindrance. Laying aside all prejudice, he eagerly turned to account the important capture of a number of zemboureks which he had just made at Kafir Kalé. He also availed himself of the military music, which, too, was mounted on camels. Profiting thus by the invention and the arms of the enemy, he formed immediately a corps, which Mirza Mehdi calls toubkhene-tchilon, (portable artillery,)* which always afterwards accompanied his person in his rapid marches, whilst the heavy siege artillery, drawn by buffalo, or by prisoners retained for this painful labor,† arrived upon the field by circuitous routes, and often after the battle had been decided, its principal service being to fire a few rounds at towns about to surrender after a long siege. If Tamasb-Kouli-Khan had possessed education with the genius nature had given him, he would probably have improved the zemboureks, instead of handing them down to us exactly as he had taken them from the Affghans. But this extraordinary man, whom the Persians are pleased to compare to the great Napoleon, had only strong natural intellect for his guide; he did not even know how to read, and learned to sign his name only after he became king.

Whilst this was passing at Khorassan, and the royal army becoming organized, a Turkish army of 60,000 men* and 70 cannon marched from Hamadan, in 1726, (1138,) upon Ispahan, under the orders of Ahmed-Pasha Seraskier. Achraff (successor of Mahmoud, the usurper of the Persian throne) marched to meet it with 30,000 Affghan troops, and 40 zemboureks mounted on dromedaries, the only artillery he could raise. (It is asserted that Achraff, surrounded by his principal ministers, and elevated, according to the custom of the kings of India, upon a throne borne by an elephant, amused himself during the battle in playing upon the flute.) Nevertheless, the Ottomans were beaten, and lost 12,000 men. The rout would have been complete if Achraff had not stopped his soldiers in their eager pursuit of an enemy with whom he preferred peace rather than war.† The Turkish general, after this defeat, was obliged to fall back on Kermauchah, abandoning his artillery and baggage to the conquerors.

---

* This author rarely uses the word *zembourek.*

† "The zemindars (noblemen who farm cantons, and sometimes even provinces of the government) shut themselves up in their fortresses, and instead of tribute, promised us cannon balls. But the army investing them, they soon surrendered at discretion. Not only were their lives spared, but even their property, on condition that they would transport the artillery to Khoda-Abad."—(*Travels of Abdul Kerim ; account of the march of Nadir Shah's army between Attek and Kandahar in* 1739.)

* M. Gardané says 120,000 men.

† Hanway, vol. II, p. 250.

The brave Tahmasb-Kouli-Khan, after great difficulties, succeeded in organizing an army of 40,000 men, which he encamped in Khorassan, and awaited, without flinching, for Achraff, who was marching against him with all the Affghan forces he had been able to assemble. This latter, presuming too much upon the valor of his troops, who, besides, were superior in number to the Persians, marched towards Damgan, a town of Khorassan, and on the 2d of October, 1729, (1141,) gave battle. Achraff resorted to the stratagem which had formerly been successful: he detached two bodies of cavalry, of 3,000 men each, who, making a wide detour for the purpose of concealing the manœuvre, were to turn the wings of the Persian line and take it in rear, whilst he, at the same time, attacked in front. But the Persian general was not a man to allow himself to be surprised. Causing his wings to fall back, for a feint, he drew on the two bodies of Affghans to the foot of a mountain, which he had fortified in advance with artillery, and behind which was posted King Tahmasb with the reserve; there, caught between two fires, the cavalry was completely destroyed. Achraff, seeing that his stratagem had been turned against himself, endeavored to force the centre with all the impetuosity of Affghan troops. He was received almost at the muzzles of the pieces, with a blaze of fire from zemboureks and musketry. "They were so enveloped in flame and smoke that they seemed to float in a sea of fire. After this discharge, the Persians advanced in good order and shot down the standard-bearer. When Achraff saw the standard of his fortunes beaten down, he fled with precipitation." The Affghans suffered much; besides a great many dead, their baggage and their camp fell into the hands of the victors.

A misunderstanding between Tahmasb and his general delayed the pursuit, and permitted Achraff to rally his troops at Veramin, upon the road from Teheran, whence he sent Aslan-Khan to defend the pass of Serdir-Khar, one of the *Caspian Gates* which crosses from east to west the mountain chain forming the spur perpendicular to the grand chain of Elbourg, and which ends in the Salt desert lying to the south.‡ "The road through it is so difficult," says a Persian author, "that ants can scarcely cross it." The Affghan general, at the head of his volunteers, established there his zemboureks, protected by musketeers, and placed his cavalry in ambuscade. "The videttes reported to the Persian general the disposition of the enemy. Immediately this lion of battle dismounted from his fiery charger, scaled the mountain on foot, at the head of five or six thousand musketeers—tigers in war—and crowning the summit of the pass with the agile artillery of the zemboureks, turned the position, delivered a plunging fire into the Affghan artillery, made himself master of it, and thus gained the possession of the pass." (*Mirza Mehdi, History of Nadir.*) This ac-

‡ "The gorge of Serdir is a road a farsang longer than that of Sialek, but less fatiguing for horses. (Sialek is a defile more to the north, and agrees better than the other with the description of Pliny.) Numerous towers, bastions, and caravanserais, surrounded by crenelated walls, attest the importance of this defile, and at the same time the facility with which the passage of an army might be disputed. The chain which this defile crosses may be turned by taking the road through the desert, but to do this one must travel over sand and salt marshes for more than thirty hours without a drop of drinkable water on the road."—(*A. Chodzko, New Annals of Travels.*)

count of the Persian author will not be thought surprising, when we consider that each of these small cannon, not weighing more than 75 pounds, could be easily carried by the artillerists to the top of the mountain.

The Affghans made forced marches towards Ispahan and established themselves in a strong position, fortified beforehand, near the village of Mourdekin-Khour. Although the Persian general found the Affghan army strongly entrenched, he determined to attack it. The Affghans defended themselves with bravery, but nothing could withstand the fury with which they were assaulted, and they left upon the field of battle 4,000 of their best soldiers. The rest took flight, and with such precipitancy that Tahmasb-Kouli-Khan could not overtake them until at Persepolis, distant more than 200 farsangs (about 795 miles) from the first field of battle.*

"Indeed, our victorious Nadir, rising, like the glorious sun, from the horizon of his prosperous fortunes, forced these rebels to imitate the owl, and to hide their heads for fear of being dazzled."

Tahmasb-Kouli-Khan, after his return from Kandahar, where he captured Achraff and chastised the Affghans with all imaginable barbarity, returned to Ispahan, deposed the king, his master, and placed upon the throne his son Abbas III, who was still in his cradle. Taking the title of Regent of the Empire, he marched with a large army to besiege Bagdad. Topal-Osman-Pacha, ex-grand vizier, was sent against him by the Sultan of Constantinople with an army of 100,000 men. The Regent determined immediately to give battle. He left in his trenches 12,000 men and all his seige artillery,† and marched with the rest of his army and his zemboureks to meet Topal-Osman-Pacha, who was encamped upon the banks of the Tigris, near the village of Samara, at a short distance from Bagdad. The battle fought on the 17th July, 1733, (1146,) was one of the most bloody ever maintained between the Turks and the Persians. The latter had at first the advantage, but the treachery of a body of Arabs whose assistance the Regent expected, but who, on the contrary, fell upon his flank, carried complete rout into the Persian army after a struggle of more than eight hours. The Regent had two horses killed under him and was thrown twice in the midst of his enemies. The Persians, who had been exposed all day to the burning rays of a summer's sun, were exhausted by heat and thirst. "The sun had so completely altered the face of nature that the waters of the fountains were changed into fire."

"The heat from the rays of the sun was so violent that the name alone of that planet would have burnt the tongue in one's mouth. If the salamander, which braves the fire itself, had approached those boiling waters, it would have been reduced to ashes."—(*Murza Mehdi,*

---

* Manuscript of Sheik Mahomed-Ali-Kazim.

† His seige artillery was necessarily limited to a small number of guns; therefore, all that could be captured were used. In a suburb beyond the Tigris there was a large tower called Kousch-Kaleci, [bird tower,] which the Persians took by surprise. In it they found a piece of artillery of prodigious weight, which the Turks had not had time to withdraw. It was put in order by the European engineers in the service of Persia, and was used against the town while waiting for the heavy artillery.

History of Nadir.) Besides a large number of dead, the Persians lost, with all their baggage, a number of zemboureks.*

Far from being discouraged by this defeat, the Regent reorganized his army, cast at Hamadan new falconets for his dromedary artillery, collected his siege artillery which was scattered through the different towns of Persia, and in less than three months was in condition to renew the war, and descended into the plains of Bagdad with an army more numerous than his first. This time the Ottoman army was, in its turn, completely beaten, and the celebrated Topal-Osman lost his life.

As we have seen, the Regent, Tahmasb-Kouli-Khan, had always in the train of his army a large number of these falconets, which, from his time, were called zemboureks, † and which rendered very important services, especially in 1733, at the siege of Guendje, and in 1734, at the battle of Bagavend, near Erivan. A Persian author relates that, in this action, the enemy's army was 120,000 strong—about eight men to each Persian.

After this last campaign, the Regent, Tahmasb-Kouli-Khan, was proclaimed King by the unanimous voice of his council and of the nobles of the kingdom. He resumed his old name of Nadir. and became Nadir-Shah. The ceremony of crowning scarcely terminated, he marched against Kandahar, and he seized it, with no other artillery than that of the zemboureks, while awaiting the arrival of his siege guns. He surrounded the town with towers so well connected by means of curtains and mounted with falconets, that the besieged were cut off from all communication with the country.

When Nadir-Shah presented himself before Delhi, his whole artillery consisted of only 12 guns ‡ of heavy calibre, and 250 zemboureks. I give an extract from a letter written by the King to his son Riza-

---

* Report of Topal-Osma-Pacha : "We remained masters of —— cannon and of a large number of falconets." It it is to be remarked that he does not state the number of cannon, for the reason that there were none of them on the field of battle, but only before Bagdad, and that their number was unknown to him when he despatched his messenger to announce the happy news to the Sultan.

Another account, coming from Turkey, said: "the Persians left upon the field of battle a great many small cannon which, apparently, are of the kind that the Persians mount upon camels, and of which the ball weighs about a pound ; they are fired from the camels kneeling." (*History of Persia, by Mamye Clairac.*)

† The Turks have attempted several times to form a corps of zembouretchis. One of these attempts, in 1825, is related by Jontanier in the first volume, page 156, of his "Voyage en Orient." On his way to Sivas, the governor, Mehemed-Pasha, invited him to a fête, which ended, as they always do in the east, with a military review. He says : "when we entered the Pasha's house, I was not a little surprised to see one of the Persian cannoneers, called zembouretchis, who manœuvred small pieces of artillery carried on the backs of camels. His uniform was complete, even to the little brass plates. Small flags were fastened upon the humps of the four camels intrusted to his care. As he recognized me, he called me to witness that in the equipment of his pieces he had conformed strictly with the Persian system. In consequence, this Persian was treated at court with a consideration beyond his condition. He was a great talker, and, in his character of soldier, chose his subjects of conversation in the last campaign in which he had served, and in which the Turks had been beaten."

‡ These even were left behind at Ambalé [twenty-five leagues from Kainal] with the baggage and the sacred harem, under the care of Feth-Ali-Khan, the afchar, master of the heavy artillery.

Kouli, whom he had left to govern in his absence as viceroy:* "All our desires have long sought this day. After providing a guard for the camp, and invoking the aid of the all powerful Creator, we mounted and marched to battle. For two hours the battle raged with fury, and a heavy fire of cannon and musketry was kept up without intermission. Then, by the aid of the Supreme Being, our heroes, lion hunters, broke the enemy's line, drove him from the field of battle, and pursued him in every direction. The battle lasted two hours, and for more than two hours and a half our soldiers, victorious, pursued the enemy. An hour before the close of day the enemy had been entirely driven from the field of battle, but, as his camp was strongly intrenched and defended by high fortifications, we could not instantly assault it."—(*History of Persia, by Sir John Malcolm.*)

From the death of Nadir Shah to the reorganization of the Persian army in our time, the artillery of the zemboureks has always been actively employed in the several wars, in which it perfectly filled the place of our field artillery. Far from requiring, as ours, scientific and exclusive(*) studies, the artillery of the zemboureks requires for its service only the simple knowledge of a common infantry soldier. The zembouretchis (artillerists) being taken from the camel-drivers, the management and care of the animal is familiar to them, so that they require only a little practice in manœuvring together, which is readily taught in camp or on the march. As for the siege of towns, which rarely embraces more than an investment to intercept provisions, this artillery would be more than sufficient, as there are in Persia only a few towns regularly fortified, and these even more so by nature than by art, the rest having only ramparts of earth flanked by turrets strong enough to resist cavalry. The following account by a Persian author will give a fair idea of these fortifications:

"In 1724, (1137,) after the reduction of Neiké-Kalé, Nadir marched against the castle of Bagvade, the stronghold of the tribe Kenderlon, and closely besieged for three months. He enclosed it with mines, which he caused to be worked with the utmost diligence. When the garrison discovered the imminent danger that threatened it, it prepared to inundate the mine, but too late; it had already been sprung. The workmen all perished, and a portion of the wall fell. Notwithstanding, the garrison held out, and crowning the breach, held it against the enemy. This attack having failed, Nadir built around the castle a dyke three cubits wide and nine high, through which he turned a river. The flow of water was so violent, that in two hours the foundations of the walls began to give way, and the fort became in the midst of the torrent like a great lake. * * * * The garrison saw its fortunate star go down in the aquatic sign."

---

* This young prince paid very dear for the precocious talent he exhibited; for, on the return of the Shah, some malcontents having fired at him, Riza Kouli was accused of complicity to his father, who had his eyes put out. Upon the execution of this barbarous order, the unfortunate young man exclaimed "Ah, sire, it is not my eyes, but those of Persia, you have put out." Afterwards, the tyrant, feeling remorse for this horrible act, and in expiation of it, slaughtered a hundred noblemen of his court accused only of having been present by his order at the cruel execution.

* This is the reason why the eastern powers have always been obliged to employ European artillery officers. Mirza Mehdi calls it " that deadly Christian invention."

This achievement, in spite of its singularity, would, it seems to me, be very applicable in Persia, if water sufficient to produce the result could be found everywhere. It is plain that this element produces more effect upon clay than bullets, which bury themselves without effecting the least caving in. Such fortifications, therefore, we see are only suitable to a dry country.*

THE USE OF ZEMBOUREKS ALMOST ABANDONED IN CONSEQUENCE OF THE NEW MILITARY ORGANIZATION.—RESUSCITATION OF THE ZEMBOUREKS.—REORGANIZATION OF THE CORPS, EQUIPMENT, MANŒUVRES.—COMPARATIVE TABLE OF THE DROMEDARY'S GAITS.

Aga-Mohammed-Khan, the eunuch, who established the present dynasty of Persia, when commencing a second expedition against Georgia, which had made an alliance, offensive and defensive, with Catherine of Russia, made a review of all his troops in the plains of Teheran. On which occasion, say the Persians, the zembouretchis escorted the person of the king.† This is sufficient evidence that it was a select corps which had rendered well known services; such only having the privilege of serving about the person of his majesty, or, as the Persians emphatically express it, of attending upon the *stirrup of victory*. The campaign against Georgia had scarcely begun when the King of Persia died, which caused a cessation of hostilities. From that time the zemboureks no longer appeared in active service, but held their post of honor in the train of the monarch, and have continued to hold it until our time.

At the beginning of this century the military organization of Persia was entirely changed by the advice of the Emperor Napoleon to Feth-Ali-Shah. French officers had first the honor of disciplining the Persian army. The Shah, adopting the political views of Napoleon, directed his forces against Russia, whose troops occupied the provinces washed by the Araxes and the Kur. At the commencement of the campaign, in 1811, the advantages and losses were reciprocal.‡ The Persians gained a signal victory over the Turks at

---

* When a heavy shower unexpectedly falls—particularly when the snow melts—it is not uncommon to see many portions of walls fallen in, mined by the water. I have myself seen, more than once, similar effects produced.

† We cannot pass over in silence the plan which this monarch wished to adopt to oppose the invasion of Russia. These are the very words of the Aga-Mohammed-Khan: "The Russian bullets shall never reach me; they shall be masters only of what is covered by the fire of their artillery; they shall not sleep; and go where they may, I will make a desert before them."—(*Malcolm's History of Persia*.) This system of warfare, apart from its barbarity, is certainly more suitable to the defence of Persia than to that of any other country, and unquestionably presents the greatest chances of success.

‡ Morier relates as follows a victory gained by the Persians at the battle of Sultaurbout: "The prince royal Abbas Mirza assembled his army near Mogan towards the last of January. It was 9,000 strong, according to the Persians, but 14,000 by the account of English officers serving in it. It was composed of Touffengtchis, the ordinary infantry (militia?) of the country; of Serbaz, or disciplined troops; of a corps of irregular cavalry; and of a train of horse artillery, consisting of twelve guns. Before passing the Araxes, the Prince learnt that the Russian troops, with their artillery, were posted at the village of Sultaurbout, a short distance from Chouché. He determined to attack them. The Russians, whom confidence had made careless, were suddenly surprised by finding themselves exposed to a fire of grape-shot, well directed, and which in a few minutes knocked over 300 men. They rallied within the walls of the village, where, however, after a short negotiation, they capitulated. One of the articles of capitulation was, that their heads should not be cut off, a common practice among the Turks and Persians. * * * * The Prince Abbas-Mirza behaved with magnanimity, for when the Russian commander, who had been wounded, was brought to him, perceiving that he wore no sword, he gave him his own, which was a very valuable one, and begged him to wear it."

Toprackalé, and another over the Pasha of Bagdad at Solimania. These successes were attributed to the new military organization, and with justice. The zemboureks, notwithstanding the signal services they had rendered in bygone days, were passed over, being used only to announce by their noisy discharges the ceremonial receptions of the court at Teheran.*

The contempt with which the artillerists of the new system regarded these small cannon which had taken no part in their victorious expeditions; the total neglect in repairing the old pieces; and above all, the irregular payment of the zembouretchis, were the causes of the dissolution of the corps. The men composing it sought other occupations more or less honorable, employing the camels in transporting merchandise, and for the most part, uniting in all the seditions and revolts which broke out in Teheran.

Such was the low condition of this arm when Hadji-Mirza-Agassi was appointed grand vizier by Mohammed Shah, the father of the present king. This minister, who joined rare ability to unlimited power, perceived, thanks to the correctness of his judgment, that it was not his policy to attempt conquests over civilized powers, but to fortify himself at home. With this object he centralized his power by drawing around the person of the king the Il-Khain, (chiefs of tribes,) who are always insubordinate, and who seize upon the slightest opportunities to raise the standard of revolt or to plunder. He built an expensive arsenal in the capital itself, Teheran; cast a large number of field-pieces of every calibre, mounting them upon carriages of the new model, and did not forget the useful zembourek. Although he expended large sums for the arsenal, which was his particular passion, he clearly perceived that a large standing army would be too onerous a burden for Persia. He felt the impossibility of paying and clothing it regularly in a state in which the taxes were irregularly collected; and in addition, saw that it would withdraw from husbandry a portion of labor very necessary in a country having no other resource than agriculture, and where the half only of the population were engaged in it.† This minister said to me one day, conversing freely, "the Persian foot soldier is brave to rashness, temperate, and a good marcher; a hunter by nature, he is intelligent to wiliness, and active from necessity." He added: "To keep up an army ready to march upon an emergency, I shall retain the organization of the army, such as it is, (composed of eighty-two battalions;) but instead of having them always under arms, they shall only be brought together from time to time for exercise. If invaded, I shall put good arms into their hands, saying to them: *March to defend your religion*

---

* M. Taucoigne, attached to the embassy of General Gardané in 1808, who aided the first attempts at reform in Persia by the French officers, Generals Taboier, Reboul, Lamy, and Verdier, was particularly well acquainted with the chief of the zembouretchis, Mahommed-Khan, whose licentious habits deprived him of any influence at court. But although the opinion of this traveller is not favorable to the zembourek, he concedes, however, that it was almost the only field artillery in Persia before the establishment by the French of a cannon foundry at Ispahan —(Vol. ii, p. 78.)

† The population of Persia is divided into tats and iliats. The first have permanent residences, and furnish the infantry; the second are nomadic shepherds, and supply the cavalry.

and your families, if you do not wish the infidel to make you the submissive witness of his triumphs." This system of *landwers* would be applied only to the infantry, as the cavalry has always been irregular, with the exception of a regiment disciplined by General Dourville in 1821, and another instructed by Colonel Jarrant in 1837, neither of which is now in existence. The zembouretchis and the artillery are the only permanent corps, as also a few battalions of guards for the protection of the king, and the security of the large towns. However imperfect such a system may at first appear, I think its entire applicability to Persia will be apparent when the nature of its resources is understood.

What confirmed the idea the vizier had conceived of reorganizing the artillery of the dromedaries, was the remembrance of the expedition of Abbas-Mirza into Kerman and Khorassan, in which the marches were delayed by the park of artillery, which, drawn by horses, was obliged to make considerable detours to find a practicable road. The unheard of sufferings endured by the troops proved sufficiently that these deserts would become vast cemeteries for regular troops, when their only means of transportation consisted of horses and mules. "The horse," says Hadji, "is the companion of the Persian; the dromedary is his slave, his faithful servant, which, deprived of every enjoyment, wears himself out in the service of his master."

The grand vizier first endeavored to use the dromedary in drawing the field-pieces. The attempt did not result as he had anticipated. Attempting to perform evolutions in the plains of Teheran with eight-pounders, drawn by dromedaries, he found that in the forward movements they went well enough, but that in wheeling about to come into battery their motions were slow and disordered. Accustomed to to turn upon the ground on which they stood, the pole of the limber struck them on the legs.*

The grand vizier requested from the India Company a model of the pieces carried by dromedaries, which the English used in their second expedition against Cabul, under the orders of General Nott. These pieces differed from the zemboreks only in calibre, and in the use of a carriage, which required two animals for the transportation of each piece with its ammunition.

Hadji-Mirza-Agassi retained the old system established in Persia, bringing to it improvements only in the fabrication of the zemboureks.

In reorganizing the corps, he began by choosing the best zembouretchis, (cannoneers,) rejecting the vicious and the aged. The new recruits were selected from among the most robust camel drivers of the tribes inhabiting Irak-Adjemi. He quartered them in new barracks, forming a large square, within which was room enough for the exercise of the troop. Around the square were the quarters of the zembouretchis. The service dromedaries were lodged in a plain adjoining the barracks; the others were placed in villages at short distances from the town.

The number of men is fixed at two hundred, including the sergeants

---

* In 1846, there was sent from Teheran, for the last expedition into Khorassan, artillery drawn by dromedaries; but they were only used for the road, in order not to fatigue the horses, which were reserved for service on coming into the presence of the enemy.

and corporals. The number of dromedaries is the same, and they must be six years old to be accepted. Each is armed with a small cannon. To complete the corps, there are also twenty-five musicians, mounted upon dromedaries superbly caparisoned, who announce with the sound of drumbs, tomtoms, trumpets, and brass drums, the reveillé, the retreat; likewise the festival days, the solemn entry of the king, and the receptions at court. Soldiers and musicians, to the number of two hundred and twenty-five, are commanded by a colonel, two majors, four captains, and eight lieutenants.

The pay of each cannoneer is about $19 a year. The uniform is as follows: jacket of blue cloth, with red facings; wide pantaloons of blue cloth; high boots of black leather; grey cloak, with long sleeves; cavalry, sabre, and pouch; white belt.

The dromedary carries a broad saddle of wood, very substantially made, and covered with black felt, and with iron stirrups. The pads are fastened to the tree by means of leather throngs tied together, and are open at top to fit the hump of the dromedary. The stuffing is of straw. In the pommel of the saddle is worked a hole, lined with iron, in which is fitted a wrought iron pivot, turning upon itself, and ending in two branches, in the manner of a fork, at the extremities of which are rings intended to receive the trunnions of a gun of twisted iron, 0m. 70 (2 feet 9 inches) long, and 80 miskal (near 14 ounces) in calibre. To the breech of this gun is attached a wooden stock 0m. 40 (1 foot 6 inches) long, shaped like that of a musket, and with a flint-lock. Two ammunition pouches of thick woolen stuff, covered with black leather, hang from the two sides of the saddle, carrying fifty ball and grape cartridges; besides twenty blank cartridges for salutes. Behind the saddle rises a staff or pike, surmounted by a red bannerol. From this staff falls a red housing which covers the ammunition pouches. Under the belly of the dromedary hangs a skin filled with water. The bridle is of common leather, and is attached to the headstall by an iron chain and toggle, passed through its rings. The headstall, breaststrap, surcingle, and girth are ornamented with fringe of red, yellow, and blue wool.

The zembouretchis, thus mounted, are arranged by fifties, which forms a *desté*, (company,) under the orders of a *soultan* (captain) and two *naips*, (lieutenants,) who are mounted on horses, and are instructed in the infantry exercise and in the school of the piece of the regular artillery. Their manœuvres are as follows: They form in one rank, with intervals of five feet between them, (when marching the interval is reduced;) the sergeants and corporals are in the same rank with the privates; the lieutenants are on the right of their sections; the captain moves where he can best oversee the execution of his commands. When the dromedaries march by the flank or in single or double file the captain is at their head, but when the nature of the ground will permit they march in line, in one rank. When marching by flank they form in line of battle to the right or left, taking the interval above mentioned, make a half face to the right and kneel down. The cannoneer dismounts, aims, fires, and reloads before mounting; sometimes he loads and fires while marching. This manœuvre executed, they fall back upon the wings of the line, and, marching in single file, take position in rear of the infantry. I grant that these manœuvres will not satisfy the rigid eye of an European tactician, neither are there any alignments nor sounds of tread which give life and animation. The fantastical caparison of the dromedaries, their ungainly figure, angular limbs, the ungraceful carrying of their long necks, and the bannerols hanging unevenly, as the animal rests upon one haunch or the other, present at first a strange sight, which recalls the artistic irregularity of the arabesque. And yet accidents are less frequent in this troop, in which there is an appearance of confusion, than in a body of regular cavalry. It is true that the Persians are never inattentive nor heedless to what they are doing, an essential quality in the management of this gigantic beast.

When the zembouretchis are to act detached from the main body, either to surprise encampments and to cut off retreat or to bring back supplies, they are escorted by irregular cavalry; sometimes a foot-soldier is mounted and rides behind. When lying in ambush the cannoneers dismount, and, making the animal kneel, get behind him, using him as a rampart.* If the ground will permit it, they detach the gun from the pommel of the saddle, and place it, upon its pivot, on the ground; the dromedaries, under a guard, are sent off a little distance to graze. In camp the place of the zembouretchis is about the person of the chief of the army or the king. The commands for their manœuvres are given either by the voice alone or by the bugle.

Besides the number necessary for mounting the zembouretchis, each corps is accompanied by twenty dromedaries, upon which cannoneers are also mounted, to replace the men or animals that may be killed. These spare animals carry also the tents and baggage of the officers and men.

Such as they are, the zembouretchis are capable of rendering valuable service. But notwithstanding all the improvements which Hadji-Mirza-Agassi has made in them, there still remains much to be done, for, there being no good iron-founders in the country, the balls are imperfectly round and very rough, scratching and injuring the bore of the piece, and consequently of too great windage, whence results much uncertainty in the firing. This inconvenience is in part remedied by placing over the ball a wad of felt, which also allows greater inclination in pointing, enabling grapeshot to be fired within range, at almost any angle, as with a swivel. The charge is small, for the piece having no recoil, might, if heavily loaded, jar the saddle violently and injure the dromedary. I shall give, in conclusion, a plan of my own for remedying these inconveniences, which I have submitted to the grand vizier.

---

* We have before us a very interesting notice by M. Jomard, member of the Institute, of the formation of a dromedary corps in Egypt by General Bonaparte. During that expedition the learned academician often witnessed similar manœuvres. "When," says M. Jomard, "a detachment of this corps was attacked by superior numbers they defended themselves in the following manner: each soldier made his animal kneel down, and, dismounting, entrenched himself behind it, and, so protected, used his weapons. Under other circumstances, the squadron, company, or detachment, drawing up in order of battle, manœuvre with precision according to a regular system of tactics, differing from those of the cavalry. On overtaking with the dromedaries a hostile tribe the soldiers dismounted, and, forming in battalion, easily conquered the Arabs."

To resume, we will add to what we have said of the zemboureks, that their name, which signifies *wasp*, indicates perfectly the kind of service they render; for it is their duty to harrass, worry, cut off, and attack at a thousand points, simultaneously, the troops against which they are directed.

I think I have adduced sufficient evidence in support of my opinion of the utility of dromedaries in an army; leaving nothing to be added to what I have said, and shall, therefore, conclude my statements with the following table:

Load of the dromedary, consisting of the armament and equipment of the zembouretchi.

Designation.	Mentabrizi.	Livres.*
Weight of the cannon, pivot, and sponge staff...............	12½	75
Weight of the saddle, saddle-cloth, girths, bridle, housing, and ornaments...	15	90
Weight of the ammunition-pouches and ammunition............	19	114
Weight of the rations of the cannoneer, consisting of three livres of bread, and of the dromedary, consisting of six livres of meal mixed with rye, and made into balls, and of twelve livres of hay or straw..	3½	21
Weight of the zembouretchi (cannoneer).....................	25	150
Total..	75	450

Comparative table of the length and velocity of the ambling step of a loaded dromedary.

Designation.	Weight of the load in livres.*	Number of steps in a minute.	Length of the step in centimetres.†	Distance traversed in an hour—metres‡
Dromedary with a full load.........	720	80	0.80	3,840
Dromedary with the zembourek.....	450	90	1.10	5,940
Dromedary with only a rider and his saddle........................	180	100	1.30	7,800

* A livre=1.0780 lbs. avoirdupois.—(Ordnance Manual, 1850; page 417.)
† A centimetre=0.039371 inches.—(Ordnance Manual, 1850; page 413.)
‡ A metre=39.37079 inches.—(Ordnance Manual, 1850; page 413.)   H. C. W.

The trot and gallop of the dromedary are very disagreeable. The first can only be used in executing manœuvres upon the field of battle; if kept up for any length of time, as, for instance, from one stage to another, the load of the zembouretchi would be completely shaken to pieces, and the man worn out with fatigue. The dromedary, we have already said, takes the gallop with difficulty, almost never when loaded, and keeps it up for a very short time. The amble is its true gait, and the only one that can be counted upon.

The swiftness of the dromedary cannot be compared with that of the horse, for he has neither his impatience nor impetuosity. Neither have they the same qualities or defects. A provident animal, the dromedary, as we see by the preceding table, regulates even the length of his steps by the weight of his burden. On taking the road he begins slowly, and by degrees comes up to the pace suited to his load, which he continues from sunrise to sunset. It would be impossible for the best dromedary to pass over 9,000 metres (about 9,842 yards) in fifteen minutes as a race horse can; but he will travel 90,000 metres (98,420 yards, about,) in fifteen hours, and that daily for a whole month, if necessary. In short, the horse is the handsome and proud noble, who expends his powers for effect; the other is the humble slave, not ambitious, and still less brilliant, but who tries to serve to the best of his ability, and constantly puts in practice the old proverb, *chi va piano va sano; e chi va sano va lontano!* He picks up the straw which the horse has trampled upon, and travels always provided with his little store of water. The one, bearing proudly *the centre of the world, the grandson of the sun, the stirrup of victory*, approaches even to the steps of the throne; the other dwells with the enterprising trader at the gates of the city. The one has all the sympathies and caresses; of the other it is only thought how his abstinence may be prolonged. The haughty Parthian cavalier never deigns to mount him; he is abandoned to the rude and rustic camel driver, to such a degree that the khan, the chief of the zembouretchis, never dismounts from his Turcoman courser to mount once his humble dromedary, which carries, however, as the Persian poets say, *an infernal dragon with fiery jaws* (the cannon.) The qualities which most recommend him to his master's care are his steadiness and patience. Therefore the prophet chose him as a sacrifice agreeable to the Great Allah, offering him as a victim at the feast of the *Courban baïram*. We can say of him, as may be said of many other useful creatures, that he is only honored after his death; for when he has been sacrificed, he is found worthy to be served upon the table of the *king of kings*.

EMPLOYMENT OF CAMELS IN NORTHERN COUNTRIES.—THE FRIGHT THEY CAUSE IN HORSES.—THE AFRICAN BREED OF DROMEDARIES TRANSPORTED INTO TUSCANY.—THEIR STRENGTH AND SWIFTNESS COMPARED WITH THOSE OF THE PERSIAN STOCK.—THEIR MAXIMUM SPEED.—MUSIC OF THE ZEMBOUREKS.

Although I wish to treat only of the Persian camel and dromedary, I must, nevertheless, add that these animals are used almost as far north as the Arctic pole, and that they flourish among us in the centre of our civilization. La Martinière tells us in his *Geographical Dictionary* (article KALMUCKS) that these quadrupeds were, at the beginning of the last century, used in transporting troops in almost the hyperborean regions of the Baltic, in a country covered with ponds and marshes, and that they contributed much towards gaining a battle. By a treaty of alliance concluded with the Kalmucks, they were obliged to furnish to the troops of Peter the Great a body of soldiers mounted on dromedaries. "This troop," says he, "contributed much to a considerable advantage gained by the late czar, near the Plasco, over a detachment of the Sweedish army immediately after the battle of Narva. These dromedaries (which I suppose were the camels with two humps, as these people have no other) which the Kalmucks used to draw and carry their baggage, are animals whose appearance frightens horses very much; when they see them for the first time they become excessively alarmed, and fly with precipitation.* The Moscovites advancing, upon the occasion we have just mentioned, to attack the Sweds, placed the Kalmucks with dromedaries in front. As soon as the Swedish horses saw them, they became frantic with fright, and broke their ranks; upon which the Moscovites fell upon them and succeeded in routing them." Dromedaries bear cold as well as heat, for they are seen in immense caravans traversing the mountains of Media in the coldest winters, when the centigrade thermometer marks 25° below zero (13° below zero of Fahrenheit.) At night they sleep upon the snow, and with the only precaution of covering their heads with a hood of felt, they support very well the extreme transitions of temperature, from the valleys warmed by the sun, to the mountains covered with ice, which they alternately traverse.

There is a very interesting pamphlet, which, although it contains nothing relating to military matters, furnishes information which naturally finds a place here. This pamphlet, by Jacques Gräberg de Hemsö, treats of a breed of dromedaries near Pisa, in Tuscany. One of the most essential particulars related of them is that the vigor which these animals of the Barbary stock have attained is analogous to that of the northern races of Persia. It is, without doubt, to the manner of raising these animals that this happy result is to be attributed. In Tuscany, the young ones are never weaned until sixteen or seventeen months old, which is the practice in the north of Persia, where the race is infinitely more vigorous than in the south of Persia, a country in which the want of resources compels the inhabitants to wean the young dromedaries too soon. M. Gräberg says that these useful animals render very important services in "the department of woods and forests," as beasts of burden, and that the work of one of them is equal to that of two horses. Each of these dromedaries carries a weight of 1,300, and sometimes 1,400 pounds Tuscany, (about from 980 to 1,050 pounds avoirdupois,) and with such loads never make less than three miles an hour, (about 3¾ miles English.) General Carbuccia says, that when in the expedition of Tiaret, under the command of General Marey-Monge, a corps of dromedaries accompanied the expedition; each of these animals carried the enormous load of 200 kilogrammes, (about 440 pounds avoirdupois.) Now this weight is not even the ordinary load of a zembourek, which is 450 livres. (See table.) We find again, p. 28: "According to what we have often observed, the large dromedary carries five to six sacks of barley of 60 kilogrammes, (about 132 pounds avoirdupois,) each; the medium sized four sacks, and the smallest sized three sacks, without counting the weight of the driver,

---

* There are horses which can never become accustomed to the sight of a camel. One of my own horses, of pure Arab blood, was of this character. For six years that I rode him, I had to be very careful whenever I had to pass through a street in which was a dromedary. Without this precaution he would wheel about and run away. In the end I succeeded in accustoming him to them a little; yet the sight of one always disturbed him; he would sidle along the walk and show much fear.

who mounts upon his beast whenever he is tired." The ordinary load in Persia is about 720 livres, (about 770 pounds avoirdupois,) and it is at this rate that they are hired, and that the packages for transportation in caravans are made up. The large dromedaries carry sometimes as much as 1,000 livres, (about 1,070 pounds avoirdupois,) the same weight as those used in Tuscany, and a third more than those used in Algiers. As for their swiftness, I have given it in the comparative table, where I say that with a load of 720 livres, and with even an addition of 280 livres for the large dromedaries, they accomplish 3,840 metres an hour, that is, 1,115 metres less than those of Tuscany, which conveniently make three miles an hour with the same load. This difference should attract the attention of the French government, which, if it would raise its own dromedaries, at the public expense, would assuredly attain the same results as have been produced in Tuscany by the same means, and would avoid the necessity of using inferior or broken down animals.

General Marey-Monge tells us that there are dromedaries in Algiers which are said to have travelled from 80 to 100 leagues a day, (from 200 to 250 miles.) M. Pottinger and M. Christie say that each chief of the Beloutchis, to execute a tchapaoul, (razia,) has under his orders a dozen dromedaries that travel very near 90 miles a day, until they arrive at the theatre of operations. The maximum speed of the dromedaries of the north of Persia is said to be 30 leagues, (about 75 miles,) a day, and I doubt much if they can exceed this rate. There are, no doubt, exceptions to this limit, but they cannot be offered as a general rule. On this point my conclusions are drawn from the following. The frequent revolts which disturb the country, and especially the despotism of the chief, which permits him to dispose of the lives of his subjects, obliges the latter to be always on the alert.* The nobles keep almost always in their stables a horse whose qualities, concealed from the public, are known only to the master and to a faithful groom. These animals, kept only for the *rowz seiah*, (day of misfortune,) are reputed to make 60 leagues, (about 150 miles,) and even more, in a day.† If the dromedaries could attain a like speed, they would, no doubt, be used for the same purpose, which is never done.‡

There remains a few words to be said about the military music of the zemboureks, a subject to be avoided but that it involves a point

---

* The *Kouroglou*, a popular song of northern Persia, which expresses by lively images the mind and character of the nation, puts these words in the mouth of the prince who has put out the eyes of Kouroglou's father: "In a moment of anger I caused his eyes to be put out, but who will dispute the right of a master to punish his servant, in order that he may afterwards heap favors upon him? Follow me, you will learn how to please me, and I will know how to recompense you." (A. Chodzko.)

† The Turcoman horses often make journeys of sixty leagues (about 150 miles) a day, which renders it impossible to overtake their horsemen when they make incursions into the Persian territory.

‡ The grand vizier whom I have had occasion to mention so often, owed his safety once to the swiftness of his horse. Taking refuge in the mosque of Shah-Abdoul-Azim, (an asylum,) his pursuers, forced to respect the sanctity of the place, sought to starve him out. I was fortunate enough to aid his escape and to save the life of one whose kind protection had so often been useful to me in my career. I have several letters from him, dated from this forced retreat, and in which, forgetting that he had just been despoiled of immense wealth, and that his life was in danger, regretted only the loss of his horse, which his personal enemy, the chief of the tribe Shah-Serene, had seized.

of some importance. It is said by some that the noise of drums and trumpets frightens the dromedaries. We affirm, with full knowledge of the matter, that these animals are accustomed, not only as easily as the horse to military music, but more, that that which precedes them is incomparably more noisy and frightening than ours. The instruments which compose it are, the *karine*, which has the form of the *tuba*, the ancient Roman horn, and which is eight feet long.* Its sound is comparable only to the bellowing of a furious bull.† The *kôous*, a large drum two feet in circumference; the *balaban;* the *houl*, a common drum ; the *nagarah*, a kettle drum ; the *cheipour*, or *nafié*, a trumpet; the *zourna*, a hautboy; and the cymbals, *zeng*. All these instruments are in twos and threes, and the band of the regiment consists of twenty-five zembouretchis, who beat and blow like madmen.‡ Mirza-Mehdi relates, "that Nadir commanded the *nagahra kanê* (military music) of his august army to rend the air with their martial strains, and took his departure on the sounding of the military instruments, which resembled the trumpet of the resurrection." We will not say, therefore, as the Englishman did: "that there was something agreeable in this music." On the contrary, we will add, that one must have Persian ears to endure the frightful uproar in which the people of this country delight. They love beyond everything the air of the Kouroglou, (son of the blindman,) a very martial song, which produces in them the same effect that our patriotic songs do upon us. One of the passages which particularly electrifies them, when words are added to the music, is the following: " Cease your boasting ! what to my eyes are thirty, sixty, or a hundred of your soldiers? What are your rocks, your precipices, and your deserts under the hoof of my courser? In me behold the leopard of the mountains and of the valleys."—(See the Oriental Review, translation from M. Chodzko.)

GENERAL REFLECTIONS.—IMPERFECTIONS OF THE ZEMBOUREKS.—DELAY IN SERVING.—NEW PACK CARRIAGE PROPOSED.—INCREASE OF THE PERSONNEL.—FORMATION OF A NEW COMPANY OF ZEMBOUREKS.—MANŒUVRES.

Before commencing this paper my intention had been to give only a few sketches of the zembureks, accompanied by slight superficial details ; such was my plan, and probably I should not have departed from it if I had not found such a mass of materials, which seemed to draw me to a greater extension of my little treatise. If I have sometimes entertained the reader with matters relating to myself, it arises

---

* There is in the national library, in the department of antiquities, a brass trumpet 1m.17 long, (about 40 inches,) brought from Colchis and presented to the library, in 1824, by M. Gamba, the consul of France at Tiflis. This is the true ancient trumpet now used in this country ; the sound of it is very piercing, and can be heard a great distance. (Magasin Pittoresque, Vol. XX, p. 36.)

† The Persian musicians have succeeded in producing from this instrument a modulated sound which resembles the pronunciation of the name of the king, Mehemed Shah, a harmonious trick which is worth to them a generous gratuity.

‡ One may imagine what such music can be when he hears that they have no written music ; that each one knows the airs by ear only, and consequently modulates them according to his own pleasure, endeavoring only to drown the noise of his neighbor by his own, in order to produce himself the greatest possible effect.

from the fact, that being in daily intercourse and in business relation with all the most powerful personages of the country during a residence of fourteen years, it has been impossible for me to speak of them without finding myself mixed up in what concerned them. There, where manners and customs are so different from ours, the European finds himself too conspicuous to avoid an active participation in most of the important occurrences. It is not to be concealed, that after the efforts and inducements held out by General Marey-Monge during his government of Algiers, and the researches as profound as judicious of General Carbuccia, that there remained but little for me to say on the subject. Indeed, this author, enlightened by his own investigations, has given us the most minute details of the usefulness of the dromedary in Africa for military transportation. His work is truly a manual which should be consulted not only by officers employed in active service in Algiers, but by those of all powers having intercourse with the East. It may one day be of great service to them; and, without any doubt, they will find in it inexhaustible resources upon the natural history of the dromedary, its hygean, and breeding. The expedition of Khiva in 1840 by the Russian army, composed of 6,000 men and of 10,000 camels, as also those made in Cabool in 1839 and 1842 by the English army, which numbered 30,000 dromedaries, prove to us the utility of this study; and the invasion which our civilization aims at over all Asia gives indisputable interest to its investigation. However, encouraged by those only who have so knowingly treated the subject, I determined to relate not only what I have seen and done, but more—the modifications I have attempted for the improvement of this portable artillery.

To understand clearly what were the improvements required by the zembourek, we must state what the arm was in its primitive condition, and how it was served.

The zembourek, with the exception of finish in the workmanship, was of the same dimensions as we have described, less the lock which now replaces the pan on the right side of the barrel. Having no recoil, and being pointed by hand, it had the great inconvenience (which it still has) of kicking violently whenever the load was increased; this was endeavored to be remedied by twisting rags around the breech, (fig. 1.) The pack (fig. 2) was made of two wooden forks—one resting upon the withers, and the other upon the croup of the dromedary, from $0^m.70$ to $0^m.75$ (from 2 feet 9 inches to 3 feet) apart, joined together by cross-bars; behind this pack were fixed vertically two staves, from which hung bannerols, one of which besides was used as a rammer, linstock, and whip. The animal was guided by means of a halter, headstall, and cordlonge.

The cannoneer wore a high sheepskin cap, ornamented with a capplate; a long coat, the flaps of which were turned back under the belt, and decorated on the breast with small pendants of metal, which, striking together during the march, produced a continued jingling. His weapon was a *cama*, or sort of long poinard. The service of the piece was performed as follows: The right guide, after the captain, placed himself at a certain distance in front of the line, and by motions with his arms and legs indicated the manœuvre, using the voice only to make some remark. To load and fire, the cannoneer, seated upon his pack, took with his right hand a powder bag from his pouch, poured out a charge into a measure, turned it over into the gun, and put over it a loose wad; then, with the left hand taking a ball or a handful of bullets he introduced them into the bore of the piece, and placed over them a felt wad, and then rammed all down with the rammer stuck up behind him. This done, seizing the powder horn which hung at his belt, he primed; and that the motion of the dromedary should not shake the priming from the pan, he held it in either with the palm of his hand, or by a rag wrapped over it. The piece was fired by a match worn over the body in the manner of a shoulder belt, the lighted end being hung, for ready use, astride of the gun, care being taken not to let it touch the dromedary's neck. This, as we may see, was the manner of doing the thing with us in the sixteenth century, and the most expert artillerist required at least three minutes to load and fire his piece. We have already said that the cannoneer, after dismounting his piece from the pack, stuck the pivot with force into the ground; this injured the trunnions, and jarred the stock so much as soon to render it unserviceable. The gun, moreover, was laid too low, affecting materially the regularity of the firing; and, kicking violently, it often happened that the cannoneer's hands were injured. Another inconvenience proceeding from the want of a carriage was the derangement of the gun by the kicking, destroying the perpendicularity of the pivot by the enlargement of the hole in which it stuck. It often occurred, as I have myself witnessed, that after the second discharge the gun was lying on the ground.

It was necessary then to modify the zembourek, and to simplify its service in such a manner as to remedy to the utmost its inconveniences, without at all impairing its particular advantages.

NEW PACK CARRIAGE.

The improvement which the grand vizier had made in the fabrication of the piece, and in the preparation of the ammunition for it, was, without doubt, a great step; and if confined to small charges of grape shot, the end was almost gained. But it was not less important that the piece should be able to fire ball with heavy charges when dismounted from the animal and placed in battery, and at the same time that the cannoneer should not be incommoded by a carriage which would interfere with his movements, and impede the animal's march by an increase of burden. I invented a pack carriage, (figs. 4 and 5,) the model of which I presented to the prime minister in May, 1847. It consists of the two forks, (D,) the branches of both being united by a curved cross tie, forming the pommel (a) and the cantle (b) of the pack. To the ends of the four branches are attached small wheels (c) for the pack to move on when it is placed upon the ground. The two branches are joined together by eight iron bars, (e,) four on each side. This forms the frame of the pack carriage. The cantle fork bears an elevating screw, (k,) and the pivot on which the gun turns passes through the pommel fork, and rests upon the curved cross tie (f) below. Two sponge hooks, (g,) staples for stirrup leathers, (h,) and one for the breast strap, (i,) all of iron, are set in. The girth is fastened, as in the old pack, to the bars; the straps (J) are used for fastening the saddle-pads (P) to the saddle-bow. A substitute is added instead of the breech plate, and behind the stock of the gun, consisting of a spring (figs. 4, 5, 6) which retains a small plate of iron with a groove, (r,) to which is fitted, when the gun is served, a plate of iron slightly arched, and fastened by a small key (l s) that enables the gun to be pointed to the right or left without moving the carriage.

This carriage requires an increase of force, which should be three men to each piece, for it is impossible to place the piece in battery, to serve it, and to hold the dromedaries without this increase of the *personnel*.

We have seen that the evolutions could not be conducted with requisite regularity, because the cannoneer had enough to do to load his gun, and so was prevented from guiding his animal. The addition of two cannoneers, mounted upon a second dromedary, remedies this defect. This dromedary, besides the burden of the two men, should also carry a double ammunition pouch containing the heavy charges with bullets, the pouch of priming tubes, the priming wire, (the lock doing away with the finger stall,) the lint stock, and the worm. The two cannoneers should be armed, both with a sabre-bayonet, a carbine, and a cartridge-box. The cannoneer mounted upon the dromedary with the piece is equipped as before, except that his cartridge-box is replaced by an ammunition pouch, to which is added a second priming wire and a priming horn. This cannoneer should be armed only with a sabre-bayonet. The ammunition in his double pouch should be ball cartridges. The bannerol is done away with. The men's rations are divided between the two dromedaries.

By this arrangement the number of men and of dromedaries for a company are as follows: 1 captain and 2 lieutenants on horseback, 4 sergeants on dromedaries, 10 corporals, 2 trumpeters, 1 adjutant, 1 quartermaster, and 50 cannoneers—in all, 71; aggregate: 46 dromedaries and 5 horses.

FORMATION IN ORDER OF BATTLE.

The company is formed in two ranks, (fig. 3.) The dromedaries of the front rank, carrying a man and a gun, are at intervals of $1^m.50$ (five feet) apart. Those of the rear rank, carrying two cannoneers sitting back to back, are three metres (about three yards) in rear of those of the front rank and covering them.

The captain's post is six metres in rear of the rank of file closers, opposite to the centre of the company; by his side are the trumpeters. The lieutenants are in the front rank on the right of their platoons. The adjutant and quartermaster, on horseback, in the rank of file closers, are three metres in rear of the centre of each platoon. The four sergeants, in the rank of file closers, are in the rear of the right and left of the sections.*

---

* These non-commissioned officers are armed with lance, sabre, and holster pistols.

When the cannoneer of the front rank loads and fires his piece mounted, his dromedary half faces to the right or left, the rear rank remaining faced to the front.

ADVANCING IN LINE OF BATTLE.

The front rank remains at a halt; the rear rank advances through the intervals of the front rank. In passing, the cannoneer of the front rank hands to the cannoneer of the rear rank, sitting faced to the rear, the longe of his dromedary. This latter leads the animal while the first busies himself with loading his piece, (fig. 7.) The captain takes post in front of the centre of his company and conducts the march. At command, the dromedaries of the front rank resume their original positions.

Other marchings are subjected to such changes as the tactician will readily conceive, and which it is not necessary to detail here.

TO PLACE THE PIECE IN BATTERY.

The dromedaries of the rear rank advance to the sides and in line with those of the front rank, and all kneel down. Two cannoneers dismount the piece and its carriage from the animal, and place it in battery in front of the line of dromedaries, whilst the third, or corporal,* overseeing the movement, prepares the ammunition for service.

SERVICE OF THE PIECE IN BATTERY.

The cannoneer of the right sponges, rams down, primes, and fires. The cannoneer of the left purveys, shuts pan, and points. The third cannoneer, placed between the two dromedaries, serves out the ammunition, and assists in purveying, (fig. 8.)

CONCLUSION.

I presume that these generalities upon the manœuvres, with the plates I have added, will suffice to give an idea of the service of the zembourek.

The improvements made permit three rounds to be fired in a minute, and the pack-carriage I have proposed has the advantage of greater solidity than the other, without any increase of weight, since it only weighs 38 kilogrammes, (about 83 pounds avoirdupois,) although made of iron. Besides, the piece mounted on the carriage can fire a double charge, and the cannoneer, more conveniently placed for pointing, can aim with greater exactness and precision. The addition of a second dromedary gives regularity in marching and in the evolutions; and the men, in addition to the duties of artillerists, act like dragoons on foot, and cover the retreat.

Notwithstanding the defects and inconveniences attending it, the services rendered by the dromedary artillery are none the less real;

---

* Each squad consists of four dromedaries, five cannoneers, and a corporal.

for we have seen that in several battles the Persians, with forces inferior to those of the enemy, gained, with the assistance of the zemboureks, brilliant successes over the Ottoman army, which left upon the field of battle several of its generals-in-chief, among them, those who had fought against Prince Eugene, of Savoy, Moncenigo, Panin, Roumianzoff, &c. This Ottoman army, moreover, was the same that gained the famous treaty made with the Czar by Balladji-Mohammed-Pasha, on the banks of the Pruth; and some years later the treaty of Belgrade, one of the most glorious ever concluded by the Porte with the Russians and the Austrians.

We know that the Ottomans, in their campaigns, have always had superabundance of arms and ammunition, and that they spare no expense in adopting the inventions and improvements made in Europe. The *toptchis* (artillerists) and the koumbaradjis (bombardiers) have always been in Turkey regular corps, (see the *memoirs of Napoleon at the siege of St. Jean d'Acre,*) instructed by European officers, such as the Baron de Tolt, and others like him, whilst the Persians, centered in Asia, have had only such teachers as chance brought to them. They have been able, then, themselves not only to quell intestine wars, but more, to reconquer their usurped provinces, and to preserve over Turkey the preponderance which has lasted to the present time. All these results were obtained by troops badly armed and inferior in numbers to their enemies, but which had the inappreciable advantages of extreme mobility and means of rapid transportation.

Most of these wars were surprises, in which the Persian army fell unexpectedly upon the enemy, at a time when he was overcome by long marches, or by heat or cold, in a country where the elevation of the sun causes extreme changes of temperature. In consequence, the Zembourek has been called upon to play among them an important part; it is an invention purely Asiatic, peculiar to and suited to the regions of Asia. It is for this reason that it has been maintained in spite of its defects, which are, however, in great part remediable.

I have mentioned the eagerness with which the Persians sought for an artillery transportable on the backs of animals. In 1846, Marshal Soult, at the request of the Count de Sartiges, minister of France to Persia, sent to his excellency the Hadji, a mountain howitzer. Immediately a number were cast like it; but although they may be found very useful in the mountainous regions of the country, they are not all that is necessary for the plains. The Zembourek will fulfil very much better both of these conditions, particularly with the improvements that may be made in it.

238 PURCHASE OF CAMELS FOR MILITARY PURPOSES.

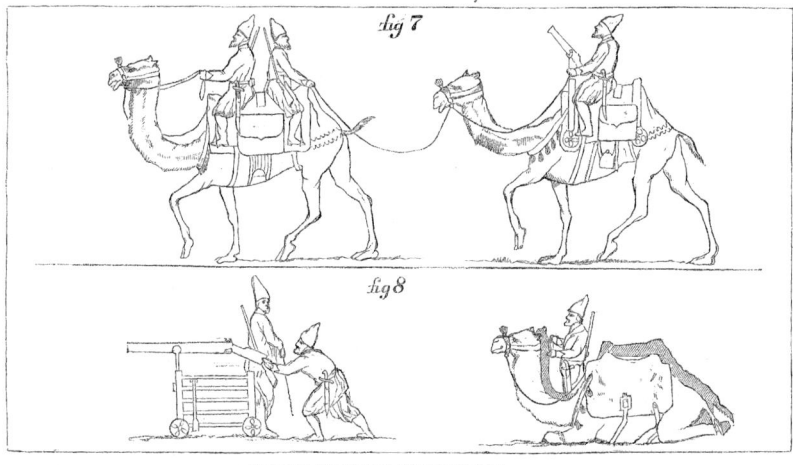

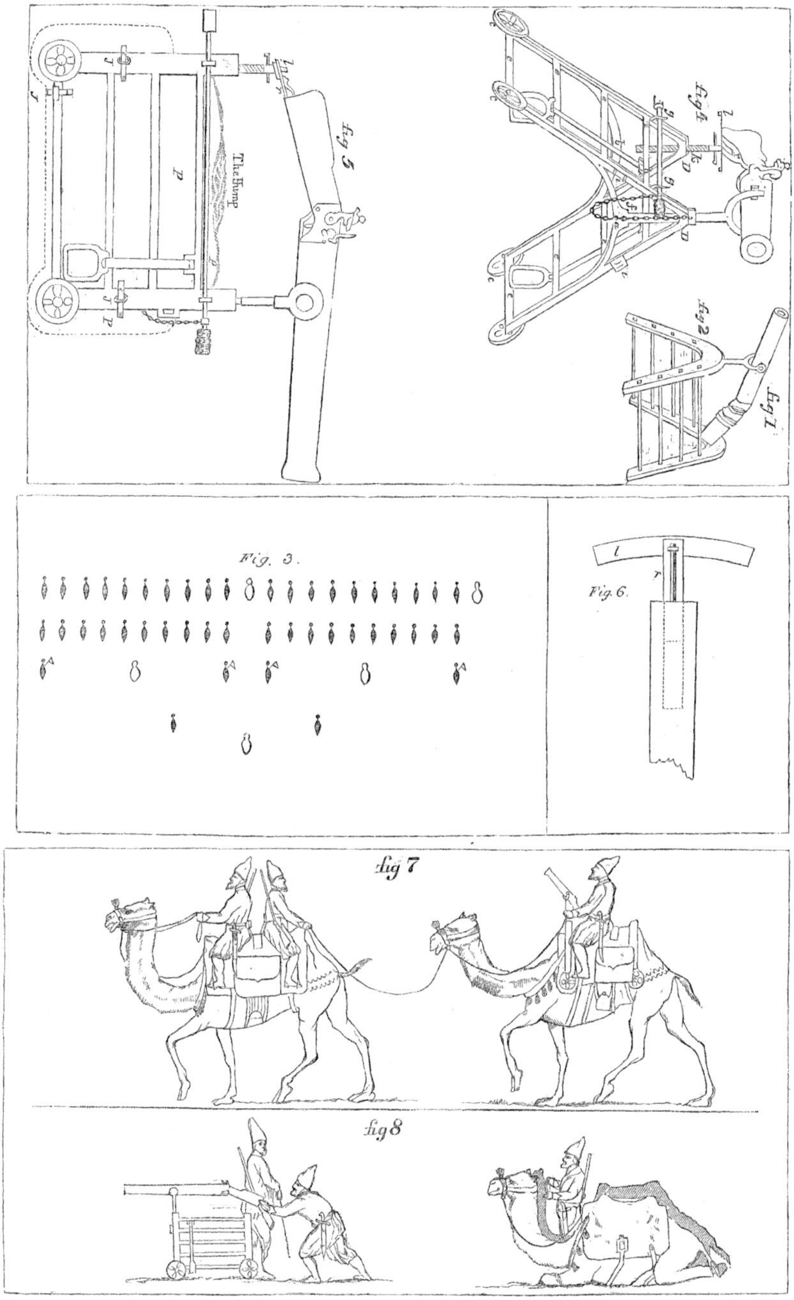

ZEMBOUREK, OR DROMEDARY ARTILLERY OF PERSIA.

DATE DUE

Printed in Dunstable, United Kingdom